Developing Sustainable Leadership

Developing Sustainable Leadership

edited by
Brent Davies

Paul Chapman
Publishing

First published 2007

Paul Chapman Publishing
SAGE Publications Ltd
1 Oliver's Yard
55 City Road
London EC1Y 1SP

SAGE Publications Inc.
2455 Teller Road
Thousand Oaks, California 91320

SAGE Publications India Pvt Ltd
B 1/I 1 Mohan Cooperative Industrial Area
Mathura Road, Post Bag 7
New Delhi 110 044
India

SAGE Publications Asia-Pacific Pte Ltd
33 Pekin Street #02-01
Far East Square
Singapore 048763

Library of Congress Control Number: 2006940470

British Library Cataloguing in Publication data

A catalogue record for this book is available from the British Library

ISBN 978-1-4129-2395-8
ISBN 978-1-4129-2396-5 (pbk)

Typeset by Pantek Arts Ltd, Maidstone, Kent
Printed in Great Britain by Athenaeum Press, Gateshead, Tyne & Wear
Printed on paper from sustainable resources

This book is dedicated to:

Dr Mark Lofthouse
for moral leadership in
difficult times.

Contents

List of figures ix
List of tables x
Editor and Contributors xi

Introduction 1
Brent Davies

1 **Sustainable leadership** 11
Brent Davies

2 **Sustaining exhilarating leadership** 26
Brian J. Caldwell

3 **Energizing leadership for sustainability** 46
Andy Hargreaves and Dean Fink

4 **Sustaining resilience** 65
Christopher Day and Michèle Schmidt

5 **Sustainability of the status quo** 87
Terry Deal

6 **Developing and sustaining school leaders: lessons from research** 97
Kenneth Leithwood, Scott Bauer and Brian Riedlinger

7 **Sustaining leadership in complex times: an individual and system solution** 116
Michael Fullan and Lyn Sharratt

8 **Leadership sustainability in an emerging market environment** 137
Guilbert C. Hentschke

9 **Sustaining leaders for system change** 154
David Hopkins

10 **Leadership succession** 175
Geoff Southworth

Index 194

List of figures

1.1	Deep learning	12
1.2	Short-term viability and long-term sustainability	14
1.3	Characteristics of successful leaders	18
1.4	Strategic conversations and strategic capacity	21
7.1	The Literacy Collaborative vision	119
9.1	Towards sustainable systemic reform	160
9.2	System leadership as adaptive work	161
9.3	The four drivers for system reform	162
10.1	Changes towards career planning	180

List of tables

2.1 Aspects of work that are exhilarating 31
2.2 Aspects of work that are boring, depressing, discouraging or dispiriting 33
2.3 How to make work more exhilarating 36
4.1 Profiles of headteachers and schools 71
7.1 Five-year span in EQAO results in YRDSB, 1999–2005 121
7.2 The Literacy Collaborative 123
9.1 A highly differentiated approach to school improvement 167

Editor and Contributors

Editor: Professor Brent Davies, Cert Ed, BA, MSc, MPhil, PhD

Dr Brent Davies is Professor of International Leadership Development at the University of Hull. He is also a Professorial Fellow at the University of Melbourne, Visiting Professor at the Institute of Education (University of London), Special Professor at the University of Nottingham and a Faculty Member of the Centre on Educational Governance at the University of Southern California. He is an Associate Director of the Specialist Schools and Academies Trust. Brent spent the first 10 years of his career working as a teacher in South London. He then moved into higher education and now works exclusively on leadership and management development programmes for senior and middle managers in schools. He was Director of the International MBA in School Leadership at Leeds Metropolitan University. He then moved to the University of Lincolnshire and Humberside to establish the first Chair in Educational Leadership and create the International Educational Leadership Centre in Lincoln. He moved to the University of Hull in 2000 to establish the International Leadership Centre. In 2004 he moved within the university to become a research professor in leadership development at the Hull University Business School.

He has published extensively, with 20 books and 70 articles on leadership and management, his recent books including: *The New Strategic Direction and Development of the School* (2003, RoutledgeFalmer), *The Handbook of Educational Leadership and Management* (2003, Pearson), *School Leadership in the 21st Century* (2004, RoutledgeFalmer), *The Essentials of School Leadership* (2005, Sage) and *Leading the Strategically Focused School* (2006, Sage).

Contributors

Dr Scott Bauer, serves as associate professor and program coordinator in the Education Leadership programme at George Mason University, Fairfax, Virginia. His research interests involve the application of organizational design and theory to the improvement of schools, and the efficacy of various strategies used to develop school leaders at all levels. His most recent publications deal with the development of teacher leaders, the organizational design of collaborative leadership strategies, and the redesign of university-based leadership preparation programmes. He is involved in a three-year study of the implementation and effectiveness of a cross-district coaching and mentoring support system for new principals. He serves on the editorial boards of *Journal of School Leadership* and *Journal of Research for Educational Leaders*.

Dr Brian J. Caldwell is Managing Director of Melbourne-based Educational Transformations and Professorial Fellow at the University of Melbourne where he served as Dean of Education from 1998 to 2004. He serves as Associate Director of International Networking for Educational Transformation (iNET), the international arm of the Specialist Schools and Academies Trust in the UK. He is co-author of several books that have helped shape policy and practice, notably the trilogy on self-managing schools. *Re-imagining Educational Leadership* was published in 2006 drawing on insights gathered in workshops in several countries. He is Deputy Chair of the Board of the Australian Council for Educational Research.

Dr Christopher Day is Professor of Education and Co-Director of the Teacher and Leadership Research Centre (T.L.R.C.) in the university of Nottingham. Prior to this he worked as a teacher, lecturer and local authority schools adviser. He is founding editor of *Teachers and Teaching: Theory and Practice*. His books have been published in several languages and include *Teachers Matter* (2007, Open University Press); *Successful Principalship: International Perspectives* (2007, co-edited, Dordrecht, Springer); *A Passion for Teaching* (1994, Open University Press); *Effective Leadership for School Improvement* (2003, co-authored, Routledge); and *Developing Teachers: The Challenges of Lifelong Learning* (1999, Falmer Press). He has recently completed directing a four-year Department for Education and Skills (DfES)-funded research on variations in teachers' work, lives and effectiveness; and is currently directing an eight-country project on successful school principalship; a nine-country European project on successful principalship in schools in challenging urban contexts; a national project on school leadership and pupil outcomes; and a national project on effective classroom teaching.

Dr Terry Deal is a former teacher, principal, cop, and administrator who received his PhD in Educational Administration and Sociology from Stanford University. He is a professor at the University of Southern California. He teaches courses in Organizations and Leadership and has previously taught at Stanford, Harvard and Vanderbilt universities. Professor Deal specializes in the study of organizations. He consults to a wide variety of organizations such as businesses, hospitals, banks, schools, colleges, religious orders and military organizations in the USA and abroad. Professor Deal has written 20 books and more than 100 articles and book chapters concerning organizations, leadership, change, culture, and symbolism and spirit. Many of these have been translated into Japanese, Korean, Chinese, Farsi, Dutch, French, Norwegian, Portuguese, German, Italian and Spanish.

Dr Dean Fink is an international educational development consultant. He is a former teacher, principal and superintendent with the Halton Board of Education in Ontario, Canada. In the past 12 years, Dean has made presentations or conducted workshops in 31 different countries. He has published numerous book chapters and articles on topics related to school effectiveness, leadership and change in schools. He is the author or co-author of *Changing Our Schools* (McGraw-Hill, 1996) with Louise Stoll; *Good Schools/Real Schools: Why School Reform Doesn't Last* (Teachers College Press, 2000), and *It's About Learning and It's About Time* (Taylor and Francis, 2003) with Louise Stoll and Lorna Earl. His new books are *Sustainable Leadership* with Andy Hargreaves for Jossey-Bass (2006), and *Leadership for Mortals: Developing and Sustaining Leaders of Learning* for Corwin Press (2006).

Dr Michael Fullan is the former Dean of the Ontario Institute for Studies in Education of the University of Toronto. Professor Fullan is recognized as an international authority on educational reform and is engaged in training, consulting, and evaluating change projects around the world. His ideas for managing change are used in many countries, and his books have been published in many languages. His recent books include *The Moral Imperative of School Leadership* (2003), *Leadership and Sustainability* (2005) and *Breakthrough* (with Peter Hill and Carmel Crevola, 2006), *Learning Places* (with Cliff St Germain, 2006); *Turnaround Leadership* (2006); and *The Meaning of Educational Change*, 4th edition (2007). In April 2004 he was appointed Special Adviser to the Premier and to the Minister of Education, Ontario, Canada.

Dr Andy Hargreaves is the Thomas More Brennan Chair in Education at the Lynch School of Education, Boston College. Prior to that, he was Professor of Educational Leadership and Change at the University of Nottingham, England and Co-director of and Professor in the International Centre for Educational Change at the Ontario Institute for Studies in Education of the University of Toronto. His most recent book, co-authored with Dean Fink, is *Sustainable Leadership* (Jossey-Bass, 2006).

Dr Guilbert C. Hentschke is Richard T. Cooper and Mary Catherine Cooper Chair of Public School Administration at the University of Southern California's Rossier School of Education, where he served as Dean from 1988 to 2000. Prior to 1988 he served in professorial and administrative capacities at the University of Rochester, Columbia University and the Chicago Public Schools. Currently he directs programmes in the business of education, and teaches in the Ed.D. programme. An author of numerous books and articles on school reform and charter schools, he teaches graduate courses dealing with markets, regulation and performance in schooling, and serves on several boards of education businesses, including the National Centre on Education and the Economy, the Education Industry Foundation, Excellent Education Development and WestEd Regional Educational Laboratory. Dr Hentschke earned his bachelor's degree in history and economics at Princeton University and his master's and doctorate in education at Stanford University.

Dr David Hopkins is the HSBC Professor of International Leadership, where he supports the work of iNET, the International arm of the Specialist Schools Trust and the Leadership Centre at the Institute of Education, University of London. Between 2002 and 2005 he served three Secretaries of State as the Chief Adviser on School Standards at the Department for Education and Skills. Previously, he was Chair of the Leicester City Partnership Board and Professor of Education, Head of the School, and Dean of the Faculty of Education at the University of

Nottingham. Before that he was a Tutor at the University of Cambridge Institute of Education, a Secondary School teacher and Outward Bound Instructor. David is also an International Mountain Guide who still climbs regularly in the Alps and Himalayas.

Dr Kenneth Leithwood is Professor of Educational Administration and former Associate Dean of Research for OISE/University of Toronto. His recent books include *Teaching for Deep Understanding* (edited with others), *Successful Principal Leadership: An International Perspective* (edited with Chris Day), *Teacher Working Conditions that Matter* and *Making Schools Smarter* (3rd edition). He is the senior editor of the first and second *International Handbooks of Educational Leadership and Administration.*

Dr Brian Riedlinger has served as Chief Executive Officer (CEO) of the Algiers Charter School Association (ACSA) since November 2005. As CEO, he opened six schools on the west bank of New Orleans educating about 3800 students in 2005–06, and opened two more schools in 2007. In addition, he serves as CEO of the School Leadership Center of Greater New Orleans – a 'principals' center' dedicated to the improvement of school leadership and therefore, student achievement, through professional development of school leaders. Previously, he was a principal in the New Orleans Public Schools for 20 years and was selected State Principal of the Year in 1999. Brian received his bachelor's and master's degrees from Louisiana State University and his doctorate from the University of New Orleans.

Dr Michèle Schmidt is an assistant professor in education and coordinator of the MEd Leadership programme at Simon Fraser University. Her research interests focus on leadership within a context of educational change and accountability. She received her PhD at Ontario Institute for Studies in Education of the University of Toronto (OISE/UT) and completed postdoctoral studies at Johns Hopkins University.

Dr Lyn Sharratt is the Superintendent of Curriculum and Instructional Services in the York Region District School Board, north of Toronto, Canada. She has taught in three other School Districts and has been an Associate Professor at York University, pre-service programme; Executive Assistant, Professional Development, with the Federation of Women Teachers Association in Ontario; and Director of Curriculum at the

Ontario Public Schools Boards' Association working with elected trustees across the Province of Ontario. She has written many articles on technology implementation, school improvement, change, leadership development, and increasing student achievement through literacy. She is an Associate at the Ontario Institute for Studies in Education, University of Toronto.

Dr Geoff Southworth is Deputy Chief Executive and Strategic Director of Research and Policy at the National College for School Leadership (NCSL). He began his career as a teacher in Lancashire, where he taught in three schools before becoming headteacher of a school in Leyland. During his headship he became involved in school management training programmes which prompted him to move into higher education in Cambridge. At the Cambridge Institute (later the School of Education) he directed management courses for heads, deputies and middle leaders. In 1997 he was appointed Professor of Education at the University of Reading. He has written many articles and chapters in books, as well as authoring, co-authoring or editing 14 books. In 2002 he moved to the NCSL to become the Director for Research. He was and continues to be responsible for the strategic direction of the NCSL's research and evaluation activities. In 2005 he was promoted to Deputy CEO working closely with the CEO and the strategic and operational directors.

Introduction

Brent Davies

Context

The drive to raise educational standards in many countries has, over the last decade, concentrated on more tightly focused curricular frameworks and testing regimes. This has resulted in improved standards as measured by test scores (Fullan, 2005). However, this raises two questions: are these results sustainable and are there other objectives that we should be pursuing? Providing answers to these questions involves moving from a short-term to a longer-term view. Achieving success for children, in terms of how they develop academically, socially, physically, emotionally and spiritually, is the aim of all schools. How do we achieve that success both in the short and long term and how do we ensure that success is sustainable?

In leadership terms, what are the challenges and pressures that individuals in schools have to cope with? How do they meet short-term accountability demands and at the same time build longer-term learning communities based on clear moral and educational values? How do individual leaders build frameworks of care and compassion so that all who work in the school (students and adults) enhance their personal and professional health? Most importantly, how can leaders support themselves both to survive and to develop as creative educationalists in an increasingly results-driven accountability climate? In brief, how do we sustain leaders and their schools to achieve that longer-term educational success without exhausting themselves and their organizations in a search for ever-increasing short-term results? It is important to understand sustainability not as a continuation of the status quo but as sustainable improvement.

Sustainability might be considered as the ability of individuals and schools to continue to adapt and improve to meet new challenges and complexity, and to be successful in new and demanding contexts. Most significantly, this should be seen in the context of improving, not depleting, individual and organizational health and well-being.

The purpose of this book is to make a contribution to the embryonic literature on sustainability and, in particular, on sustaining leaders in the complex and challenging environment in which they work. There are two existing works in the field. Michael Fullan's (2004) *Leadership and Sustainability: System Thinkers in Action* takes a broad educational system view at national and state level with a perceptive section at the individual leader level. Second, Andy Hargreaves and Dean Fink (2005) have published *Sustaining Leadership*. These authors develop their thinking further and contribute significant chapters with new ideas in this 2007 book. This book brings together some of the leading educational thinkers and writers to offer unique perspectives that will add to a field which is receiving increasing attention. The book aims to provide a diverse but coherent account written for the reflective practitioner.

The chapters in the book

In Chapter 1 I build on my research work in strategic leadership and expound the view that if strategic leadership is to be successful it has, almost by definition, to be sustainable. In this chapter I define sustainable leadership as follows:

> *Sustainable leadership is made up of the key factors that underpin the longer-term development of the school. It builds a leadership culture based on moral purpose which provides success that is accessible to all.*

The challenge for leaders in schools is how to deal with the immediate running of the school and the demands of the current year while at the same time building longer-term capacity. The danger of imposed simplistic external targets, such as test scores and inspection outcomes, is that they are one-dimensional, measuring the school on tests that value shallow rather than deep learning and failing to appreciate the complexity of the school. It is both desirable and feasible to look at longer-term development and shorter-term targets as complementary rather than conflicting strategies. To examine the key features of building longer-term sustainability, I outline nine key factors. These are: (1) measuring outcomes and not just outputs, (2) balancing short- and long-term objectives, (3) thinking in terms of processes not plans – the way that leaders involve their colleagues is more important than the documents that they write – (4) having a passion for continued improvement and development, (5) developing personal humility and professional will as a means of building long-term leadership capacity, (6) practising strategic timing and strategic abandonment, (7) building capacity and creating involvement, (8) developing strategic measures of success and (9) building in sustainability.

I hope that these factors will start a dialogue and develop perspectives on how we can, in the educational community, support schools as they try to build sustainable learning organizations. Core moral values and a discussion of the purpose of education cannot be separated from the 'how' of operating the school; they must underpin it. The deep values of success for all and being members of a caring community are ideals that need sustaining just as much as the fabric of the school.

In Chapter 2 Brian Caldwell writes about sustaining exhilarating leadership. Although I had read and admired his work before then, I first met Brian 16 years ago in San Francisco at an American Educational Research Association (AERA) conference. Since then I have been able to draw on his ideas and insights to underpin much of my own work and this support has been very significant in my professional development. It is an honour to be a Professorial Fellow with Brian at the University of Melbourne. Brian draws on research with headteachers to ask three key questions:

1. What aspects of your work as leader are exhilarating?
2. What aspects of your work as leader are boring, depressing, discouraging or dispiriting?
3. What actions by you or others would make your work as leader more exhilarating and less boring, depressing, discouraging or dispiriting?

For each of the first two questions, Brian draws out the key factors that either make work exhilarating for headteachers or those that make work discouraging or dispiriting. He then takes the significant step in building sustainable leadership by what he calls 'shifting the balance to exhilaration' where he takes the 'leadership voices' of headteachers in his research to establish six factors that would build in sustainable success.

These focus around personal factors, professional factors, resource factors, autonomy, community, recognition and networking. To add to his own analysis of the situation, Brian draws on the expert views of three leading educationalists to unpack the importance of exhilarating leadership. In the final section Brian develops a critique of the implications for policy and practice in education.

Andy Hargreaves and Dean Fink have become a significant writing team that challenges current orthodoxies. I have had the privilege of working with both of them for over a decade and have drawn on their ideas as a key element in my professional life. In Chapter 3 Andy and Dean develop their earlier work on sustainable leadership by using three new concepts of energy restraint, energy renewal and energy release. With energy restraint they consider five factors that are working against sustainable leadership and four factors that could alleviate the problem. In considering energy renewal the authors argue passionately for the building of trust, confidence and happiness as a combination that is the source of human resourcefulness. The final part of their framework is that of energy release. They see that releasing the energy for productive educational change can only be achieved through the 'teacher as the igniting force' which is able to 'unlock students' energy'. However, it is necessary to release the vast potential energy of our teachers as a precursor of the process. They conclude: '*Improved achievement needs to renew the energy of the people responsible for securing it* through high-trust, confidence-building change principles that are undertaken *by* schools, *with* schools in transparent processes of committed improvement, that connect short-term success in immediate action to long-term transformations in teaching and learning.'

Chris Day has developed an enviable reputation as a researcher and I was delighted to work with him as a Visiting Professor at the University of Nottingham. Chris and Michèle Schmidt report on a research project that they have undertaken on successful and sustainable leadership in UK schools. Early in Chapter 4 they quote Michael Fullan, a quotation that is worth replication: '*You cannot move substantially towards sustainability in the absence of widely shared moral purpose*. The reason is that sustainability depends on the distributed effort of people at all levels of the system, and meeting the goals of moral purpose produces commitment throughout the system' (Fullan, 2005: 87). In building resilient leaders that are driven by moral purpose Chris and Michèle outline five major categories for their research:

1. Care, consultation and responsibility.
2. Justice and advocacy: the courage of conviction.
3. Being learning- and learner-focused.
4. Activist leadership.
5. Sustaining resilience.

They consider that their research,

> *although small scale, suggests that despite pressures from multiple policy implementation accountabilities, social disadvantage and changing expectations, successful headteachers who demonstrate resilient leadership are those whose values cause them to place as much emphasis upon people and processes as they do upon product ... Improvement for headteachers in this research was broadly rather than narrowly defined. It included the academic achievement of the pupils against quantitative measures (for example, results of national tests and examinations) and qualitative indicators (esteem, relationships, expectations, behaviour, participation, engagement with learning). These heads demonstrated a clear and abiding concern for learning, care, justice.*

In Chapter 5 Terry Deal provides a thought provoking commentary on the 'sustainability of the status quo'. Terry is a remarkable writer, consultant and practitioner in the education and the business world in the field of organizational culture. His reflections on organizational culture are unique and compelling. Spending some time with him in his home overlooking a vineyard and the mountains in San Luis Obispo in California does allow detached reflection! Terry argues that most educational reform imposed from outside fails to use the talents and skills of the staff in organizations and fails to be fully effective because of this. As a result, he looks at the remarkable staying power of the established way of doing things and alternative approaches to sustaining organizational change. He concludes with an interesting analysis:

> *There are some interesting explanations for this remarkable staying power which this chapter attempted to highlight. To the extent that we can accept plausible reasons for maintaining things as they are we can capture the craft knowledge of those who labour in the trenches year after year. They know a lot more than we think they do.*

> *The real challenge is how to encourage local talent to draw upon lessons they have learned and harnessing it to renew and revitalize education. An acupuncturist assumes energy in the human body and then uses needles to reduce blocks and stimulate the energy flow. That notion may be more apt than we think in our efforts to improve schools from within rather than trying to reform them from outside.*

This is very powerful insight.

Ken Leithwood has established himself as one of the pre-eminent scholars in educational leadership today. I have been delighted to have his perceptive contribution to this and other publications that I have organized. Ken, working with Scott Bauer and Brian Riedlinger, reports in Chapter 6 on research from the USA on developing and sustaining school principals. They draw together 10 lessons on how to develop a framework for this. The lessons are:

1. Dramatic individual change is possible.
2. One good experience can 'jump start' the adoption of a continuous learning ethos.
3. Ongoing support is needed if leaders are to influence student learning.
4. Training should encompass the team as well as the individual principal.
5. Direct, practical help in data-driven decision-making is especially critical in the current policy environment.
6. Practise what you preach (and be nice).
7. A little bit of money goes a long way.
8. For a long-term impact, build a community of leaders.
9. Use the community of leaders to retain successful leaders.
10. Use inspiring leadership models to recruit new leaders.

As the authors unpack each of these lessons they combine a clear analysis with practical leadership advice that will enable readers to benchmark their own leadership development practices in their schools to ensure that they are sustainable.

How do we build in sustainability? In Chapter 7 Michael Fullan and Lyn Sharratt take a research project and tease out the key factors that make change and development sustainable and the lessons for leadership. I first met Michael Fullan when we both addressed the New Zealand Principals Conference in Sky Harbour Casino in Auckland. Not only was his address inspiring, but his blackjack was impressive as well!

This piece of writing with his colleague Lyn Sharratt is equally impressive. They take a major curriculum initiative, that of developing literacy, and build four propositions that drive sustainable success. These are:

Proposition One:	Sustainability is not about prolonging specific innovations, but rather it is about establishing the conditions for continuous student improvement.
Proposition Two:	Sustainability is not possible unless school leaders and system leaders are working on the same agenda.
Proposition Three:	Proposition Two notwithstanding, sustainability is not furthered by school and system leaders simply agreeing on the direction of the reform. Rather, agreement is continually tested and extended by leaders at both school and system levels putting pressure on each other. Sustainability is a two-way or multi-way street.
Proposition Four:	We have a fair idea about what makes for sustainability within one district under conditions of stable leadership over a five or more year period, but we still do not know how sustainability fares when district leadership changes, or when state leadership changes direction.

These are powerful concepts and frameworks that make this chapter a valuable response.

In Chapter 8 Guilbert (Gib) Hentschke's is one of the three final chapters that take alternative perspectives to examine sustainability. I first visited the University of Southern California to meet Gib in 1990 and, ever since, his ability to conceptualize the relationship of business thinking to educational leadership has made an outstanding contribution to my thinking. Gib correctly identifies the increasing impact of market forces in education. He suggests that leadership and organizational behaviour is a feature of the organizational environment. Given that schools are gravitating to that market environment, then an examination of sustainability in market environments gives clues as to the future of schools and their leadership. He articulates the view that most businesses have not sustained themselves and, indeed, 'creative destruction' is a term that has come into the language. In this vein he makes an incisive conclusion to his chapter:

> *While sustainability may well provide a useful normative framework for improving education, its utility as a descriptive framework will likely be lessened as education gravitates more into a market environment. Large-scale studies of the continuity of (mostly very large, publicly traded, multinational) for-profit businesses provide significant descriptive understandings of the factors which enable a relatively small number of them to outlast their competitors, making the point that most do not. Although schooling is moving towards that market environment, it will likely be a very long time before the environment of the compulsory schooling industry could conceivably reflect the environment of those corporations.*

Nonetheless, educators and their organizations will more frequently face some of the commonplace realities associated with organizational life in a market environment. Perhaps the more intriguing question at this point is, however, whether sustainability as a prized attribute and goal for education leaders and the institutions within which they labour will ever be replaced with the normative goals such as flexibility, responsiveness, adaptability, short time to market, innovative and productive.

David Hopkins brings a unique set of skills as someone who is a leading academic, a principal adviser to Secretaries of State at the DfES and a mountain guide! Although I have known David for over a decade, I have over the last two years been able to work with him, as a Visiting Professor, on his project to build an international leadership and learning framework through his HSBC and iNET Chair at the Institute of Education in London. In Chapter 9, building on his internationally renowned work on school improvement, David puts forward the powerful moral leadership point that you cannot sustain individual schools at the expense of others. I believe that you cannot be a successful school leader if the school next door to you is failing. We need to take responsibility collectively for schools in our area. David builds a case for system leaders in education to take responsibility and action to sustain high-quality education. His chapter on system leadership focuses on system leaders, highlighting four dimensions, those of: (1) personalised learning, (2) professional teaching, (3) networks and collaboration and (4) intelligent accountability. He sees system leadership as the catalyst for systemic change. To use his words

At its heart, therefore, system leadership is about improving the deployment and development of our best leadership resources, in terms of both:

- *greater productivity: with successful leaders using their own and their staff's knowledge and skills to improve other schools; and,*
- *social justice: by using our most capable leaders to help deliver a national system in which every child has the opportunity to achieve their full potential.*

The final chapter, Chapter 10, takes the perspective of sustaining leadership by a coherent process of leadership succession, rather than of sustaining the individual leader. Geoff Southworth is well known as a researcher and more recently as Deputy Director of the National College for School Leadership. In this latter role he is charged with addressing the looming shortage of headteachers in the UK. Geoff outlines three causes of the shortfall. First, demographics mean that a large number of current headteachers are reaching retirement at the same time. Second, the post of headteacher is not always perceived as desirable by those in middle and senior leadership roles and, third, recruitment to headship is inadequate. In a response to this challenge, Geoff outlines five ways in which capacity might be built. First, there is an urgent need to increase the supply and flow of those ready to become headteachers. This can be addressed by working with those in middle and senior roles to see leadership as a desirable role. Second, there is a need to address how headship is perceived and to link this to supporting headteachers more effectively in their role. Third, key to the first two points is the need to remodel headship and see it in a number of guises from executive headship to shared headship. Fourth, increasing support is needed, especially for new heads, in terms of improved mentoring and other strategies. Finally, leadership learning communities must be developed in order to enhance a pool of talent. This is a perceptive chapter in moving on to sustain the flow of leaders.

Conclusion

It has been a delightful experience for me working with such an outstanding group of educationalists. My learning journey has been immeasurably enriched by their ideas and contributions. I thank them all. It has been significant that many of them use the work of Jim Collins (2001), *Good to Great*. Sustainability is not about maintaining what we do but moving on in a way that supports and values leadership communities. In that context I hope that the leaders who read this book will be inspired by the ideas and that this will enable them to continue on the 'good to great' journey for their school.

References

Collins, J. (2001) *Good to Great*. London: Random House Business Books.

Fullan, M. (2005) *Leadership and Sustainability: System Thinkers in Action*. Thousand Oaks, CA: Corwin Press; Toronto: Ontario Principals Council.

Hargreaves, A. and Fink, D. (2006) *Sustainable Leadership*. San Francisco, CA: Jossey-Bass.

Chapter 1

Sustainable leadership

Brent Davies

The emphasis on short-term accountability measures has often prioritized the use of short-term management strategies to meet test and Office for Standards in Education (Ofsted) measures. However, the longer-term sustainable development of the school requires leadership that is embedded in a culture focused on moral purpose and the educational success of all students. Moving away from short-termism to more fundamental consideration of sustainable leadership is the focus of this chapter. Sustainable leadership can be considered to be made up of:

> *the key factors that underpin the longer-term development of the school. It builds a leadership culture based on moral purpose which provides success that is accessible to all.*

A useful analogy is that of a tree where the roots (sustainable leadership) underpin all the school's activities.

While it would be naive or unrealistic to suggest that school leaders do not have to respond to short-term accountability targets and managerial imperatives, it is important that these responses are set against sustainable leadership factors. Just as the fellowship of the nine set out in *The Lord of the Rings* (Tolkien, 1991: 268) to battle with the forces of Mordor, so I propose nine sustainable leadership factors that should be developed and deployed to battle with the dangers of managerial short-termism! These factors have been drawn from recent research of sustainable and strategically successful schools.

1. Outcomes not just outputs

The importance of deep learning outcomes and not just short-term test outputs is the first underlying principle of sustainable leadership. While test scores in terms of standard assessment tasks (SATs) results and General Certificate of Secondary Education (GCSE) are important indicators, they are just that: indicators. They do not sum up the school or provide a holistic view of where the school is going. The downside of output measures is that schools reorientate their approaches to achieve yet higher and higher results. The danger of this is that education merely becomes an information transmission system that the recipients replicate in test conditions. External testing should provide a floor to standards and not be the ceiling. What is critical is that 16-year-olds enjoy reading, they have a positive view of school, they engage in problem-solving in a creative way with their peers; these are the outcomes of education. These skills are not necessarily measured by GCSE results! What we need is leadership that, while addressing accountability demands, focuses on deep learning and fundamental educational outcomes and values. This often takes courage in an era where the culture of working harder and harder to improve pass rates often ignores the real purpose of education.

The nature of learning poses a major strategic challenge to schools because of the attributes of short-term accountability and standards frameworks. If we were to think of learning moving from shallow learning to complex learning and then to deep learning we could characterize this as in Figure 1.1:

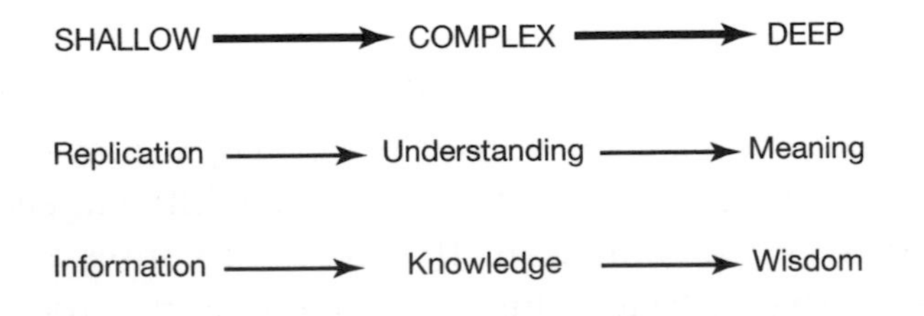

Figure 1.1 *Deep learning*

The challenge for schools is that the short-term accountability demands tend to require the replication of information with some attributes of complex learning, but assess little of the learning on the complex to deep end of the spectrum. Deep learning requires that we develop in children both the love of learning itself and some understanding of the meaning of complex knowledge so that they can exercise wisdom to make informed choices in their lives. I would argue that high-level outputs can be achieved by deep learning and the outcomes associated with it. However, it has to be a conscious choice by leaders to develop sustainable learning approaches.

In essence, sustainable leadership is inextricably linked to deep learning. It is the framework that allows deep learning to develop. It has at its core a set of beliefs about learning allied to personal and professional courage that allows those beliefs to be implemented and flourish. The slavish response to short-term demands can destroy the ability to build long-term capacity. A balance has to be struck where deep learning structures and approaches are developed that can deliver measurable outputs but those outputs are seen as indicators of deeper learning and abilities and not as ends in themselves. Sustainable leadership sets as its target the building of a culture of learning in the school that establishes a framework that can move the child's understanding from the shallow through the complex to deep learning.

2. Balancing short- and long-term objectives

There is an assumption that strategy is about the long term and is incompatible with short-term objectives. This, I believe, is inappropriate for a number of reasons. The situation should not be seen as an either/or position. It is of little value trying to convince parents that this year their child has not learnt to read but that 'we have plans in place that may remedy the situation in the next year or two'. Most children's experience is short term in relation to what they do this week, this month or what they achieve this year, and which class they are in next year. Success in the short term is an important factor in their lives, as is success in the long term.

There are some basic things that an education system should provide for children. It should provide them with definable learning achievements that allow them to function and prosper in society. Where children are not making the progress we expected for them, they need extra support and educational input to help them realize their potential. This, by necessity, requires regular review against benchmarks. Thus Hargreaves and Fink's disdain for 'imposed short-term achievement targets' (2006: 253) is difficult to support. However, I recognize the danger of seeing short-term benchmarks as the outcomes and not indicators of progress. Indeed, if annual tests were seen as diagnostic and generated learning plans for children rather than outcome scores for schools, the problem of testing may be solved overnight. What needs to be done is that the short term should not be seen as separate from the long term or as being in conflict with it, but as part of a holistic framework where short-term assessments are seen to guides on the long-term journey.

This balanced view of the short-term and long-term perspective was shown in Figure 1.1. It is of little use having a long-term strategic plan if it ignores the short term, as we see in Figure 1.2. The result in the bottom-right quadrant will be that short-term crises will prevent the long term ever being achieved. Similarly, merely operating on a short-term perspective, the top-left quadrant, will prevent long-term sustainability ever being achieved. What is needed is a balance between the short and long term as witnessed in the quadrant at the top right.

Operational processes and planning **(SDP and target setting)**			
	Effective	Functionally successful in the short term but not sustainable long term	Successful and sustainable in both the short term and long term
	Ineffective	Failure inevitable both in the short and long terms	Short-term crises will prevent longer-term sustainability
		Ineffective	**Effective**
		Strategic processes and approaches	

Figure 1.2 *Short-term viability and long-term sustainability (based on Davies, B.J., 2004)*

The challenge for headteachers is to be both leaders and managers. Vision that cannot be translated into action has no impact. Similarly, continuing to manage the now without change and development is not building capacity for the future. We need to balance both the long- and the short-term approaches. Derek Wise, headteacher of Cramlington High School, has a delightful expression, describing himself as 'pragmatopian'. By this he means that he has his head in the clouds to see the future (utopian) but is pragmatic enough to have his feet on the ground to make sure everything is working in the short term. This balancing of the short term and the long term is a key factor in a sustainable leadership approach.

3. Processes not plans

Why is the idea of process so important? John Novak from Canada, in his work on invitational leadership (Novak, 2002), contrasts the 'done with' approach to the 'done to' approach which often leaves the staff 'done in'. The reason that strategically focused schools spend a great deal of time and effort on processes to involve staff is that involvement:

- allows a wider range of talented people to contribute;
- draws on expertise and experience;
- builds consensus and agreement;
- builds transparency and understanding;
- articulates challenges and invites solutions.

Schools are living systems made up of people who can choose to contribute or not contribute, or choose to be positive to change or negative to change. Which choices they take can be influenced by the strategic leaders in the school. Strategic change takes time and effort, and leaders often report to me that they underestimate the time and effort needed. The approach should be to work with the 'willing' to start the strategic conversations, build ideas and visions, and then slowly draw the reluctant members on the staff to join in. Schools are a network of individuals linked together through a series of interconnections largely based on conversation. This is powerfully illustrated by Van der Heijden (1996: 273): 'Often much more important is the informal learning activity consisting of unscheduled discussions, debate and conversation about strategic questions that goes on continuously at all levels in the organisation.'

What is required to create an effective individual and institutional conversation? The first way is for leaders to model behaviour. How do they interact with colleagues on a day-to-day basis? Do they just react to the current demands or do they engage people in thinking and talking about the future? Leaders need to take the informal opportunities to interact with others both to discuss the problems of the present, but also to engage in a dialogue about the challenges of the future. The conversation over coffee or walking to the car park can be just as important as more formal meetings. It is also necessary to work with other leaders in the school to encourage them to do likewise so that the culture in the school builds reflection and dialogue.

How we structure meetings has a critical impact on the ability to engage in strategic conversations. When I meet successful leaders in the course of my research, I find that their schools separate out strategic and operational matters, and that they structure separate meetings to deal with those items. This gives the formal forum to deal with discussions and conversations to run alongside the informal discussions. Davies (2006) talks about articulating a vision and engaging in conversations with colleagues, as a means to build participation and motivation to enhance strategic capacity in the school. The critical test of strategy is to ask a teacher what they are doing in their classroom this week that has been driven by the school plan. If they cannot articulate a view then it is likely that the plan is on a shelf in the headteacher's office and used only for external evaluation. What should happen is that, because they have been part of the process, staff can articulate the four or five major development themes of the school.

4. Passion

Passion is often seen in terms of a passion for social justice, passion for learning, passion to make a difference. It is the passion to make a difference that turns beliefs into reality and is the mark of sustainable leadership. Beliefs are statements or views that help us set our personal views and experiences into context. My own passion for education would be based on the fact that:

- I believe every child can achieve;
- I believe every child will achieve;
- I believe that all children are entitled to high quality education;
- I believe that we collectively and individually can make a difference to children's learning.

Passion works on the emotional side of leadership. Bolman and Deal (1995: 12), in their inspirational book *Leading with Soul* emphasize the emotional side of leadership: 'Heart, hope and faith, rooted in soul and spirit, are necessary for today's managers to become tomorrow's leaders, for today's sterile bureaucracies to become tomorrow's communities of meaning'.

Passion must be the driving force that moves vision into action. Bennis and Nanus (1985: 92–3) argue that the creation of a sense of meaning is one of the distinguishing features of leadership:

> *the leader operates on the emotional and spiritual resources of the organisation, on its values, commitment, and aspirations ... Leaders often inspire their followers to high levels of achievement by showing them how their work contributes to worthwhile ends. It is an emotional appeal to some of the most fundamental of human needs – the need to be important, to make a difference, to feel useful, to be part of a successful and worthwhile enterprise.*

Sustainable leadership establishes a set of values and purposes that underpin the educational process in the school. Most significantly it is the individual passion and commitment of the leader that drives the values and purposes into reality. Values without implementation do little for the school. It is in the tackling of difficult challenges to change and improve, often by confronting unacceptable practices, that passionate leaders show their educational values.

What skills does sustainable leadership require to translate passion into reality? Deal and Peterson (1999: 87) see that school leaders take on eight major symbolic roles:

1. Historian – understanding where the school has come from and why it behaves currently as it does.
2. Anthropological sleuth – seeks to understand the current set of norms, values and beliefs that define the current culture.
3. Visionary – works with others to define a deeply value-focused picture of the future for the school.
4. Symbolic – affirms values through dress, behaviour, attention and routines.
5. Potter – shapes and is shaped by the school's heroes, rituals, traditions, ceremonies, symbols; brings in staff who share core values.
6. Poet – uses language to reinforce values and sustains the school's best image of itself.
7. Actor – improvises in the school's inevitable dramas, comedies and tragedies.
8. Healer – oversees transitions and changes in the life of the school; heals wounds of conflict and loss.

As we saw at the start of this section, a passion for social justice, learning and, most importantly, to make a difference will only become meaningful if the leader develops the skills to get into the deep underlying culture of the school to effect deep-rooted change.

5. Personal humility and professional will

We can make use of the ideas of an influential writer in the leadership field here. Jim Collins, in his book *Good to Great* (2001), outlines a number of factors that allow good companies to become great companies over a significant period of time. The central factor is that of leadership and in particular what he calls Level 5 leadership. In reporting his research on leadership in his book he identifies that levels of leadership work through five stages of: highly capable individual, contributing team member, competent manager, effective leader and executive. The challenge is to move from Level 4 leaders who are highly effective but see themselves as the sole factor in success and see the 'I' of achievement as more important than the 'we' of the organization. They often leave the organization without effective leaders to succeed them. Level 5 leaders 'channel their ego needs away from themselves and into the larger goal of building a great company. It's not that Level 5 leaders have no ego or self-interest. Indeed, they are incredibly ambitious – *but their ambition is first and foremost for the institution, not for themselves*' (Collins, 2001: 21; original emphasis). Collins summarizes two sides of leaders who have been successful in the long term: professional will and the personal quality of humility that goes with it. He demonstrates the dimensions of these categories in Figure 1.3.

Professional Will	Personal Humility
Creates superb results, a clear catalyst in the transition from good to great.	Demonstrates a compelling modesty, shunning public adulation; never boastful.
Demonstrates an unwavering resolve to do whatever must be done to produce the best long-term results, no matter how difficult.	Acts with quiet, calm determination; relies principally on inspired standards, not inspiring charisma, to motivate.
Sets the standard of building an enduring great company; will settle for nothing less.	Channels ambition into the company, not the self; sets up successors for even greater success in the next generation.
Looks in the mirror, not out the window, to apportion responsibility for poor results, never blaming other people, external factors, or bad luck.	Looks out the window, not in the mirror, to apportion credit for the success of the company – to other people, external factors, and good luck.

Figure 1.3 *Characteristics of successful leaders (Collins, 2001: 36 from* Good to Great *© 2001 by Jim Collins. Reprinted with permission from Jim Collins)*

In my research, the leaders that have emerged as being successful over the longer term are those that have a passion for children and their learning, and see the school as the way to facilitate this. They talk of 'our' school and what 'we' are doing, and have the determination to take on difficult decisions for themselves to improve the organization. Indeed, challenging poor performance is a characteristic of the professional will of transformational leaders. They are transformational leaders and not transactional leaders. But, most significantly, they have been modest about their role and credit the team they have built. Sustainable leadership develops these attributes throughout the wider staffing group that undertakes leadership roles in the school.

6. Strategic timing and strategic abandonment

A key question for sustainable leadership is when to make changes and what to give up to make space for the new activity. The leadership challenge of *when* to make a significant strategic change is as critical to success as choosing what strategic change to make. The issue of timing can rest on leadership intuition (Parikh, 1994) as much as on rational analysis. When individuals in the school are ready for change, when the school needs the change, and when the external constraints and conditions force the change, all have to be balanced one against the other. Such judgement is manifested in not only *knowing what* and *knowing how* but also *knowing when* (Boal and Hooijberg, 2001) and, as important, knowing *what not to do* (Kaplan and Norton, 2001). Therefore we could add to this list knowing *what to give up or abandon* in order to create capacity to undertake the new activity.

There is a useful distinction between 'Chronos' time and 'Kairos' time (Bartunek and Necochea, 2000). The former is the normal ticking of the clock and the passage of time; the latter points to those intense moments in time when critical actions and decisions take place. There are critical points at which strategic leaders can make successful interventions. Leaders in my research projects have commented to me: 'You have to pick the right moment but also be careful that you don't wait for every single detail to be in place'; and 'I learnt very early on to spend as much time on *how* you implement as to *what* you implement and I spend a lot of time on what is the best way to do it'.

In addition to the critical skill of strategic timing is that of strategic abandonment. If a school adopts a new way of doing things or adopts a new strategic priority, how that fits into an already crowded agenda has to be considered. The result is that leaders have to downgrade the importance or abandon existing strategies, not because they are wrong in themselves, but they have become less significant in comparison to new factors. As one school leader in my research said to me:

> *I see abandonment as being two different issues. One is the abandonment of things that are not working and actually taking people's time and energy. That's easy to do. The other side of it was to actually say OK this is working well and we are really comfortable with it and it is getting the results we want, but actually there is another strategy here that takes us onto the next stage but we can't run them both together. This has to be suspended or abandoned in order to give the other one time to grow.*

This concept of strategic abandonment is a very powerful one. The difficult aspect of strategic abandonment occurs where the school has to give up acceptable current practice to make capacity available for future improved practice. Thus sustainable leadership is working toward sustainable change and development by judging the effective time to make a change and creating the capacity to undertake that change by abandoning other activities.

7. Building capacity and creating involvement

A key challenge for sustainable leadership is getting the right team and establishing the leadership capacity for the school. Jim Collins (2001: 13) argues persuasively:

> *'First Who ... Then What'. We expected that good-to-great leaders would begin by setting a new vision and strategy. We found instead that they first got the right people on the bus, the wrong people off the bus, and the right people in the right seats – and then figured out where to drive it. The old adage 'People are your most important asset' turns out to be wrong. People are not your most important asset. The right people are.*

The message from this example is the right people in the right posts is key. This is not always that straightforward in the education sector. However, leaders who transform their schools, challenge poor or inappropriate performance and move staff. Sustainable leaders face this difficult challenge. Once this structural challenge has been met the second challenge is to involve all the staff in the school. Indeed we need to think not just of teaching staff but all staff in the school as well as students and governors. My research suggests that strategic conversations play a major role in this.

If we assume that schools are made up of different individuals who think about their role and the nature of the school in different ways, it may also be reasonable to assume that the school is not just a collection of these views but that, through the interaction of these individuals, a unique and powerful perspective can be developed to enhance the school. Schools are a network of individuals linked together through a series of interconnections largely based on conversation. How leaders encourage and develop both formal and informal conversations within the school is critical in:

- establishing a common vocabulary;
- understanding how individuals could make things happen;
- consensus building;
- outlining individual visions;
- building reflection;
- keeping everyone involved;
- carrying everyone forward.

This can be seen diagrammatically in Figure 1.4.

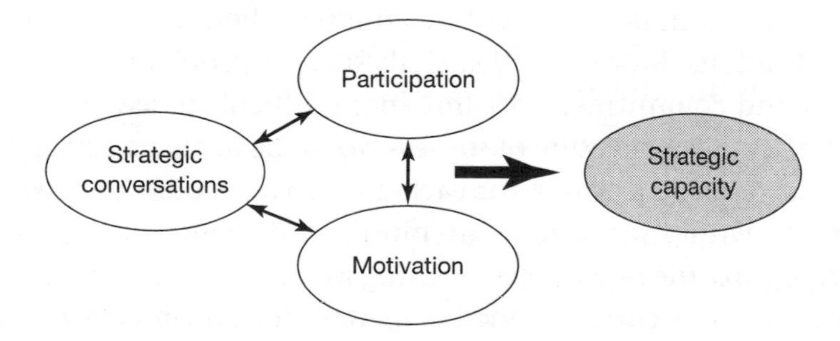

Figure 1.4 *Strategic conversations and strategic capacity*

Strategic conversations are conversations that move away from the day-to-day operational matters and move on to the fundamental discussions of the nature and direction of the school. Sustainable leadership focuses on developing these conversations.

8. Developing strategic measures of success

What would a sustainable strategically focused school look like? How would it know if it was successful in five or seven years' time? One of the ways of answering these two questions would be that a strategically focused school would have established strategic measures of success. In setting success criteria, the temptation could be to extend some of the short-term measures of success that are currently used in the league-table culture. However, this would commit two errors. One would be the use of measures of 'shallow' learning, those of easily replicable knowledge, rather than profound or deep learning. The second would be that this approach would be one of planning forward, not utilizing the idea of planning backwards from a future success target. Another challenge is that of measurement. The standard maxim that we 'value what we can measure' rather than 'we measure what we value' is a useful starting point here. It draws into the debate the balance between qualitative and quantitative measures. Results of responses to standardized tests can be reported in a relatively straightforward way. While such results can be indicative of underlying ability, they are only 'indicative'; they do not define deep understanding, motivation to learn or love of the subject area. Other more complex learning, such as social learning, can be witnessed by children's behaviour to each other or towards adults. More complex skills such as problem-solving, determination and commitment became more difficult to assess.

The core strategic measure of success would be to create active involvement in sustainable learning for each child. This would start with valuing learning within the school community but, significantly, each child would recognize the need to see learning as an ongoing process throughout their life. The current concern in the UK, and many westernized countries, regarding the increase in obesity in children and in adults and the lack of sensible exercise and diet undertaken is a case in point. The obsession in the USA with team sports and competitive sports, and to a degree the culture of team sports in UK schools, has set up a culture of reward and success for the few and humiliation for the rest. The success criterion for secondary school sport may not be 'Did the hockey or football team win the cup?' but 'How many children are actively engaged in physical exercise five years after they have left school?' I would hazard a guess at less than a quarter and that could be an overestimate!

So strategic measures of success might be some of the following:

- Staff are reflective practitioners – they stay after school and discuss ideas with colleagues and build professional learning communities.
- There is a 'no blame culture' where individuals try new things and learn from their mistakes.
- Curriculum and learning pedagogy are seen as areas of change and development and are not set in stone.
- Collaborative cultures are established within the school and between neighbouring schools, where staff share success and failures and learn from other.
- Individuals in the school take responsibility for their roles – they take decisions rather than having decisions forced on them.
- Learning outcomes consistently improve as deep learning improves the way staff and students work at learning challenges.

The challenge for sustainable leadership is to create a series of strategic measures of success; in Steven Covey's words: 'Begin with the end in mind' (1989: 95).

9. Building in sustainability

Sustainability is all about creating an achievement culture that lasts. Sustainability is not the same as maintainability. It can be defined as:

> *the ability of individuals and schools to continue to improve to meet new challenges and complexity in a way that does not damage individuals or the wider community but builds capacity and capability to be successful in new and demanding contexts.*

Sustainable leadership seeks to move the school on from its current situation to a desired and improved future state. In doing so, it needs to ensure that the changes which are embarked on are not transitory but are embedded within the organization, and will continue as patterns of working. They should not be dependent on a single leader. Initially, the single leader may be the catalyst for the change. However, only if new strategic direction and practices are adopted by wider groups of leaders and staff in the school will they be sustainable. What general principles of sustainability can we bring to the debate about developing a strategically focused school?

Hargreaves and Fink (2006: 18) outline seven principles of sustainability; I shall use three of their perceptive headings as a means of examining what factors need to be present for strategic change to be successful and sustainable. The three factors are discussed in the following paragraphs.

First is the concept of *depth*. This means that sustainable strategic change must affect the deep and underlying principles of the school's moral purpose and its learning imperative. Sustainable change would focus on developing areas and activities that affect the life opportunities of the children it serves, and the deep learning skills and knowledge that they need to develop. It must also affect all areas of the school. The rhetoric of the values and beliefs contained in documentation of the school needs to be enacted and witnessed in the behaviour and attitudes of children to each other, the behaviour and attitudes of the staff to each other, and the interrelationships between each other. Profound strategic change that lasts must reach down to all aspects of the school's activities and behaviours.

The second concept is that of *length*. By this Hargreaves and Fink mean that strategic change lasts over time. In particular the change is fundamental and desirable, and is not dependent on a single leader. Leadership changes should enhance provision in strategically focused sustainable schools and not result in abandoning one set of practices in favour of the opposite. One primary school I work with has, over more than a decade of the introduction of the National Curriculum, resisted a single-subject approach and maintained its integrated cross-curricular topic approach, because the teachers saw that as central to their understanding of learning and their strategic purpose. It is a strategic competency of the school.

The third concept is *breadth*. This is an interesting concept because it means not only spreading new ideas across the staff and students within the school, but in other ways. It certainly means extending the strategic vision, direction and understanding of strategic change across the wider school community of parents and those in the local community. It also means building alliances for strategic change across other schools in the region to support and create a demand for change in the local educational community that will contribute to the long-term enhancement of children's learning opportunities.

Sustainable leadership examines how to embed change at the start of the process and not as an afterthought after initial implementation.

Conclusion

The challenges outlined in this chapter are focused on the need to build enduring capacity to provide successful learning and educational opportunities for children. Short-term measures of success are important but they are just that, short-term. Sustainable leadership sees those short-term measures as indicators and balances them with the need to build long-term capacity. Leaders are the individuals charged with linking the current realities to an improved and sustainable educational future. Reflecting on the nine points should assist leaders build the capacity to achieve long-term success by embedding sustainable leadership in their schools.

References

Bartunek, J.M. and Necochea, R. (2000) 'Old insights and new times', *Journal of Management Inquiry*, 9(2): 103–13.

Bennis, W. and Nanus, B. (1985) *Leaders*. New York: Harper and Row.

Boal, K.B. and Hooijberg, R. (2001) 'Strategic leadership research; moving on', *Leadership Quarterly*, 11(4): 515–49.

Bolman, L. and Deal, T.E. (1995) *Leading with Soul*. San Francisco, CA: Jossey-Bass.

Collins, J. (2001) *Good to Great*. London: Random House Business Books.

Covey, S. (1989) *The 7 Habits of Highly Effective People*. New York: Simon and Schuster.

Davies, B. (2006) *Leading the Strategically Focused School*. London: Paul Chapman Publishing.

Davies, B.J (2004) *An investigation into the Development of a Strategically Focused Primary School*. EdD Thesis, University of Hull.

Deal, T. and Peterson, K.D. (1999) *Shaping School Culture*. San Francisco, CA: Jossey-Bass.

Hargreaves, A. and Fink, D. (2006) *Sustainable Leadership*. San Francisco, CA: Jossey-Bass/John Wiley and Sons.

Kaplan, R.S. and Norton, D.P. (2001) *The Strategy-Focused Organization*. Boston, MA: Harvard Business School.

Novak, J. (2002) *Inviting Educational Leadership*. London: Pearson Education.

Parikh, J. (1994) *Intuition – The New Frontier of Management*. Oxford: Blackwell.

Tolkien, J.R.R. (1991) *The Lord of the Rings*. London: HarperCollins.

Van der Heijden, K. (1996) *Scenarios – The Art of Strategic Conversation*. New York: Wiley.

Chapter 2

Sustaining exhilarating leadership

Brian J. Caldwell

Attracting and sustaining appointments to the position of principal (headteacher) is a matter of concern in many countries. Also of concern is the level of achievement of students, in absolute terms but also as far as disparities in levels of success among different categories of student are concerned. The first concern may in fact be a consequence of the second, as policy-makers respond to the student achievement issue by demanding more of the principal, to the point that the role is no longer sustainable. Sustainability in leadership is quite properly at centre stage among issues in education at this time (Davies, 2006; Fullan, 2005; Hargreaves and Fink, 2006).

It is astonishing under these circumstances that some leaders find their work to be exhilarating. It is the purpose of this chapter to explore the conditions under which leadership can be experienced in this way. The findings will challenge many of the orthodoxies about schools and school systems and the manner in which they are led.

The crisis in leadership

Evidence of a crisis in school leadership may be found in surveys of school principals, either of their views about the role or, in simple statistical terms, about the number of vacancies and the paucity of applicants. In Victoria, *The Privilege and the Price* (Department of Education and Training, 2004) reported on workload in government (public) schools and its impact on the health and well-being of the principal class. On workload, for example, the number of hours per week for principals in Victoria was similar to that for headteachers in England, as reported in a survey at about the same time, being about 60 hours per week. In both places, this is well above the average of leaders and managers in other professional fields in several European nations (about 45 hours per week). The report contained disturbing evidence of the impact on the emotional and physical well-being of principals.

Even more disturbing is the evidence from England about the number of vacancies and the number of acting appointments to the position of headteacher. The issue is not the number of positions falling vacant each year. On average, a school seeks a new head once every seven years, which means about 14 per cent of schools advertise each year. The number of schools advertising in 2005 was 12 per cent. Of deep concern is that more than one-third of schools were not able to make an appointment after the initial advertisement. Education Data Surveys (EDS) reported that re-advertisement reached record levels. Education Data Surveys' John Howson suggested that: 'the 2005 results are alarming, especially for secondary schools. In all the time I have been conducting this survey, I cannot recall the problem being this bad'. The seriousness of the situation is affirmed in a report of the National Audit Office (NAO) that blamed the shortage of headteachers for holding back progress in the most challenged schools (Smithers, 2006).

The interim report of a two-year study conducted by the National Association of Head Teachers (NAHT), the Eastern Leadership Centre (ELC), the University of Cambridge, the National College for School Leadership (NCSL) and the Hay Group (NAHT et al., 2005) found that 'the number of quality candidates to choose from is often seen as too small or nonexistent'. It drew attention to the fact that headteacher salaries had risen on average by 34 per cent between 1998 and 2003. Salaries exceed £100,000 per annum for heads of secondary schools in London; a level likely to make them the highest paid principals of public schools in the world. The report canvassed a range of good practices in recruitment, drawing on approaches from England and other countries. At the same time, it acknowledged that recruitment and appointment of headteachers is an international concern.

Setting the scene

As shall be demonstrated in the pages that follow, leadership can be exhilarating in all senses of the word, as reflected in the synonyms provided by *Roget's New Millennium Thesaurus*: animating, bracing, breathtaking, electric, elevating, enlivening, exalting, exciting, eye-popping, gladdening, inspiring, intoxicating, invigorating, quickening, rousing, stimulating, stirring, thrilling, uplifting, vitalizing. The antonyms of exhilarating from the same source are boring, depressing, discouraging, dispiriting. Leaders who are exhilarated may encounter such moments but they have found ways to work around them or, if they cannot do so, their sense of exhilaration overrides them. They acknowledge that there are challenges to be addressed and problems to be overcome but dealing with them is an aspect of their work they find exhilarating.

This chapter is about such leaders. It explores the circumstances under which the balance can be changed to achieve that exhilaration. It exhorts policy-makers to create an environment in which this can occur without giving any quarter on an agenda for transformation, that is, change that ensures high levels of achievement for all students in all settings, especially under challenging circumstances, thus contributing to the well-being of the individual and the nation.

Exhilaration in leadership was reported in the third of a series of three publications. In *Re-imagining the Self-Managing School* (Caldwell, 2004) it was demonstrated how the best practice of self-management had far outstripped its initial conception. Self-management, or school-based management, refers to decentralization to the school level of authority and responsibility to make decisions on significant matters within a centrally determined framework of goals, policies, curriculum, standards and accountabilities. It was found that a remarkable change was under way and this was the subject of nine workshops over nine weeks from February to May 2005 in Australia (1), Chile (2), England (5) and New Zealand (1). Conducting such workshops was itself an exhilarating experience and the outcomes were reported in *The New Enterprise Logic of Schools* (Caldwell, 2005). The concept of 'new enterprise logic' was derived from the work of Zuboff and Maxmin (2004). The main features of the new enterprise logic of schools are:

1. The student is the most important unit of organization – not the classroom, not the school and not the school system.
2. Schools cannot achieve expectations for transformation by acting alone or operating in a line of support from the centre of a school system to the level of the school, classroom or student. The success of a school depends on its capacity to join networks to share knowledge, address problems and pool resources.

3. Leadership is distributed across schools in networks as well as within schools.
4. Networks involve a range of individuals, agencies, institutions and organizations across public and private sectors in educational and non-educational settings. Personnel and other resources are allocated to energize and sustain them.
5. New approaches to resource allocation are required under these conditions. These take account of developments in personalizing learning and the networking of expertise and support.
6. Intellectual capital and social capital are as important as other forms of capital.

In each of these nine workshops, school leaders described a transformation. One or more of the six characteristics were addressed. A striking impression was that these leaders were exhilarated, despite the challenges and the problems, even though aspects of the work were boring, depressing, discouraging or dispiriting.

Five workshops followed the publication of *The New Enterprise Logic of Schools* in June 2005. These were conducted in Queensland and Victoria from July to October 2005. The findings are presented in the pages that follow, with implications drawn for policy and practice. A more detailed account is contained in *Exhilarating Leadership* (Caldwell, 2006a). These publications were combined, updated and expanded in *Re-imagining Educational Leadership* (Caldwell, 2006b).

Leader voice

Listening to 'student voice' has been a priority in the movement to personalize learning. It is a stepping stone to addressing the first element in the new enterprise logic of schools: 'the student is the most important unit of organisation, not the classroom, not the school and not the school system'.

It seems sensible to listen to 'leader voice' if the work of school leaders is to become more exhilarating and less boring, discouraging, depressing or dispiriting. Listening to leaders and acting on what is heard may be an important stepping stone to addressing the problems of leader stress and premature departure from the ranks.

Five workshops were conducted over 12 weeks in two states of Australia. Most of the 185 participants were principals, with a range of leadership positions among those who were not. They came from a representative cross-section of schools, with most from government or state schools, and the others from non-government subsidized schools, either Catholic systemic schools or independent schools. They came from a variety of socio-economic settings. There was a balance of male and female participants.

Participants were invited to respond to three questions:

1. What aspects of your work as leader are exhilarating?
2. What aspects of your work as leader are boring, depressing, discouraging or dispiriting?
3. What actions by you or others would make your work as leader more exhilarating and less boring, depressing, discouraging or dispiriting?

Participants were given a list of synonyms for exhilarating drawn from *Roget's New Millennium Thesaurus*: animating, bracing, breathtaking, electric, elevating, enlivening, exalting, exciting, eye-popping, gladdening, inspiring, intoxicating, invigorating, quickening, rousing, stimulating, stirring, thrilling, uplifting, vitalizing. Antonyms from the same source were included in questions 2 and 3.

Participants were given five to eight minutes to respond to each question using an interactive technology that collected responses from each of 12 keyboards around the room. Groups ranged in size from three to eight. In some instances participants entered their individual responses; in others a group discussion was held and one member of the group listened and entered responses as they were generated. The atmosphere for this part of the workshop was itself exhilarating as participants generated a very large number of responses very quickly, and these were all displayed simultaneously on a large screen so that everyone could see what was unfolding. The largest number of responses generated in a five to eight minute period was 162 by the 55 participants at one workshop for question 2 – one new response on screen every three seconds, with each participant generating on average three responses.

Themes among the responses were identified by the participants as a group when all responses for each question were displayed. After the workshop, the themes were refined by the author who then placed each of the 1,413 responses in one of the 21 themes that were generated in this way – seven themes for each question. Summaries are contained in Tables 2.1, 2.2 and 2.3 and discussed below. Implications for policy and practice are drawn in the final section of the chapter.

Work that is exhilarating

Participants in the five workshops generated 509 responses to the question 'What aspects of your work as leader are exhilarating?' Responses are summarized in Table 2.1.

There are some striking features in the pattern of responses. Each of the three top-ranking themes attracted at least 20 per cent of responses, together totalling 67 per cent. Each is concerned with good outcomes. Top ranking (26 per cent) is exhilaration associated with success in a particular project, challenge, problem or grant; second ranking (21 per cent) is associated with good working relationships with and among staff; the third for experiencing and celebrating the accomplishments of students (20 per cent). The dominant pattern is therefore associated with the core purpose of schooling that can be summarized as 'success in tasks related to learning and the support of learning, characterized by fine working relationships with staff, and enjoyment that accompanies good outcomes for students'.

Table 2.1: *Aspects of work that are exhilarating*

Rank	Theme	Illustrative responses	Number	%
1	Success	Achieving success with a particular project; successfully solving a problem or meeting a challenge; realizing a vision; preparing a curriculum; winning grants and other resources for school; absence of complaints	130	26
2	Staff	Working with staff; observing staff as they address issues or adopt new practices; mentoring staff including beginning teachers; school-based research and development; dreaming together; having fun together	106	21
3	Students	Experiencing and celebrating the accomplishments of students, especially when needs are met; engaging with students	104	20

4	Personal	Personal development; passion for the moral purpose of schooling; success in the personal exercise of leadership; thinking quickly; personal reflection; receiving positive feedback; being challenged; living on the edge; never a dull moment; diversification in the work; participation in debate; experiencing a great meeting	69	14
5	Collaboration	Witnessing collaborative efforts of different stakeholders: staff, parents, students and others in community; experience in a learning community; enthusiasm of staff working together	47	9
6	Community	Working with parents and other members of the community; winning the support of the community for aspects of the school programme; seeing them understand the 'big picture'	46	9
7	Networks	Working with others in a network or cluster of schools	7	1
Total			509	100

Middle ranking (14 per cent) among the seven themes is a more personal response by leaders to the work situation, with words like passion, challenge, living on the edge, great meetings and reflection. It should be borne in mind that each participant generated on average between two and three responses to this question, so that this theme is unlikely to have been the sole response of any particular person.

The last three themes are associated more with external matters, with community mentioned in 9 per cent of responses and networks by only 1 per cent. Nine per cent referred to exhilaration experienced at being part of or witnessing the collaborative efforts of different stakeholders, conveying a sense of a learning community.

These patterns were generally the same for participants in each workshop. Where there were differences in rankings they were generally of one or two ranks only. It was not possible to discern an explanation for variations when the different locations and characteristics of respondents were taken into account. They are most likely chance variations. Most important, however, is the striking pattern of the three top-ranked themes, and some implications are drawn in the final section of the chapter.

Work that is boring, depressing, discouraging or dispiriting

Antonyms for exhilarating are boring, depressing, discouraging or dispiriting, and participants were invited to describe aspects of their work that had these characteristics. A total of 527 responses was received, slightly more than the number of responses about aspects of work that are exhilarating (509). Responses are summarized in Table 2.2.

Table 2.2 *Aspects of work that are boring, depressing, discouraging or dispiriting*

Rank	Theme	Illustrative responses	Number	%
1	Performance of staff	Staff not making an effort; resist change; blockers; use outdated pedagogy; make complaints	126	24
2	Administrative work	Filling in forms or reports or surveys, email; including those required for legal purposes; preparing timetables; unnecessary meetings; governance issues; online recruiting procedures (government schools in Victoria)	122	23
3	Lack of support	Lack of support from different levels of the system; poor understanding at higher levels of nature of schooling; unfairness or inadequacy in allocating resources to school; complexity in hierarchy or bureaucracy; lack of feedback	115	22

4	External factors	Factors outside control of school or leader including culture of blame; unmotivated or disengaged students; lack of support from parents; purposeless meetings; death of student; having to reinvent the wheel; party politics; need for marketing to maintain enrolments, imposed curriculum	81	15
5	Personal factors	Lack of time, difficulties in communication; personal judgements not suited to school context; tiredness; absence of challenge; enormity of task; workload; loneliness; tough decisions; sitting in front of computer; meetings	59	11
6	Constraints	Constraints on school in performance management; unions; work environment	23	4
7	None	One participant found no aspect of work had these characteristics	1	0
Total			527	99

As in Table 2.1, there is a striking pattern among the themes that are ranked most highly in the analysis. Each of the top three themes attracted at least 20 per cent of responses, with a narrow range of 22–24 per cent, and a total overall of 69 per cent. The top-ranked theme is described as 'performance of staff' (24 per cent) and this described the way respondents experienced the work of some of their colleagues: not making an effort, resisting or blocking change, not keeping up to date, or complaining. Second ranking was accorded to 'administrative work' (23 per cent), referring to such matters as form filling, surveys, email, unnecessary meetings and, in one workshop in Victoria, the use of online recruiting procedures. Third rank was accorded the perceived lack of support (22 per cent) from different levels of the system, lack of resources, complexity in bureaucratic arrangements, and lack of feedback.

The middle rank among themes for responses to this question is described as 'external factors' (15 per cent), being a range of matters that were perceived to be outside the control of the school. Reference was made to culture, student characteristics, party politics and imposed curriculum

It is noteworthy that 11 per cent of responses were related to perceptions of self or matters that were immediately concerned with the work of the leader. In some instances, these could well have been characterized as 'administrative tasks' but they were classified as personal in nature if the wording suggested this rather than the alternative. Included here were lack of time, problems in getting a message across, tiredness, absence of challenge, sitting in front of a computer or through meetings, loneliness and the enormity of the workload.

The sixth ranking theme was characterized as 'constraints' (4 per cent), referring to matters related to the performance management of staff, with instances cited of barriers to selection and removal of staff. There were a few references to unions and the overall work environment.

As with the responses to the first question, there were no differences in rankings among participants in the different workshops that warrant observations that could be sheeted home to differences in the characteristics of the five settings.

In general, the overarching theme is the influence of matters considered by participants to be either outside their control or due to the actions of others. Indeed, 89 per cent of responses are covered by this statement. Some might say there is a familiar pattern here. The early studies of satisfaction and dissatisfaction by researchers such as Frederick Hertzberg were sometimes criticized on the basis that it is a human response to attribute satisfaction to achievement of success (as in patterns of response to question 1) and dissatisfaction to the actions of others (as in patterns of response to question 2). However, the reader is invited to take the patterns at face value, or suspend judgement, until those for question 3 are considered. There are some surprises!

Shifting the balance to exhilaration

Question 3 was 'What actions by you or others would make your work as leader more exhilarating and less boring, depressing, discouraging or dispiriting?' The 377 responses were organized according to seven themes, as summarized in Table 2.3.

The biggest surprise, running counter to the criticism of findings of research on satisfaction and dissatisfaction reported above, is that the largest category of response reflected the view that the keys to shifting the balance to exhilaration lay in their own hands. It calls for a personal response. With 33 per cent of responses, this is the strongest theme of any for the three questions posed in the workshops. Items illustrated in Table 2.3 reveal two kinds of personal response. One refers to personal lifestyle to become more tolerant, secure a better balance in life and have fun. The second referred to the way participants carried out their work. A frequently mentioned item here was to delegate more. Others could see the benefit of mentoring and coaching and seeking greater clarity in their role. There are important implications here, and these are taken up in the final section of the chapter.

The second ranked theme is described as 'professionalism', with 21 per cent of participants seeing the need for greater accountability, enthusiasm, openness, willingness to take risks and innovate, teamwork and a capacity for strategic planning among their colleagues. One might argue that this is another area where the leader can take action without recourse to new policies, although the fourth-ranked theme of autonomy does express this view.

Table 2.3 *How to make the work more exhilarating*

Rank	Theme	Illustrative responses	Number	%
1	Personal	Achieve better balance in personal life; become more tolerant and sensitive; more time to have fun; study leave; delegate more; improve internal communication and relationships within the school; greater clarity in role and supervision (of self); mentoring; coaching; saying no	125	33
2	Professionalism	There needs to be a higher level of professionalism among some staff, with accountability, enthusiasm, openness, shared values, willingness to take risks and innovate; teamwork; strategic planning	78	21

3	Resources	Additional resources to allow greater focus on students; reduction in class size, shift funds from centre to schools; getting sense of priority; more time; full time deputy; building a capacity to focus on meeting the needs of individual students; support in times of crisis and trauma	73	19
4	Autonomy	Fewer constraints on schools, including industrial; more careful thought at the system level about policies before requiring implementation in schools; separation of education and politics; less administration ('administrivia' or 'ministrivia') unless clearly connected to learning outcomes; greater sensitivity to schools; greater capacity at the school level to select, manage and reward the performance of staff	34	9
5	Community	Higher level of support from community in sponsorship, marketing, goodwill and communication	23	6
=6	Recognition	More recognition of achievements of self and school and less blame and cynicism by others toward the school	22	6
=6	Networking	Networking with other schools for mutual support	22	6
TOTAL			377	100

Taken together, the two-top ranked themes on personal and professional matters account for 54 per cent of responses. The remaining 46 per cent are more clearly connected to actions by others. The third-ranked theme is concerned with resources, with 19 per cent calling for additional resources to enable them to give more attention to meeting the needs of students, if necessary shifting more funds from the centre of the system to schools. Resources may be in the form of emotional support, with several participants referring to times of crisis and trauma, as experienced with tragedies that occur from time to time.

It is noteworthy that just 9 per cent of participants called for greater autonomy for the school, especially in respect to personnel matters and freeing the school from 'administrivia' and 'ministrivia', with the latter a term coined in the one workshop to refer to demands for action or information that are made by ministers of education.

The remaining themes drew relatively few responses, with 6 per cent for each of community (for higher levels of support), recognition (of achievements of self and the school) and networking (to seek mutual support).

Expert commentary on the findings

The author invited three high profile leaders who are exemplary in the way they communicate a sense of exhilaration in their work to comment on the findings reported in Tables 2.1, 2.2 and 2.3. The first was shared in correspondence with Sir Iain Hall, honoured for his leadership at Parrs Wood High School in Manchester, a specialist Arts and Technology College, serving more recently as consultant to the Specialist Schools and Academies Trust and the National College for School Leadership. The others emerged in extended conversations with two leaders who were invited to join the author in the interpretation of responses. One was Steve Marshall, Director of Education, Lifelong Learning and Skills for Wales, following his successful experience in transforming leadership as Chief Executive of the Department of Education and Children's Services in South Australia. The other was Jim Spinks, co-author in the self-managing school series (Caldwell and Spinks, 1988; 1992; 1998). Jim was a successful school principal and is now a skilled consultant on aligning resource allocation in education with expectations for learning, and the nature, needs and aspirations of students. The insights of these three leaders provide new perspectives that may help shape strategies to shift the balance to exhilaration.

Sir Iain Hall

Sir Iain Hall, former head at Parrs Wood High School in Manchester, and now a consultant on school leadership, affirmed the major themes that emerged in responses to the question: 'What aspects of your leadership are exhilarating?' Sixty-seven per cent of workshop participants associated exhilaration with good outcomes, such as success with a particular project, high achievement by students and staff who work together to make it all happen. Sir Iain also highlighted the importance of talking up the exhilarating aspects of the role rather than dwelling on workload:

It is important that we describe leadership as exhilarating, for far too long the negative aspects of workload have obscured the debate and sent out the wrong messages to our developing leaders. I hope that I have always been a headteacher who placed individual learning at the centre of my energies. The real exhilaration comes not when you see your ideas and strategies taken up in school but when you stumble upon them being taken even further than you imagined, with new initiatives and innovations springing from the original thoughts. Suddenly, you see these being laterally transferred across subject boundaries and the excitement growing. No longer are they your ideas but theirs! The 'buzz' in the school and the excitement in the students responding to these new initiatives make it all worthwhile.

Steve Marshall

Steve Marshall held senior leadership positions in Victoria before returning to South Australia as Chief Executive of the Department of Education and Children's Services in South Australia, where he began his career in education. He has a Master of Educational Administration and a Master of Business Administration and is undertaking research on school renewal for a Doctor of Philosophy. He is up to date with current writing about education and the general literature about leadership and change, often exploring the deeper aspects of personal engagement and motivation. He seems always to have a book in his hand or in his briefcase. Apart from his track record of successful transformation, he is an exemplar for the second part of his title as Director of Education, Lifelong Learning and Skills for Wales. Exuberance and exhilaration are apt descriptions of how others see him, but there is also a steely determination to lead a team that will create a world-class system of public education.

Steve Marshall reflected on the early stages of analysis of responses to question 1, 'What aspects of your work are exhilarating?', and question 2, 'What aspects of your work are boring, depressing, discouraging or dispiriting?' He suggested there was broad consistency with Maslow's hierarchy of needs. Responses to question 1 indicated that higher-order needs were being met (self-actualization; the esteem needs of self-esteem, recognition and status; and the social needs of sense of belonging and love), while those for question 2 suggested that lower-order needs were not being met (especially safety needs of security and protection). In reference to exhilaration (question 1) he also noted the sense of moral purpose and the importance of interdependence and alignment with a vision for the school that underpinned the responses. He referred to much of the language in responses to question 2 as 'toxic' in the sense that there were many references to 'what can't be done'. The dominant theme in responses to question 3, 'What actions by you or others would make your work as leader more exhilarating and less boring, depressing, discouraging or dispiriting?', was personal, that is, the balance can be shifted to exhilaration through the personal efforts of the leader. Steve Marshall affirmed such a strategy while acknowledging the importance of support that can be provided from within the school system.

Jim Spinks

Jim Spinks is also a leader who communicates a sense of exhilaration. He served as principal for many years in remote locations in Tasmania, most famously as head at Rosebery District High School, where he developed a model for self-management that underpinned our publications and led to his influential work around the world in recent decades. He has made an important contribution to the transformation of school management. He models an attribute that many participants in workshops believed to be important if they were to shift the balance to exhilaration, namely, a balance in life. He has been a wilderness guide and has travelled to the Antarctic on several occasions.

Jim Spinks affirmed that 'in 27 years as principal I mostly lived on adrenaline through exhilaration'. He was struck by the words of one workshop participant who referred, in his response to question 2, to leadership that is 'emetic', meaning 'an agent that induces vomiting'. While some may read the comment as a devastating reflection on levels of stress in school leadership, Jim Spinks put an entirely different construction on it:

> *If you want to experience exhilaration, you've got to do something extraordinary: either you've got to attempt something extraordinary or you've got to achieve something extraordinary. You've also got to be daring, and you've also got to take a risk that you might fail. When you look at leadership in schools, for quite a large percentage of principals, the last thing they want to do is fail, and so they tend to step back from what is courageous, what is daring, what is high risk.*

Jim Spinks referred to the tendency in responses to question 2 for participants to refer to external factors. He used the example of those who referred to 'party politics'. 'Any principal who thinks that education can take place without it being in a political environment has got rocks in their head!' Without denying the importance of being an active player, he referred to the example of his wife, Marilyn Spinks, also a highly successful principal and now a partner in their consultancy, who displayed the Serenity Prayer of Reinhold Niebuhr on the wall of her office: 'God grant me the serenity to accept the things I cannot change; the courage to change the things I can; and wisdom to know the difference'. He suggested that there were 'people looking for exhilaration but who too often were really focusing on things they had no capacity to change. If you focus on that, you've no time left, no energy left to pursue the things that require courage'. He mentioned two leaders in his experience who never had the opportunity to experience exhilaration, despite successful experience in teaching, one 'who spent 95 per cent of his time decrying decisions made by government and the department', and another who immersed himself in what many participants in the workshops described as 'administrivia', in this instance spending much of his time monitoring power usage in different parts of the school.

Discussion turned to how people chose to enter or were selected to the principalship. A key question is whether sufficient attention is paid to personal factors. Jim Spinks highlighted the traditional culture of teaching that is now inconsistent with capacities that are required for transformation and leadership that is exhilarating. 'In the past there was a culture where you entered the public service because it was safe and secure. As a kid from the bush, we were encouraged to go into the public service in education because it was a government job, it was secure, with very good holidays, and working conditions were pleasant'. However, 'it attracted people who were not necessarily daring risk takers'. He referred to efforts to attract the right people into the principalship through raising salaries, but the other way 'is to try and change the culture'. He referred to his own experience as principal at Sheffield District High School, following his appointment at Rosebery, when he accepted the challenge of raising levels of literacy, setting a target of 100 per cent of students meeting the standard. Success was achieved through the efforts of a brilliant young team leader on staff. He referred to the reaction of fellow principals: 'Half of them just got so angry. The other half got so excited.' The difference seemed to be associated with views about what was possible and a willingness to set high standards under challenging circumstances, fulfilment of which called for courage and daring action.

Jim Spinks believes that courageous leaders outside education ought to be encouraged to pursue a career in schools but 'they must have some understanding about learning and about teaching. Most of all, they must have compassion for children'. He expressed 'grave doubts' about efforts to set standards for school leaders by developing lists of criteria against which aspirants or incumbents should be measured. He reported unsatisfactory experiences with the approach in Tasmania. 'None of them talked about courage, none of them talked about risk taking or daring. I think they stepped away from those things and therefore stepped back into mediocrity'.

Implications for policy and practice

Spinks's views raise an important issue. Are the people needed to lead schools in times of challenge and complexity attracted to or screened out of the processes of appointment? Terrence Deal, Guilbert Hentschke and others provide an interesting account of leadership in the *Adventures of Charter School Creators* (Deal et al., 2005). This book has international significance even though it is about a uniquely American project in school reform. There are barely 3,000 charter schools in America. Along with magnet schools, they represent a tiny fraction of the total number of schools. Despite this, observers in other countries follow developments with great interest, since the issue of school choice transcends national boundaries, as does concern for how levels of achievement can be raised for large numbers of students in challenging circumstances.

Deal and Hentschke are the lead authors and they are mindful, however, of the range of views about charter schools. They acknowledge that there are many unanswered questions.

> *Do partnerships undergirding charter schools portend a new definition of public responsibility and promise new kinds of schooling consonant with 21st century urban America's needs and demands? Or, alternatively, are they precursors of a form of privatisation unresponsive to the welfare of underserved children? Answers to these questions are important but as yet unclear. (Deal et al., 2004: 9–10)*

Having framed the book in this manner, Deal and Hentschke leave the stage to leaders of 13 charter schools to tell their stories. These leaders are remarkably frank in their accounts of the challenges and conflicts. What appeared at the outset to be a shared vision and a common commitment to the way it would be achieved would often give way to debilitating debate that threw doubt on whether the venture would survive. Kathleen O'Connor wrote about this in her story of the Odyssey Charter School in Los Angeles. The charter was approved on 25 May 1999 but 'the first wave of discontent ... was in February 2000 ... by the end of May, there was an attempted mutiny initiated by seven families who enlisted the aid of those who had the power to end our journey' (Deal et al., 2004: 47). These stories are superb sources for analysis of leadership using frames or lenses that help 'figure out what is going on': human resource, structural, political, symbolic (Bolman and Deal, 2003).

Some charter schools enjoy international as well as national renown, notably the Vaughn Next Century Learning Centre in Los Angles. As she has done on seemingly countless occasions, Yvonne Chan tells how it was achieved. Hers is undoubtedly one of the most remarkable achievements in leadership in any setting. What stood out in her account on this occasion are the kinds of sacrifice that were necessary to get the venture off the ground. 'When no government funds flowed to us in July, when our year-round school began, I mortgaged my house. All staff agreed not to be paid until August' (Deal et al., 2004: 65).

The book does not set out to provide evidence that the charter school project is a success as far as educational outcomes are concerned. It is essentially a book about leadership under conditions of extraordinary complexity and uncertainty. The final chapter by Deal and Hentschke is one of the most important statements about leadership to appear in recent times. They pose three questions. 'Does starting a charter school from scratch require fundamentally different leadership skills than taking a position in an existing suburban public school? If so, how do those leadership requirements vary? If not, what are the generic characteristics of school leadership relevant across the range of situations?' (Deal et al., 2004: 247). They conclude that the leadership is different in charter schools to that in regular public schools. It is the opportunity to create and shape that is 'enormously heady and compelling ... like the rush that drives an entrepreneur who believes she or he has a novel idea for the marketplace' (Deal et al., 2004: 250). They complete the analysis with concise descriptions of the kinds of decisions that characterize such leadership: decisions about what business to be in, how to organize and operate service delivery, the kinds of people to employ and their compensation, about customers and clients to be served, and how to allocate operating revenue.

After reading the heroic accounts of leadership in 13 charter schools, the reader might expect Deal and Hentschke to conclude that the role is beyond most people or that few will be attracted to it. This is not the case. They suggest that those who have taken on the role are not the kind of people who are attracted to leadership in a regular school. 'Far from being more demanding and less attractive, charter schools are attracting people to school leadership who seem to thrive on "daunting opportunities"' (Deal et al., 2004: 256). The challenge for policy-makers and other key stakeholders is therefore to 'extend an invitation to entrepreneurs with a passion for fulfilling the most sacred calling of all – to create places where every child can learn and grow' (Deal et al., 2004: 250).

It is reassuring that the large majority of participants (67 per cent) in the workshops reported that exhilaration was associated with success in the core business of the school, summarized in the statement: 'success in tasks related to learning and the support of learning, characterized by fine working relationships with staff, and enjoyment that accompanies good outcomes for students'. The major implication is the importance of building the capacities of leaders and their colleagues to maximize the probability that they will experience such success. These capacities are concerned with curriculum, pedagogy, strategy formation, vision building, alignment of staff and the community to the vision, working well with colleagues, and having fun along the way. Programmes for leadership development and ongoing professional learning should be concerned with these matters.

There was similarly a large majority (69 per cent) in views about aspects of work that participants found boring, depressing, discouraging or dispiriting, with roughly similar numbers reporting concerns about the performance of staff, administrative work, and perceived lack of support. Taken at face value, a major implication is that actions by leaders and others should seek to minimize these concerns through policies that strengthen the hand of the school in selection and performance management of staff, minimizing the amount of administrative work, and providing more support, through additional resources and greater sympathy and understanding of those who are in a position to provide support.

References

Bolman, L. and Deal, T. (2003) *Reframing Organisations*. San Francisco, CA: Jossey-Bass.

Caldwell, B.J. (2004) *Re-imagining the Self-Managing School*. London: Specialist Schools and Academies Trust.

Caldwell, B.J. (2005) *The New Enterprise Logic of Schools*. London: Specialist Schools and Academies Trust.

Caldwell, B.J. (2006a) *Exhilarating Leadership*. London: Specialist Schools and Academies Trust.

Caldwell, B.J. (2006b) *Re-imagining Educational Leadership*. Camberwell: ACER Press and London: Sage.

Caldwell, B.J. and Spinks, J.M. (1988) *The Self Managing School*. London: Falmer.

Caldwell, B.J. and Spinks, J.M. (1992) *Leading the Self-Managing School*. London: Falmer.

Caldwell, B.J. and Spinks, J.M. (1998) *Beyond the Self-Managing School*. London: Falmer.

Davies, B. (2006) *Leading the Strategically Focused School*. London: Paul Chapman Publishing.

Deal, T.E., Hentschke, G.C, Kecker, K., Lind, C., Oshman, S. and Shore, R. (2004) *Adventures of Charter School Creators*. Lanham, MD: Scarecrow Education.

Department of Education and Training (Victoria) (2004) *The Privilege and the Price*. Melbourne: Department of Education and Training.

Fullan, M. (2005) *Leadership Sustainability*. Thousand Oaks, CA: Corwin Press.

Hargreaves, A. and Fink, D. (2006) *Sustainable Leadership*. San Francisco, CA: Jossey-Bass.

National Association of Head Teachers (NAHT), Eastern Leadership Centre (ELC), University of Cambridge, National College of School Leadership (NCSL) and Hay Group (2005) *Leading Appointments: A Study into and Guidance on Headteacher Recruitment*. Interim Report. Available on the NAHT website at www.naht.org.uk.

Smithers, R. (2006) 'Headteacher vacancies expose schools crisis', *Guardian*, 12 January.

Zuboff, S. and Maxmin, J. (2004) *The Support Economy*. New York: Penguin Books.

Chapter 3

Energizing leadership for sustainability

Andy Hargreaves and Dean Fink

The leadership shortfall

Headlines in the *Times Educational Supplement* in the United Kingdom (UK) have announced 'Stressed heads admit to making mistakes' (TES, 2005); 'Heads driven out by OFSTED' (Paton and Stewart, 2005); 'Governors want Superman or Wonderwoman' (TES, 2005). One anguished school head declared that 'stress of job and unrealistic targets have made the job unbearable', and another, who had opted for early retirement, asserted that 'the paper work mountain has grown to the extent that it now ruins the real work of a head' (TES, 2005). In Canada, under the headline 'Being a Principal Can Be Punishing Work', the President of the Ontario Principals' Council proclaimed that, 'principals are finding it very stressful to balance all the needs and concerns of parents, kids, taxpayers and the province' because of struggles with life–work balance, students' anti-social behaviour, and increasingly unrealistic expectations of what schools should and can do (Healey, 2006: A6).

At the turn of the twenty-first century, when we interviewed Ontario secondary principals working in what was then a highly accelerated and extremely pressured reform environment, they were exhausted and exasperated by unrealistic accountability requirements, unbearably all-consuming workloads, and increasingly overwhelmed and embittered teaching staffs (Goodson, 2003; Hargreaves and Fink, 2006). These principals felt they were 'carrying the whole world', in a policy climate where 'the rules change, day by day in terms of what we can and can't do' and 'implementing policies I do not agree with'. Within just three years of completing our study, most of the principals we interviewed had clearly had enough and had moved up into the district office, across to the private sector, out into graduate studies and early retirement, or away to mental health care facilities!

Even in more optimistic climates of educational reform, where accountability regimes are less punitive and hierarchical, and improvement processes are more professionally inclusive, engaging and even exciting, the sheer pace and urgency of efforts to raise student achievement can be overwhelming for educational leaders. This has been evident in an evaluation one of us has conducted of a network of more than 300 underperforming schools striving for improvement (Hargreaves et al., 2006). The good news is that two-thirds of the schools improved within two years as a result of networking with each other, accessing expertise from mentor schools, and circulating practical strategies for short-, medium- and long-term change among each other. But the difficulty is that although very many of these short-term strategies were praised by leaders and their teachers when they saw them in action, because they were so 'gimmicky and great', the energy demanded from engaging in networking, innovation and implementation under considerable time pressures was so intensive, that headteachers and assistant heads ran severe risks of burning out.

> *It's been the hardest year I've ever had, this year, because I've just been pulled in so many directions. I've really enjoyed doing the job, but you get a little bit of overload, because you go to conferences and you hear all of this stuff that's being done. And you think 'oh, we're not doing that! And how do we do? We need to go back and perhaps need to do some things.' So you get that pressure, that you think 'Oh, wow – are we as good as we really are? Should we really be here?' ... The other schools are really, really high-flying schools. And then I have the dreadful pressures from the head of department. And guilt ... And so I feel I've been very torn this year ... And I'm rushing – just rushing from place to place.*

These examples are not unusual or isolated. There is a disturbing international crisis in leadership succession in the schools of many western countries. Leadership roles in education and particularly the job of the principal have become 'greedy work' because schools, school districts and educational reform expectations now make 'total claims on their members and attempt to encompass within their circle the whole personality' (Gronn, 2003: 5). Many of the increasing numbers of women leaders entering principalship, for instance, find they are turning into middle-level 'emotional managers' and motivators of unwanted, hierarchically imposed and stereotypically masculine, test-driven change agendas (Blackmore, 1996).

Jurisdiction after jurisdiction has separated out principals from the teachers' unions and teachers have noticed the difference! Analysing our data on more than 200 teachers' changing perceptions of their principals over 30 years in Ontario and New York State, we found that in the 1970s teachers saw their principals as larger-than-life characters (in a good or a bad way) who stayed with their schools, knew everyone within it, and were seen as being loyal to the school and its people. As accountability requirements began to increase in the 1980s, while some principals overprotected their staff from the intensifying reform agenda, others were still able to stay close to their teachers and work with them collegially to finesse the implementation of change so it did not damage, and indeed actively enhanced, the goals and purposes of the school community. But from the mid-1990s, when the standardized reform agenda had become all-encompassing and all-consuming, teachers in both countries now saw their principals as anonymous and interchangeable managers rather than leaders, who were less visible around the school, moved in and out of it more quickly, and seemed to be more loyal to the district and more interested in their own career than committed to the long-term future of the school (Fink and Brayman, 2006). In the words of one of the study's long-serving teachers, in the 1970s and 1980s, the school's principals:

> *were totally committed to the overall program of the school. Their Number 1 focus was the school. As times went on and principals changed, the principal was less interested in the school and more interested in his own personal growth. You could tell as some of these other principals came in; they spent more time outside the school than they did inside the school. I get to (Principal x in the mid 1990s) and his Number 1 focus wasn't on (the school). It was on the next step to be a superintendent, and that's what he is right now.*

Tragically and sometimes heartrendingly, this is not how leaders see themselves. But once principals had been officially segregated from teachers, and teachers began to work to rule (contracted hours) in protest against imposed reforms, this systemically created perception of principals-as-enemy drove one male assistant principal in our study to tears, when he came to school early, day after day, to prepare equipment for his teachers so they could teach effectively despite a constantly 'late' start, only to be served with a pile of grievance letters from them at the end of the day, on the instructions of the teachers' union.

Existing and potential leaders are therefore questioning leadership roles as they are presently defined and asking themselves whether they are worth their time, energy and commitment. We seem to be able to get teachers to qualify for middle-level leadership, and even to take up assistant principalship, but they then resist moving into the principal's or the district office. The closer they get to the principalship, and the more they see of it, the less likely they are to want to do it (Pounder et al., 2003). Indeed, in Spain, where principals are elected by their teacher colleagues, the majority of jobs cannot be filled because the leaders then have to press their peers into implementing unwanted external reform demands – an utterly unenviable responsibility (Bolivar Moreno, 2006).

While a significant part of this paradox is the 'greedy' nature of the work, demographics also play a major role. For the last two decades, our schools have been run by a Baby Boomer demographic of leaders, who have aged with their institutions and are now retired or about to retire. They are being replaced by the much smaller Generation X. In the USA, more than 40 per cent of its 93,000 public school principals are expected to retire within the next five years. Many districts are already feeling the crunch: a San Jose superintendent had to take 33 trips across the country to find four principals with whom he was satisfied; New York City's schools began the same year with 163 temporary principals; and 39 per cent of Chicago's principals are already eligible for retirement (Stein, 2001).

Some regions of England are also experiencing similar shortages for some types of schools. A study of the frequency of newspaper advertisements for heads (principals) and deputies (assistant principals) concluded that the number of advertisements for headteachers was above the average for the past 10 years and the highest recorded for four years. Many schools still failed to appoint a new headteacher after the first advertisement (Howson, 2005). A survey of local authorities by the UK's National Association of Head Teachers reported that 'there are hundreds of schools and thousands of children and young people in schools without permanent leadership teams' (NAHT, 2006: 1). Similar patterns have been appearing in Canada (Williams, 2001), Australia (Gronn and Rawlings-Sanaei, 2003) and New Zealand (Brookings et al., 2003).

In time, the sheer shortfall of leaders may resolve itself, because waiting in the wings to succeed Generation X is the demographically larger Generation Y (born between 1978 and 1984). Sometimes referred to as the 'Millennials' (Howe and Strauss, 2000) or the 'Baby-Boom Echo' (Foot, 2001), this generation is very different from their Baby Boom parents, and its Generation X older siblings. 'This generation is more interesting, more confident, less hidebound and uptight, better educated, more creative, in some essential fashion, unafraid' (Quindien, 2000, cited in Tulgan and Martin, 2001: 3), 'Masters of the internet and P.C ... They're blunt. They're savvy. They're contradictory' (Tulgan and Martin, 2001: xi).

We are already learning what this new, demographically dominant generation is bringing to the profession of teaching. In her study of the new generation of teachers, Susan Moore Johnson finds that many 'Millenials' have been entering the profession not as enthusiastic ingénues, straight from college, but after working and sometimes leading in other fields and walks of life (Johnson et al., 2004). In England, these 'new professionals' have had less curriculum freedom than their Baby Boomer predecessors, they are more likely to accept the given frameworks of curriculum prescription and testing in which they master their craft, and their professional ambitions are more likely to focus specifically on caring for students and on competent instruction, rather than on also trying to transform the world (Troman and Woods, 2000).

This generation may barely have mastered teaching before it is drawn into leading. While the numbers from which to choose new leaders may be sufficient, are the candidates interested? Will they be ready? Can they be properly prepared? If we can successfully attract these new entrants to educational leadership, they will be demographically different from the people they replace (Kauffman et al., 2004). New leaders will be younger. More of them will be female and many will have young families. They will calculate their options, negotiate their careers, manage their time and think about their lives more carefully than those they have replaced. In view of this shift, the challenge of generational leadership succession will therefore not only be to find new leaders, but also to define new leadership. If we want to find and keep more and better educational leaders, the work of educational leadership is going to have to change. The evidence of our own research and school improvement work is clear – the present principalship is an unsustainable job, locked into an unsustainable model of school reform.

Sustainable leadership

There is a better way – a more sustainable way – that does not push improvement forward at the cost of wearing out the leaders who are responsible for it, and of deterring a new generation of leaders from taking up the challenge. How can we achieve sustainable improvement if we cannot sustain the leaders of improvement?

To understand this conundrum, and how we must extricate ourselves from it, it is important to understand the meaning of sustainability itself. Sustainability means much more than maintainability (keeping things going) or affordability (improvement on the cheap). Lester Brown, founder of the World Watch Institute, first coined the term *sustainability* in the environmental field in the early 1980s (quoted in Suzuki, 2003). He defined a sustainable society as one that is able to satisfy its needs without diminishing the opportunities for future generations to meet theirs. The key and most widely used definition of the slightly different but closely related idea of sustainable development appears in the Brundtland Report of the World Commission on Environment and Development in 1987: 'Humankind has the ability to achieve sustainable development – to meet the needs of the present without compromising the ability of future generations to meet their own needs' (World Commission on Environment and Development, 1987: 51). Adapting this definition, we have argued that 'Sustainable educational leadership and improvement preserves and develops deep learning for all that spreads and lasts, in ways that do no harm to and indeed create positive benefit for others around us, now and in the future' (Hargreaves and Fink, 2003: 694).

Drawing on the environmental and corporate literature in a study of change over time in eight US and Canadian secondary schools through the eyes of the teachers and leaders who worked there in the 1970s, 1980s and 1990s (Hargreaves and Goodson, 2006), we have created an explanatory framework of seven principles of sustainable leadership (Hargreaves and Fink, 2006).

Sustainable leadership is characterized by *depth* of learning and real achievement rather than superficially tested performance; *length* of impact over the long haul, beyond individual leaders, through effectively managed succession; *breadth* of influence, where leadership becomes a distributed responsibility; *justice* in ensuring that leadership actions do no harm to and actively benefit students in other schools;

diversity that replaces standardization and alignment with networks and cohesion; *conservation* that builds on the best of the past to create an even better future, and *resourcefulness* that conserves and renews teachers' and leaders' energy and does not burn them out. These principles are a meal, not a menu. You cannot pick and choose; they all work together.

At the same time, the seven principles are not mandates or dictates. They are certainly moral imperatives, but they also contain challenging moral dilemmas, that require creative and courageous as well as morally principled thinking and action. For example:

- *Depth* – How do we promote and protect deep and broad learning that lasts in a climate that insists on immediate, tested results?
- *Length* – How do we remain steadfastly committed to the long-term goals for authentic improvement while attending properly to the urgent needs of underachieving children right now?
- *Breadth* – How do we distribute leadership more widely and more wisely and also retain a sense of the distinctive leadership gifts that we contribute ourselves?
- *Justice* – How do we help other people's schools and children without sacrificing and short-changing our own?
- *Diversity* – How do we accommodate, include and connect the rich diversity of our students' learning and teachers' teaching, and also retain focus, direction and cohesion in our efforts to improve?
- *Conservation* – How do we innovate for a better future by building on the firm foundations of the past without staying stuck in the past or wallowing in nostalgic memories of it?
- *Resourcefulness* – How do we engage people's energy and motivation for urgent improvement without wearing them out?

Too much educational reform in recent years has neither grappled with these dilemmas, nor even acknowledged the moral imperative of sustainability. It has sacrificed depth of learning to the achievement appearances of standardized testing. The political expediency of short-term achievement targets has immersed educators in an overwhelming present and impeded their ability to plan and prepare for a more sustainable future. Inspirational and distributed leadership in cultures of hope where improvement becomes everyone's responsibility has been short-circuited by top-down management of unwanted reform agendas in cultures of fear. Schools have been pitted against each other in unjust market competition for the higher-achieving students who will bring them better results. Diversity has been destroyed by standardization. The achievements of the past have been derogated by governments who want to claim responsibility for measured improvement in the future. And instead of energizing teachers and leaders to achieving lasting improvement, educators have been treated as if they are bottomless pits that will never run out of gas. It is this last issue of energy and resources – the seventh principle of sustainable leadership – that is our focus in the remainder of this chapter.

Energizing leadership

There are three basic understandings of sustainable energy use – energy restraint, energy renewal and energy release.

Energy restraint

The first environmental view of sustainable energy concentrates on the finite nature of planetary resources. Fossil fuels are disappearing, greenhouse gases are intensifying and we are running out of time and space. We have to stop producing and consuming more and more because within a century or less, more prosperous countries and their people will have reached the limits to growth. If we want to protect and preserve nature's legacy, along with our own survival within it, the people of more prosperous countries will have to restrain their appetites and start to come to terms with the meaning of *enough* (McKibben, 2003).

The finite view of energy draws on the second law of thermodynamics in physics. This states that once energy is transformed, it is no longer a resource available for work in the future. The two laws of thermodynamics are succinct:

1. The energy of the universe is constant.
2. The entropy of the universe tends to a maximum.

As energy moves from high to low temperatures, it is not as capable of doing useful work. The energy spreads out, it is not as useful (even though it is still conserved), and so it tends towards disorder or increasing *entropy* (Goodstein, 2004).

Entropy is nature's penalty for energy transformation (Rifkin, 1981). Human and natural systems are in a perpetual state of dissipation until they reach equilibrium where all the energy is transformed and ultimately expended, resulting in death. A look in the mirror as we age gives evidence of entropy, as do air pollution and toxic waste. We can only slow down entropy, not stop it. So we exercise, recycle, donate money to poverty groups, and so on. The process of entropy goes from *cradle to grave*. The ecological implications of entropy are clear and widely understood – slow down the damage, conserve your fuel, reuse and recycle, be prudent and self-sacrificing, limit your appetites, do less bad things.

In terms of human resources, our energy and long-term effectiveness become depleted when we:

- have no time to sleep, relax or exercise properly;
- feel constantly overwrought and/or emotionally disengaged from those around us in a world where we have no time for proper relationships;
- are always having to think too quickly or superficially;
- are disconnected from and unable to pursue or fulfil our own morally compelling purposes (Loehr and Schwartz, 2003).

Loehr and Schwartz (2003) acknowledge that some organizational and work environments are toxically energy-depleting. In educational change and leadership, these have been abundantly evident where:

- *a hurried and narrowing curriculum* allows no space for depth and breadth of learning or teaching;
- externally imposed and annually inescapable *short-term achievement targets* make teaching and learning like an enforced and everlasting sprint;
- insistence on an accountability agenda of *endless improvement* makes schools look more made-over than Michael Jackson;
- *subjecting schools to the repetitive change syndrome* of bureaucratic overwork and innovation overload produces exhaustion, insecurity and lack of opportunity for reflection, replenishment and renewal (Abrahamson, 2004);
- *shaming and blaming* schools labelled as underperforming, leaves their teachers with diminished confidence and depleted commitment.

These excesses of mechanically driven reform in an overly pressurized environment have led to epidemics of teacher stress, loss of confidence and emotional withdrawal in many parts of the world (Dinham, 2004).

The wasted contributions of teachers are reflected in the wasted lives of principals who experienced excessive stress, 'unnecessary paperwork' and jobs that have too much management and not enough leadership (Green et al., 2001: 23).

In the age of standardization, and the push to meet short-term achievement targets, teachers and leaders have been treated by governments as if their energy resources are limitless. In response, some governments and system leaders are saying 'Enough' and starting to slow down the entropic process of depletion and waste by:

- infusing additional resources and extra energy into the system for better buildings, smaller class sizes, increased numbers of support staff, and additional in-school time to prepare and to plan (Teachernet, 2005); in this view, there is no achievement without investment;
- replacing externally imposed with internally agreed targets for improvement (Alberta Learning, 2004; Hargreaves and Shirley, 2006);
- reducing the speed and scope of reform implementation and also the relentless and insatiable pace of expected improvement, as a way of accepting that there are human limits to the rate of progress (including raising educational standards);
- substituting the emotionally depleting strategies of shaming and blaming underperforming schools and their teachers and leaders, with support strategies that rebuild confidence, competence and pride among the educators who will be responsible for arresting the decline in performance and for securing improvement instead (Fullan, 2007).

Sustainability through energy restraint, then, means being less ruthlessly exploitative of teachers' and leaders' energy reserves, and more prepared to conserve and replace some of this energy by injecting additional human and fiscal resources into the system.

Energy renewal

Nobel Prize-winning physicist, Ilse Prigogene, found the perspective of entropy and energy dissipation somewhat depressing. It was, he said, contrary to how living systems evolve in an opposite way to entropy: from simple to complex, from disorder to order (Rifkin, 1981). He suggested that some parts of the universe are closed systems, which behave in mechanical ways, and are subject to the law of entropy. But most social and biological systems are open because they exchange energy, matter and information with their environments. Open systems in nature include brains, immune systems, cells and ant colonies (Capra, 2002). In open systems, energy need not be dissipated, but can be exchanged, replenished and renewed. In this *cradle-to-cradle* approach, resources are never lost, but renewed and replenished to promote regeneration and improvement (McDonough and Braungart, 2002).

While energy restraint urges us to be less bad and avoid or limit wearing out people or things, energy renewal inspires us to do more good things and find ways to re-energize people or exchange energy more efficiently within the system. Schools and educational systems are also open systems that exchange energy, matter and information with their environments. They can renew, restore and rejuvenate. Losers can become winners, failures can become successes, and the weak can become strong.

In open systems, energy need not be dissipated; resources are never lost, but renewed and replenished to promote regeneration and improvement. Reform is not necessarily renewal. Reform originates outside schools, 'beyond time and space' (Goodlad, 1994: 218). It does not 'accommodate the nature and circumstances of schools' (Goodlad, 1994: 218). Traditional large-scale reform efforts assume that something is wrong and that system-wide restructuring must take place to create what Goodlad has called standardized 'McSchools'. Renewal, however, is ecologically grounded in the lives of schools and the people who work within them, 'Schools are cultures seeking to maintain a state of equilibrium that allows them to function in the face of perturbations from without. They are ecosystems within larger ecosystems' (Goodlad, 1994: 218).

Renewal, Goodlad argues, is a 'cottage industry'. It is about specific people and places that are linked to other cottage industries through common purposes and cultural ties. Each school becomes an ecosystem within a district ecosystem, and renewal occurs through networked interaction where schools and districts work co-operatively towards common goals (Goodlad, 1994). 'In a good school these interactions are healthy, enabling the school both to conduct its daily business effectively and to cope with exigencies. In a poor school, these interactions are unhealthy, making the conduct of business difficult. Bad schools are in a constant state of crisis or near crisis' (Goodlad, 1994: 219). This ability to maintain equilibrium while dealing with dissonance is at the heart of school renewal. 'The language of school renewal is multidimensional, relatively free of good guys and bad guys and of ends, means and outcomes linearity. The language and the ethos are of the people around and especially in schools acquiring the efficacy and developing the collaborative mechanisms necessary to (produce) better schools' (Goodlad, 1997).

Enhancing resourcefulness is partly a matter of slowing down entropy, conserving energy and, in the drive for ever-escalating standards, sometimes being prepared to say 'Enough'. Slowing the pace of change, improving the emotional tone of reform, injecting financial and building resources into the system, and generally exercising *restraint* in how far we exploit people's reserves of energy – these are essential elements of resourcefulness. So too is the commitment to replenishment and *renewal* among school and system leaders – of purposes, learning, commitment, personal and professional development, emotional capacity and sheer physical regeneration.

Renewal and restraint are not either/or choices in our challenge to develop resourceful sustainability. Renewal *and* restraint, exchanging energy *and* slowing down entropy, change in the system *and* action by individuals – all these *both/and* combinations are needed in our efforts to rethink sustainable leadership and improvement. The power of these combinations can be seen in three sources of human resourcefulness in educational change: trust, confidence and happiness.

- *Trust* creates and consolidates energy, commitment and relationships. When trust is broken, people lessen their commitment, withdraw from relationships and entropy abounds. High-trust systems in which teachers, leaders, students and parents together actively commit and trust each other to secure improvement, in systems which trust their capacity to do so, lead to improved student achievement. Low-trust systems that are driven by test scores, short-term targets, punitive inspections and cultures of fear, produce lower levels of achievement over time (Bryk and Schneider, 2004; Spillane, 2006).
- *Confidence* 'consists of positive expectation for favourable outcomes. Confidence influences the willingness to invest – to commit money, time, reputation, emotional energy, or other resources – or to withhold or hedge investment' (Kanter, 2004: 7). *Confidence* – in oneself, in team members or colleagues, in the structures and policies of the organization, and in the external environment that provides

resources – produces and feeds on winning streaks that fuel people's energy and redouble their efforts to persevere for the long haul, especially at moments of doubt and difficulty (Hargreaves et al., 2006).

- *Happiness* renews energy when people have some choice, but not too much – a warning against completely open educational markets and overly prescribed reforms (Schwartz, 2004); when people feel included and have control over their own destiny – an argument against imposed and arbitrary achievement targets (Haidt, 2005); and when people are able to achieve their purposes, especially via attaining incremental goals along the way (Haidt, 2005; Lazarus, 1994), a case for setting short-term targets and interim goals collaboratively.

At the school level, leadership of and through professional learning communities creates measurable improvement through energy renewal. Schools that operate as strong professional learning communities where teachers work and learn together, using evidence and experience to improve student learning, have demonstrable and measurably positive effects on student achievement (Dufour and Eaker, 1998; McLaughlin and Talbert, 2006: Ch. 2). Professional learning communities renew teachers intellectually by enhancing and increasing the ways they can learn and improve from one another, informed by evidence about the impact of their efforts on student achievement (Hargreaves, 2007). They renew teachers emotionally by building high-trust/high-challenge environments of mutual encouragement and support (Stoll and Louis, 2007). And they renew teachers morally and spiritually, by rekindling shared commitment to the purpose of improving student achievement and overall well-being (Fullan, 2005).

At the system level, energy renewal drives further improvement when schools are networked with others in high-trust systems of mutual professional learning and transparent commitment to student learning, that value proven practitioner experience as well as 'objective' measurable evidence of successful practice. The 300 underperforming schools networked with each other and linked to mentor schools in the UK's Specialist Schools and Academies Trust Raising Achievement/Transforming Learning project (Hargreaves et al., 2006), and many elements of the Ontario Liberal Government's Educational Reform strategy (Fullan, 2007), comprise compelling examples of effective, high-trust, confidence-building processes of improvement *by* schools, *with* schools, rather than reform imposed *on* schools.

Energy release

A third type of energy is atomic energy. Powerful yet dangerous, atomic energy is the enormous potential energy that is contained within the atom; energy that awaits the precise technology and ingenious intervention that can release it along with all its awesome power. The successful and effective release of atomic energy would enable humans to acquire all the energy they needed. At the same time, if used carelessly, or placed in the wrong hands, atomic energy can just as easily destroy the planet on which our survival depends.

In their remarkable book on the link between Einstein's theory of relativity and the complexities of educational reform, Nobel Prize-winning physicist Stanislaw Glazek and octogenarian educational change theorist Seymour Sarason describe what they believe to be more than an analogous relationship between splitting the atomic nucleus and releasing the energy of educational reform (Sarason, 1996).

First, they say, releasing the energy for productive educational change 'can only be achieved through a teacher as the igniting force' (Sarason, 1996: 12). Second, 'The purpose of the educational reform is to unlock students' energy, which will fuel the motivation to learn, and do more than before the reform started ... The reformer seeks to unlock student energy and motivation that will alter that existing state of affairs' (Sarason, 1996: 12). Third, 'changes in students are impossible' unless the 'organizing nuclear force' of the teacher also changes and becomes a 'better igniting force' (Sarason, 1996: 12). In other words, if we are to release the immense potential energy of our students, we must also release the vast potential energy of our teachers.

Yet, releasing the latent energy of students and teachers is seen by many as potentially dangerous, just as there are those who fear what may happen with the unconstrained release of atomic energy in the physical world. We live in a society that seems increasingly frightened of its own children (Dudley-Marling et al., 2006), distrustful of its teachers and suspicious of its educational leaders. So governments have built elaborate bureaucratic structures replete with 'laundry lists' of competencies, invasive and often oppressive accountability procedures, and inflexible organizational structures that are designed more to regulate and channel people's existing energy rather than release the potential energy that could fuel further improvement.

In fearing the danger of the energy that might be released, governments and bureaucracies drain and try to contain the diminishing energy that already exists. Yet, paradoxically, in the UK's Raising Achievement/Transforming Learning project, one of the most turned-around schools significantly improved its performance with a group of struggling early-secondary students by releasing the students' and teachers' energy together (Hargreaves et al., 2006). The school's head-teacher (principal) invited some of his ageing late-career staff to release the learning energy of students by abandoning the constraining prescribed curriculum and the preoccupation with standardized tests – and by drawing instead on their own locked-up energy and wisdom from their early careers in the 1970s and 1980s of how to create and invent a curriculum that would excite students by engaging with their diverse lives. This transformation was brought about by releasing the energy of teachers who had become increasingly embittered by standardized reform, so that they, in turn, could increase and release the learning power of their diverse students (Oakes and Lipton, 2006).

Conclusion

If the quest to improve achievement rests on cynical strategies to raise test scores, the result will be educationally unsupportable and unsustainable. Apparent improvements will largely be temporary and quickly reach a plateau; they will register as improvements only in what is directly tested; they will often be artefacts of increasingly easier test items; they will improve performance largely in the lower rather than higher areas of learning proficiency; they will bring gains mainly to those students already very close to the pass mark rather than those whose struggles are most serious; they will be secured at the expense of other important areas of learning, achievement and enjoyment; and the price of their forceful and fearful implementation will be exacted on the health and energy of present leaders and the aspirations of potential ones, on whom all our improvement efforts ultimately depend.

Improvement needs energy. *Improved achievement requires increased investment* that puts more financial and human resources into the system, as well as more prudent, patient and restrained use of the human resources that already exist. *Improved achievement needs to renew the energy of the people responsible for securing it* through high-trust, confidence-building change principles that are undertaken *by* schools, *with* schools in transparent processes of committed improvement, that connect short-term success in immediate action to long-term transformations in teaching and learning. *Improved achievement also needs to release rather than restrict* the energy, talent and learning power of our students, teachers and leaders in cultures of hope, that do not fear the power of the learning that will be released.

In the face of immediate and imminent climate change, the world is finally waking up to the reality of its global energy crisis and the need for greater restraint, more renewal and perhaps even nuclear release of the planet's energy reserves. After years of inauthentic improvement, and in the face of a massive recruitment and retention crisis in educational leadership, we now need an equally compelling strategy of energizing, sustainable leadership and improvement in educational change.

References

Abrahamson, E. (2004) *Change without Pain: How Managers can Overcome Initiative Overload, Organizational Chaos, and Employee Burnout*. Boston, MA: Harvard Business School.

Alberta Learning (2004) *Improving Student Learning: Alberta Initiative for School Improvement*. (Edmonton: Alberta Learning).

Blackmore, J. (1996) 'Doing "emotional labour" in the education market place: stories from the field of women in management', *Discourse: Studies in the Cultural Politics of Education*, 17(3): 337–49.

Bolivar Moreno, J.M. (2006) 'Between transaction and transformation: the role of school principals as education leaders in Spain', *Journal of Educational Change* (7), 1–2 March: 19–31.

Brooking, K., Collins, G., Court, M. and O'Neill, J. (2003) 'Getting below the surface of the principals' recruitment "crisis" in New Zealand primary schools', *Australian Journal of Education*, 47(2): 146–59.

Bryk, A.S. and Schneider, B.L. (2004). *Trust in Schools: A Core Resource for Improvement*. New York: Russell Sage Foundation Publications.

Capra, F. (2002) *The Hidden Connections: A Science for Sustainable Living*. New York: HarperCollins.

Dinham, S. (2004) 'The Changing Face of Teaching', *Professional Educator*, 3(2): 2–3.

Dudley-Marling, C., Jackson, J. and Patel Stevens, L. (2006) 'Disrespecting childhood', *Phi Delta Kappa*, 87(10): 748–55.

Dufour, R.E. and Eaker, R. (1998) *Professional Learning Communities at Work: Best Practices for Enhancing Student Achievement*. Bloomington, IN: National Educational Services.

Fink, D. and Brayman, C. (2006) 'School leadership and the challenges of change', *Educational Administration Quarterly*, 42(1): 62–89.

Foot, D. (2001) *Boom, Bust and Echo*. Toronto: Stoddart.

Fullan, M. (2005) *Leadership and Sustainability: System Thinkers in Action*. Thousand Oaks, CA: Corwin Press.

Fullan, M. (2007) *Turnaround Leadership*. San Francisco, CA: Jossey-Bass/Wiley.

Goodlad, J. (1994) *Educational Renewal: Better Teachers, Better Schools*. San Francisco, CA: Jossey-Bass.

Goodlad, J. (1997) 'Beyond McSchools: a challenge to educational leadership', Centre for Educational Renewal website, http://depts.washington.edu/cedren/CER.htm (accessed 7 November 2006).

Goodson, I.F. (2003) *Professional Knowledge, Professional Lives: Studies in Education and Change*. Maidenhead: Open University Press.

Goodstein, D. (2004). *Out of Gas: The End of the Age of Oil*. New York: W.W. Norton.

Green, R., Malcolm, S., Greenwood, K., Small, M. and Murphy, G. (2001) 'A survey of the health of Victorian primary school principals', *International Journal of Educational Management*, 15(1): 23–30.

Gronn, P. (2003) *The New Work of Educational Leaders: Changing Leadership Practice in an Era of School Reform*. London: Paul Chapman Publishing.

Gronn, P. and Rawlings-Sanaei, F. (2003) 'Principal recruitment in a climate of leadership disengagement', *Australian Journal of Education*, 47(2): 172–85.

Haidt, J. (2005) *The Happiness Hypothesis*. New York: Basic Books.

Hargreaves, A. (2007) 'Sustainable professional learning communities', in L. Stoll and K.S. Louis, (eds), *Professional Learning Communities: Divergence, Depth and Dilemmas*. Maidenhead: Open University Press.

Hargreaves, A. and Fink, D. (2003) 'Sustaining leadership', *Phi Delta Kappan*, 84(9): 693–700.

Hargreaves, A. and Fink, D. (2006) *Sustainable Leadership*. San Francisco, CA: Jossey-Bass/Wiley.

Hargreaves, A. and Goodson, I. (2006) 'Educational change over time? The sustainability and non-sustainability of three decades of secondary school change and continuity', *Educational Administration Quarterly*, 42(1): 3–41.

Hargreaves, A. and Shirley, D. (2006) 'Data-driven to distraction', *Education Week*, 26(16): 1–2.

Hargreaves, A., Shirley, D., Evans, M., Johnson, C. and Riseman, D. (2006) *The Long and the Short of Raising Achievement: Final Report of the Evaluation of the 'Raising Achievement, Transforming Learning' Project of the UK Specialist Schools and Academies Trust*. Chestnut Hill: Boston College.

Healey, D. (2006) 'Being a principal can be punishing', *Hamilton Spectator*, 11 June: A6.

Howe, N. and Strauss, W. (2000) *Millennials Rising: The Next Great Generation*. New York: Vintage Books.

Howson, J. (2005) *20th Annual Survey of Senior Staff Appointments in Schools in England and Wales*. Oxford: Education Data Surveys.

Johnson, S.M., Kardos, S.M. (2004) *Finders and Keepers: Helping New Teachers Survive and Thrive in Our Schools*. San Francisco, CA: Jossey-Bass.

Kanter, R.M. (2004) *Confidence: How Winning Streaks and Losing Streaks Begin and End*. New York: Crown Business.

Kauffman, D., Liu, E. and Donaldson, M.L. (2004) 'The support gap: new teachers' early experiences in high-income and low-income schools' *Educational Policy Analysis Archives*, 12(61). Available from http://epaa.asu.edu/epaa/v12n61/v12n61.pdf (accessed 7 November 2006).

Lazarus, R. (1994) *Emotion and Adaptation*. Oxford: Oxford University Press.

Loehr, J. and Schwartz, T. (2003) *The Power of Full Engagement: Managing Energy, not Time, is the Key to High Performance and Personal Renewal*. New York: Free Press.

McDonough, W. and Braungart, M. (2002) *Cradle to Cradle: Remaking the Way We Make Things*. New York: North Point Press.

McKibben, B. (2003) *Enough: Staying Human in an Engineered Age*. New York: Times Books.

McLaughlin, M. and Talbert, J. (2006) *Building School-Based Teacher Learning Communities*. New York: Teachers College Press.

National Association of Head Teachers (NAHT) (2006) 'NAHT press release survey confirms deepening crisis of recruitment to headship, National Association of Head Teachers', 26 April, available at www.naht.org.uk/news/web_news_view.asp?ID=2140andsectionid=3.

Oakes, J. and Lipton, M. (2006) *Teaching to Change the World*. New York: McGraw-Hill College.

Paton, G. and Stewart, W. (2005) 'Heads driven out by OFSTED', *Times Educational Supplement*, 9 September, available at www.tes.co.uk/search/?story_id+2131152.

Pounder, D., Galvin, P. and Shelton, P. (2003) 'An analysis of the United States educational administrator shortage', *Australian Journal of Education*, 47(12): 133–45.

Rifkin, J. (1981) *Entropy: A New World View*. New York: Bantam.

Sarason, S. (1996) *Revisiting the Culture of the School and the Problem of Change*. New York: Teachers College Press.

Schwartz, B (2004) *The Paradox of Choice: Why More is Less*. New York: Harper and Row.
Spillane, J. (2006) *Distributed Leadership*. San Francisco, CA: Jossey-Bass.
Stein, J. (2001) 'How to fix the coming principal shortage', *Time*, 20 July, www.time.com/time/columnist/goldstein/article/0,9565,168379,00.html.
Stoll, L. and Louis, K.S. (2007) *Professional Learning Communities: Divergence, Depth and Dilemmas*. Maidenhead: Open University Press.
Suzuki, D. (2003) *The David Suzuki Reader: A Lifetime of Ideas from a Leading Activist and Thinker*. Vancouver: Greystone Press.
Teachernet (2005) 'School workforce remodelling', www.teachernet.gov/uk/wholeschool/remodelling/.
Times Educational Supplement (TES) (2005) 'Governors want Superman or Wonderwoman', 9 September, www.tes.co.uk/search/?story_id+2131161.
Troman, G. and Woods, P. (2000) 'Careers under stress: teacher adaptations at a time of intensive reform', *Journal of Educational Change*, 1(3): 253–75.
Tulgan, B. and Martin, C. (2001) *Managing Generation Y: Global Citizens Born in the Late Seventies and Early Eighties*. Amherst, MA: HRD Press.
Williams, T. (2001) *Unrecognized Exodus, Unaccepted Accountability: The Looming Shortage of Principals and Vice Principals in Ontario Public School Boards*. Toronto: Ontario Principals Council.
World Commission on Environment and Development (1987) *Our Common Future*. New York: Oxford University Press, www.are.admin.ch/imperia/md/content/are/nachhaltigeentwicklung/brundtland_bericht.pdf?PHPSESSID=e3c6f1426e270560d671dd1b93fc8fc2.

Chapter 4

Sustaining resilience

Christopher Day and Michèle Schmidt[1]

Introduction

Drawing from research on successful and sustainable leadership in education and extensive interviews with five successful headteachers in primary (elementary) and secondary schools in the UK, this chapter focuses upon the contribution of resilience to the capacities of successful headteachers to sustain their success. It suggests that resilience (defined as the capacity to continue to 'bounce back', to recover strength or spirit quickly in the face of adverse circumstances) is closely allied to a strong sense of moral purpose, and that moral purpose itself is fundamental to both an ethic of social justice and a concern for promoting achievement in all aspects of students' and staff's lives. Texts based on empirical leadership research, either emphasize qualities of passion and commitment (Sugrue, 2005), strategic direction (Leithwood and Jantzi, 1999), or, more recently, principles of sustainability (Davies, 2006; Day, 2005; Fullan, 2005; Hargreaves and Fink, 2006). However, in doing so, they acknowledge only implicitly the need for such headteachers (and teachers) to be resilient as they face persistent and potentially eroding challenges of personal, professional and organizational, social and demographic change over time in varying personal, professional and organizational circumstances.

The school which a headteacher inherits on appointment may be very different from the one he/she leads in five or 10 years' time. The headteacher her/himself may also have changed during this period. Indeed, if research on headteachers' professional life phases is taken into account (Day and Bakioglu, 1996; Ribbins, 1999; Weindling, 1999) many headteachers will experience changes in family circumstances, energy and health and, even, commitment levels during their tenure. Concomitant with these, will be policy and demographic changes. As Hargreaves and Fink point out, 'sustainable improvement depends upon successful leadership, and for this, courage is needed to be a leader of learning in sometimes uncongenial conditions dominated by school rankings, test scores, and short-term achievement targets ... [with] ... firm convictions about and unwavering commitment to enhancing deep and broad learning, not merely tested achievement, for *all* students' (2006: 28). (See also, Day and Leithwood, 2007.) However, our research indicates that sustaining such firm convictions demands not only courage but, more importantly, a capacity for resilience; and that this is closely associated with strength of moral purpose.

Moral purpose

'You cannot move substantially towards sustainability in the absence of widely shared moral purpose. The reason is that sustainability depends on the distributed effort of people at all levels of the system, and meeting the goals of moral purpose produces commitment throughout the system' (Fullan, 2005: 87). Moral purpose is not a new concept, and the body of research relating to this continues to grow (Leithwood and Duke, 1998). Moral purposes are often associated with humanistic and transformational leadership (Greenfield, 1991; Hodgkinson, 1991; Leithwood and Jantzi, 1999; Sergiovanni, 1993; Starratt, 1994), and they apply to all leaders whose educational vision encompasses notions of a 'good' society, participative democracy and the fulfilment of all individuals' intellectual, social and emotional potential. Many researchers have provided instances where morals and values constitute the core of leadership and administrative practices, however contingent these may be (Bates, 1993; Beck, 1992; 1994; Day, Harris, Hadfield, Tolley and Beresford, 2000; Evers and Lakomksi, 1991; Greenfield, 1991; Maxcy, 1995; Sergiovanni, 1993; Starratt, 1994). Having a core moral dimension (Bogotch, Miron and Murray, 1998) acknowledges that classroom teaching and school leadership at their best are more than the skilful acquisition, communication and application of knowledge and skills, that they go beyond technical solutions and include a sense of care and social justice for all members of the community (Beck, 1994; Noddings, 1992; Starratt, 1991).

Successful leaders look inwardly as well as outwardly (Day et al., 2000), attending to what some have called the state of their own 'souls' (Starratt, 1991) in the knowledge that their work includes modelling, dialogue, practice and affirmation as well as monitoring, being 'data-driven' and, where appropriate, critical. Modelling for these educators means demonstrating to students and teachers that they are cared for. Dialogue involves open spaces that allow for diverse ideas and divergent thinking as well as spaces for listening. Such an approach allows head-teachers to show they care by listening and responding fully to their students and teachers. Care involves relationships with others and the responsibilities that accompany those relationships. Moral leaders who care, nurture a school culture within which students (and teachers) feel cared about and consequently experience a sense of being valued and respected (Kohn, 1996). Caring, from this perspective, becomes the fundamental organizational value, which helps determine a school's priorities and directs school decision-making. Furthermore, it relates to Hargreaves and Fink's (2006) principle of resourcefulness where sustainable leadership develops and does not deplete material and human resources. It renews people's energy. Bryk and Schneider (2002) and Hargreaves and Fink (2006) speak specifically of the importance of trust and confidence as important features of renewal and achievement. Trust 'amounts to people being able to rely on each other' (Spillane, 2006: 212); and it is this value which often drives 'distributed leadership' agendas in schools which aspire to become learning communities. Confidence refers to belief 'in oneself, in team members or colleagues, in the structures and policies of the organization, and in the external environment that provides resources' (Spillane, 2006: 216).

In sum, leaders with moral purposes are values-led. They put the principles of responsibility, care and justice, alongside their determination to ensure that students leave their schools with the best possible life chances. These values are at the forefront of their decision-making processes, their perceptions of the purposes of schooling, their understanding of the concept of education and their choice of 'right' or 'good' actions.

From a perspective of social justice, successful leadership involves equity and fairness in relation to individual and community choice. How a school is governed is a crucial part of justice. An ethic of social justice demands that headteachers serve as advocates for students and teachers: 'To promote a just, social order in the school, the school community must carry out an ongoing critique of those structured features of the school that work against human beings' (Starratt, 1994: 194). Such leaders see themselves as 'responsible not just as professionals to their own students' learning but also as citizens, community members, and ethical human beings to all those whom their actions affect or might affect' (cited in Hargreaves and Fink, 2006: 151). Perhaps the most critical and lasting moral principle of sustainable leadership is having such learner and learning-centred perspectives as a key focus for the school's philosophy and teachers' practices.

> *Sustainable leadership, like sustainable improvement, begins with a strong and unswerving sense of moral purpose. The core meaning of sustain is 'to hold up; bear the weight of; be able to bear (strain, suffering, and the like) without collapse.' Inner conviction, unshakeable faith, and a driving, hopeful sense of purpose that stretches far beyond the self – these are the inalienable elements of moral character that truly sustain people during times of overwhelming difficulty and almost unbearable suffering. (Hargreaves and Fink, 2006: 23–4)*

The challenge, then, is how to sustain moral purpose within an ever-changing environment, demanding government mandates and shifting demographics in schools. We maintain that headteachers who are able to lead with moral purpose, must rely upon their own resilience to do so.

Resilience

Resilience is not a quality that is innate. On the contrary, with Bernard (1991), we believe, and this research will show, that it is more than a set of personal traits. While the concept of resilience originated in the disciplines of psychiatry and developmental psychology with a focus on internal factors within the individual (Waller, 2001), the notion of resilience that is presented by the social work literature, interests us most, and advances a perspective that views resilience as multidimensional and multi-determined and is best understood as a dynamic within a social system of interrelationships (Walsh, 1998). Within particular and changing environments, resilience encompasses the individual's capacity to deal effectively with stress and pressure, to cope with everyday challenges, to rebound from disappointments, mistakes and adversity, to develop clear and realistic goals, to solve problems, to interact comfortably with others, to treat oneself and others with respect and dignity, and to have the ability to meet life's challenges with thoughtfulness, confidence, purpose, responsibility, empathy and hope (Brooks, 2005). Thus, although we may be born with an innate capacity for resilience, the capacity to be resilient and retain hope in different negative circumstances, whether these be connected to personal or professional factors, can be enhanced or inhibited by the nature of the settings in which we work, the people with whom we work and the strength of our beliefs or aspirations (Bernard, 1991; Henderson and Milstein, 2003; Luthar, 1996; Oswald, Johnson and Howard, 2003).

Fredrickson (2004) has developed a 'broaden-and-build' theory of positive emotions. She suggests that, 'through experiences of positive emotions ... people transform themselves, becoming more creative, knowledgeable, resilient, socially integrated and healthy' (Frederickson, 2004: 1369); that 'the personal resources accrued during states of positive emotions are durable, [outlasting] the transient emotional states that led to their acquisition' (2004: 1369); and that, 'positive emotions may fuel psychological resilience' (2004: 1372);. In other words, they serve as resources which assist people to cope with adversity.

It is not difficult to relate these research findings to the focus of successful school leaders upon building learning communities, for such learning communities thrive essentially because they build positive emotional climates in which people's interests, contentment, joy and love of learning are nurtured. So it is with the 'communities of practice' (Wenger, 1998) and so it is in classrooms which encourage 'authentic' learning. Fredrickson concludes: 'When positive emotions are in short supply, people get stuck. They lose their degrees of behavioural freedom and become painfully predictable. But when positive emotions are in ample supply, people take off. They become generative, creative, resilient' (2004: 1375). Each of the headteachers in this study could be characterized by 'positive emotionality' (Tugade, Frederickson and Feldman, 2004: 1173). Their positive emotions meant that resilience had become, for them, an enduring professional resource.

Methodology

A key reason for our focus upon the nature of resilience lies in the testimonies of five leaders of schools in this study who were deemed to be effective by independent external inspection reports. Within this context, since the notion of success and what it means to be successful is contested, the researchers recognized the importance of selecting the schools on the basis of a wide range of contexts and leadership challenges. The selection of the case study schools and their headteachers was, therefore, conducted around four main criteria:

1. Schools working in different phases (for example, primary to secondary and including special schools) in a range of communities (urban/suburban/rural, different socio-economic groupings, regional spread).
2. Schools in which publicly acknowledged successful leaders had spent different amounts of time.
3. Headteachers who had been identified by independent external inspection reports.
4. Schools in which student measurable achievement levels had been raised in ways which were attributed to the quality of headship.

The sample comprised three female (secondary, primary, nursery/infant) and two male headteachers (secondary, junior/primary) who had been in their current position between six and 22 years. They had all raised the levels of measurable pupil attainments in their schools and were highly regarded by their peers. All of the schools were publicly owned and maintained by local education authorities in England. Three of the schools served communities which comprised predominantly ethnic minority populations. Two of the schools had a 30 per cent or higher level of special educational needs (SEN). Four of the schools comprised students from low socio-economic backgrounds from single-parent homes or families facing unemployment, while one primary school comprised 80 per cent Pakistan-Muslim families. Details of the five headteachers and characteristics of their schools are shown in Table 4.1.

Findings

The findings are presented under five themes which emerged from the data analysis and which, together, constitute the key principles and practices by which these headteachers contributed to the cognitive, emotional health and academic successes of the school community, through the sustained exercise of moral purpose and resilience:

Table 4.1 *Profiles of headteachers and schools*

Head-teacher	Gender	Years as head-teacher	Teaching specialty	School description	Student/ demographic population	Family background	Ofsted
Adams	F	13	Geography	▪ Secondary Inner city ▪ Low attainment on entry ▪ Challenging behaviour ▪ Specialist status school	▪ 93% ethnic ▪ 58 languages ▪ 1500 students ▪ 680 ESL (English as a second language) ▪ 41%	▪ High unemployment rate ▪ Main employer – Ford; catering; semi-skilled occupations	▪ 1993 – HMI ▪ 1997 – Improving school ▪ 2003 – Good
Bott	M	10	Science	▪ Secondary (grs. 7–11; 11–16 years old) ▪ 50 teachers ▪ High crime district	▪ 803 students ▪ 70% low income ▪ 30% SEN (special educational needs) population ▪ 6% statement population	▪ Single-parent homes ▪ 34% unemployed; nuclear plant (BNF); British Aerospace; small companies	▪ 2003 – Very good
Calder	M	22		▪ Junior primary (7–11-year-olds) ▪ 20 teachers	▪ 480 students ▪ 80% Pakistan-Muslim ▪ 15% SEN ▪ 90% from community	▪ Professional ▪ Wealthy ▪ Own business, factories ▪ Property prices rising	▪ 2 inspections: (a) Very good (b) Better than very good

Table 4.1 *Continued*

Denman	F	8		■ Primary ■ 8 teachers	■ 205 students ■ 26% SEN ■ 51% FSM	■ Unemployed ■ Low income area Single-parent homes ■ Drug use	■ 1996 – Special measures ■ 1999 – Improved ■ 2001 – Excellent
Elwood	F	6		■ Nursery, infants ■ 10 teachers (80 in nursery, 150 infants)	■ 230 students ■ 42% FSM ■ 40% Single-parent homes ■ 50% from outside the community ■ High % SEN	■ White collar (e.g. postman) ■ More generally low income ■ Drug use ■ High absenteeism	■ 1996 – Failing ■ 2000 – Very good

1. Care, consultation and responsibility.
2. Justice and advocacy: the courage of conviction.
3. Being learning and learner focused.
4. Activist leadership.
5. Sustaining resilience.

Care, consultation and responsibility

A prime focus for the headteachers was their relationship with others. Day's research (2005) highlights themes that guide headteachers who are able to sustain success in schools in challenging circumstances. These include: performativity, vision and resilience; building an inclusive community and sustaining involvement; values, beliefs and the ethical dimension; trust; moral purpose, agency and a culture of courage; expectation and achievement; leaders who learn, who build internal capital and who have passion and commitment. Collectively, these principles of sustainability highlight leaders who 'place as much emphasis upon people and processes as they do upon product' (Day, 2005: 581). It is not surprising then that a prime focus for the headteachers was to be their relationship with others. There seemed to be an importance placed on building a nurturing school culture that demonstrated what the people in the school cared about: co-operation, teamwork, trust and respect. Rather than expressing power over their staff, the heads employed approaches that incorporated relational and distributed dimensions. Headteacher Bott promoted relations and unity with his staff: 'We take our jobs very seriously and I believe we do a good job, but we're all together; we look after each other.'

The heads placed a high value on distributing leadership among their staff as a way of encouraging teachers and others to take responsibility and ownership of their work. When asked how she would describe her school culture, headteacher Elwood emphasized collaboration and responsibility among her staff and students:

> *A lot of collaboration. I know I have mentioned that teachers work in year group teams, and they collaborate. Teaching assistants, I try to place them so they are working mainly in one team and they feel they are linked in and well embedded in that team and this is to do with getting back to everybody feeling valued and having a place.*

This same headteacher introduced the notion of collective responsibility 'where people can take responsibility and by that I don't just mean staff, but children as well. They all have opportunities to take on responsibilities, even from a young age'.

Denman stressed the importance of consulting with her staff so that there was open communication, which gave her a sense of what responsibilities her staff could handle and when:

> *We work very much as a team ... we can argue amongst ourselves and we can discuss things, but once we have decided, we all put our weight behind it, even if it isn't what you particularly want. If it has been decided by the people together, then you go with it. And you give it your best shot.*

Indeed, the headteachers demanded from and relied on the trust and confidence of their staff (Bryk and Schneider, 2002). Thus teachers, support staff and students alike were included in this process. The same applied in reverse. The heads had the confidence and trust of the teachers, students and parents. Bott explained that without the trust of his staff, he would not be able to run the school in the way he would like:

> *It has no end of advantages both for me and the staff because the school cannot run with just one person; it runs with the whole staff. What it has enabled for me is that I am able to concentrate on the things I should be concentrating on. And I can leave other people and trust them to do a good job in other things really. But that has an effect on them too because it builds on their self-esteem; it builds up their confidence.*

Although the heads revealed their concern for the welfare of their schools in general, and their students and teachers specifically, it was clear that this concern did not exclude their mission for academic achievement. They emphasized the personal and the functional (Fielding, 2001).

Care, as defined by Noddings (1992) and Starratt (1994), involves confidence and trust. Indeed, the headteachers relied on the trust and confidence of their staff, not just teachers but also support staff and students alike, and vice versa, that is, the confidence and trust teachers, students and parents had in them as heads. We might conclude then that, for these heads, being a leader was a form of stewardship, and the responsibilities of stewardship required that obligations and commitments born from values and ideas were to be met with resilience, regardless of obstacles.

Justice and advocacy: the courage of conviction

Alongside care, consultation and responsibility, what seemed to be of immense value to these headteachers was the pursuit of equitable allocation, access and balance of resources of time; a sense of fairness dealing with teachers; and maintaining high standards in the recruitment and retention of teachers. First and foremost, the heads worked hard at removing practical and policy obstacles for teachers in their efforts to promote positive environments for learners and teachers. Calder had a concern for how much time and energy teachers had to devote to new externally generated initiatives without compromising the school culture and vision. He explained how he communicated to external authorities that some initiatives would just have to wait, since his teachers were not ready to implement something new:

> *I don't allow some of the pressures [from the local authority] to actually come in at all. I just sort of say, 'Well, we're not doing that one. So I'm not even going to put that in front of you'. I'm not doing anything for show that I don't need to do; I'm going to do what the parents want me to do, which is to see that their children get the best education.*

Illustrations of respect for the people around them in schools were widespread. For example, Denman was adamant about her feelings of not asking teachers to do something that she herself would not be prepared to do: 'If I have new staff, I will go in and teach and I will go and observe them as I am not asking them to do anything that I haven't done or can't do myself. And I think that is important – staff have to have a regard and respect for you as a teacher for you to be a headteacher.'

The heads seemed to place primacy on being advocates for their students and teachers by promoting an ongoing critique of what quality education looks like (Starratt, 1994). For example, many of the headteachers had a vision or had something 'up their sleeve' that they hoped to implement in the school to further the academic and personal growth opportunities for their students. Their decisions about allocation of funds in their schools were based on a clear understanding of the relative values of the choices involved (Stringfield et al., 1996). They were invariably asking themselves: 'Who will benefit from this?' 'What values do my objectives express?' 'How do they relate to other people's values?' and 'How do I decide which goals are valuable ones to pursue?' These questions of value or moral purpose, are part of establishing and responsibly pursuing any educational improvement purpose (Stringfield, Ross and Smith, 1996). For the heads in this research, being learning and learner focused was part of their moral purposes.

Being learning and learner focused

All the headteachers were ambitious to continue to improve the learning opportunities for their students which were specific to their needs. Denman said: 'I think I have a very clear vision and I suppose I have strong opinions about what's right and wrong, so I know exactly where I want us to go and I don't think we are complacent as a school.' These longer-range improvement purposes were not intended to be quick fixes for learning. Denman valued the use of whiteboards:

> *The use of ICT in school [is critical]. I don't want to use ICT for the sake of it, but I also don't want them to be an add-on, hence we all have electronic whiteboards in the rooms which is quite threatening to some staff. I saw the potential of it, and other schools say to us, well why and how have you got all those. Because I prioritized it. I took all of my money and put it in that because ... this is what we need to put our money into. These are perfect tools for the children and for the staff. These are going to make life better and may have because the resources that are there are in their hands, and the motivational factor they have for the children, the application of the life that they have for the children and any jobs in the future. All need computer skills. They are all valid.*

Bott's vision for enhanced learning was a little different. He wanted to transform the school into a 'specialist college'.[2] 'Yes, it's common knowledge what it is. I want this school to get specialist college status. And I want it to be a science college, not because I'm a scientist, I have to say that. It's going to be science and math and those two departments are exceptionally strong.' Adams invested in a consultant to address the behavioural issues in her school:

> *We actually have a system in place. About four or five years ago, we were looking at behaviour in lessons and around the school and it was a sort of panic about behaviour and all schools have them, even though behaviour isn't different. And anyway, what I did was, I did a questionnaire, and you know, I was taking notice of my staff, and then I got a consultant in, and what came out of his work, because he did a lot of*

interviews with staff, was the real issue was not with behaviour, it was with consistency with staff. So we worked really hard with consistency

Perhaps the most critical and lasting moral principle of leadership is integrity for learning. These headteachers all made the advancement of deep and broad learning for all a key focus for the school's philosophy and teachers' practices.

Activist leadership

The heads were unanimous in their concerns about the negative impact of national policy demands on their visions for learners, learning and capacity for success. Calder commented: 'I think one of the main challenges for any headteacher now is to balance the demands made nationally against your own school agenda and your own staff and it's taking into account the staff collectively, the staff individually and what you can reasonably expect them to move towards.'

It seemed then that, where resilience was particularly necessary was when moral purposes conflicted with governmental mandates. Bott recounted his experience as a head 10 years earlier, when he was much more conscious of 'toeing the party line':

When I was first appointed as head you're under incredible pressure to toe the party line – that's the DfES [Department for Education and Skills] line, [and] the LEA [local education authority] line and so you're supposed to do everything. And I very rapidly came to the conclusion, going back 10 years, that workload was ridiculous. They just throw initiatives at you one after the other and it's nonsense.

He went on to say that over the years he resisted 'jumping through hoops' and had become more thoughtful about implementing government initiatives:

I won't jump through hoops [anymore]. I don't care who sent the directive down. If I don't like it, I don't do it. And now after years of experience, I've got the confidence to do that and say, 'Hang on. No. That doesn't fit this school and we're not doing it.' Something else comes along and I'll say, 'Yep. That's a great idea. We'll do that.'

While it seemed that the heads viewed the government initiatives as political nuisances, they did not openly resist these accountability measures, but rather mediated them (Day et al., 2000). They were passionate about the values they held and their moral purposes regarding their organizations.

It seems then, that in their efforts to sustain their organizations, moral purposes were most explicitly put to the test when the heads were faced with implementing governmental mandates. They all seemed to be grappling with what they believed was successful in relation to nationally imposed assessment criteria, which often conflicted with their own notions of success. They managed successfully a number of 'dilemma[s] associated with ... instance[s] in which compliance with a formal organizational rule, policy or directive conflicts with school-level concerns of students, parents, or teachers or perhaps with good pedagogical practice' (Crowson, 1989, cited in Capper, 1993: 276).

When we did ask what factors determined success in their schools, the heads would often put governmental success indicators as secondary to school success indicators. Denman commented that her criteria for success were often different from governmental organizations:

> *I do sometimes have a problem with, for instance, target setting because I'll get the LEA who say to me your targets this year should be such and such because that then will bring us in line with our base line target from the government. So for the LEA to get their target, schools have to have this target and I say, 'No, these are children you are talking about'.*

To these heads, well-being was associated with the capacity to achieve success. Calder's comments illustrate this well:

> *Well, I think if we go backwards in priority, the top priority would be parents and children ... and then there's Ofsted. Ofsted in a sense gives you guidance in what they expect to see and how the school should be run. And so obviously you want to meet ... you want to become as close as you can to doing what the people who are judging you are judging you against. And then after that would be the LEA and after that it would be the DfES in terms of additional things.*

This head, like others, viewed her obligation to government policies as no more important than her obligation to her students, staff and community. In essence, the heads did not dispute the need for public accountability. Rather, they themselves had higher expectations and aspirations for the personal, social and academic achievement of their students. They understood that in order to achieve success within an organization, a clear sense of moral purpose, care and justice is needed; and to sustain success required resilience of staff and students.

Sustaining resilience

> *'Leaders are the stewards of organizational energy ... They inspire or demoralize others, first by how effectively they manage their own energy and next by how well they manage, focus, invest and renew the collective energy of those they lead' (Loehr and Schwartz, 2003: 5).*

The leadership challenges the heads faced required them to display the ability to 'bounce back' in adverse circumstances, and this was not always easy. Elwood relayed her own difficulties when dealing with incompetent teachers. She found the whole process emotionally draining and demoralizing for the teachers involved, and dreaded these scenarios. She described one situation where, 'there was one teacher who we had to start down the route of competency, but that is a terrible route to go ... it is terribly demoralizing. I mean, I hated it. It is something I would never want to do again, but I would if I had to'.

In order to honour their commitment for a collaborative and distributive form of decision making, the heads remained resilient when goals they believed were important were not necessarily supported by their staff. This required patience, tenacity and faith on their part that the right things would happen to the betterment of the school.

Denman described the importance of working together with her teachers to maintain morale during those stressful times when their school was evaluated by Ofsted:

> *The school cannot run with just one person. It's run with the whole staff ... [this] builds on their [the teachers'] self-esteem; it builds up their confidence and that was so important when we were in special measures ... So in that instance, you have to be careful that your morale does not let you down – that you keep that up.*

Indeed, researchers claim that individuals who perceive themselves to be supported by others exhibit more positive physical health, mental health and longevity than those who perceive themselves as not having support from others (Cutrona and Russell, 1990; Hobfoll and Stevens, 1990).

The heads all engaged in activities that allowed them to get away from the stresses of work and refresh themselves outside of the workplace by travelling, reading, shopping, train-spotting, exercising at the gym, or cycling. In fact, the heads endeavoured to separate their work from their personal lives – some more easily than others. Bott had trained himself to 'switch off' work: 'I've had to train myself to do that ... I can switch off. I do sleep well ... You get terribly frustrated at times, like you do in all jobs, but you learn to live with it.'

In sum the heads all relied on support networks within and outside their schools, furthered their learning and took time out to reflect on their practice. Most importantly, they entered their assignments with a positive mindset. They garnered much experience over the years and developed resilience-conserving strategies to make sure their values were clearly articulated and understood by others. Calder revealed some of his strategies gained over 22 years of experience, which included simply learning from one's mistakes and moving on:

> *I'm one of those people who learns by experience so if I think, well, that didn't work last time and I don't do that again ... I can remember someone once saying to me, M ..., if you've got a problem with somebody don't deal with it on a Friday because they just get the weekend to go over it and get steamed up about it.*

Adams remarked on her ability to move ahead incrementally, realizing that setbacks are inevitable. She used a metaphor of building blocks that require time to set: 'You have to put a building block in then you go up a bit more; you've got another building block in [and] it is that sort of ... and if you look at the results when we have done that, the plateaus have got shorter.' Denman added that: 'You give it your best shot ... I think of myself like a ball. I bounce back ... I have tried to bounce back as well no matter how hard you hit, you bounce back and sometimes the harder you hit, the better you bounce back.'

The heads acted rather than reacted. They routinely took the offensive in situations of adversity. Despite their challenges, they remained focused on what they cared about by maintaining a strong sense of purpose and organizational values. Bott sustained his focus on school goals despite the governmental mandates that at times seemed to jeopardize what was valued in the school by feeling confident enough to prioritize what was important:

> *Well, if I want to do something, I try to think what's reasonable. I say 'We'll do so many [changes] this year and so many next year.' I don't feel obliged to do things for people just to get them done. I think what we've got to do, what is reasonable in the time and they are just as important so we might go for those. So I try to prioritize for the benefit of the school.*

One characteristic of headteachers who continue to 'bounce back' from negative emotional experiences in response to changing situational demands is hope, an 'affirmation that despite the heartbreak and trials that we face daily ... we can see that our actions can be purposeful and significant' (Sockett, 1993: 85). To be resilient is to retain hope, to possess a disposition 'which results in them being positive about experience or aspects of that experience ... the belief that something good, which does not presently apply to one's own life, or the life of others, could still materialize, and so is yearned for as a result' (Halpin, 2003: 15).

Positive emotions have received less attention in the research on resilience than have negative ones (Fredrickson, 2004: 1367). The same might also be said about the plethora of research in schools which highlight the negative effects of various reform environments rather than the positive ways in which many whom they affect have responded. Yet, experience of positive emotions prompts individuals to engage with their environments. Rather than fight against or ignore change, resilient headteachers and their staff will absorb, mediate and, where appropriate, adapt, in the belief that they can continue to contribute positively to broadly rather than narrowly defined educational purposes.

Discussion

What, then, do our findings tell us in response to our question: 'How do headteachers, who are deemed successful leaders, sustain themselves and their schools?' The government-imposed results-driven agenda in the UK, with its focus upon measurable pupil achievement and the monitoring of teaching standards, has had the effect of bringing into sharp relief the tensions which arise in managing complex, interrelated and sometimes contradictory moral and instrumental purposes of schooling. The apparent focus of these standards upon rational forms of management planning with an emphasis upon performativity through target setting, assessment and measurable achievement was found by these headteachers to limit their capacities to achieve success.

The vision of what is needed to achieve better examination results failed to encompass their concerns to provide educational processes which would benefit the individual and society.

This research, although small scale, suggests that despite pressures from multiple policy implementation accountabilities, social disadvantage and changing expectations, successful headteachers who demonstrate resilient leadership are those whose values cause them to place as much emphasis upon people and processes as they do upon product (Day, 2005; Day and Leithwood, 2007). Improvement for headteachers in this research was broadly rather than narrowly defined. It included the academic achievement of the pupils against quantitative measures (for example, results of national tests and examinations) and qualitative indicators (esteem, relationships, expectations, behaviour, participation, engagement with learning). These heads demonstrated a clear and abiding concern for learning, care, justice. Their practices involved modelling and promoting respect for others; advocating fairness, equality and justice; caring for the well-being and whole development of students and staff; displaying and also demanding honesty and integrity; placing primacy on a positive school climate; nurturing learner-centred teaching; and promoting high standards. Regardless of external pressures, they were constantly vigilant about building and sustaining their schools as caring, values-led, and collaborative communities. Within their management of competing tensions and dilemmas, they remained vision oriented and people-centred, and did so with a sense of moral purpose, at the centre of which was a focus upon care, justice, learning and learners. In common with successful principals in a longitudinal study of schools in challenging contexts in North America, these successful headteachers, 'refused to cave in (in the face of external demands for more public accountability through pupil test results), to trade their core values for unquestioning compliance, or to abandon authentic achievement for cynical attempts to boost test score gains' (Hargreaves and Fink, 2006: 31).

Previous research indicates that such purposes and processes are often inextricably intertwined with the professional and personal moral purposes of the headteacher (Day et al., 2001; Jackson, Boostrom and Hansen, 1993; Sergiovanni, 1992; Tom, 1984). This research suggests, however, that these headteachers' success relied on their resilience; and that their capacity to be resilient was closely related to the strength of their moral purposes.

Note

1. The authors shared equally in the writing of this.
2. This status is awarded by government to schools which meet required specialist standards in a particular curriculum area, for example, PE; Arts; Sciences. The school must raise £50,000 from local businesses and this is matched by government funding.

References

Bates, B.M. (1993) 'On knowing: cultural and critical approaches to educational administration', *Educational Management and Administration*, 21(3): 171–6.

Beck, L. (1992) 'Meeting the challenge of the future: the place of a caring ethic in educational administration', *American Journal of Education*, 100: 454–96.

Beck, L. (1994) *Reclaiming Educational Administration as a Caring Profession*. New York: Teachers College Press.

Bernard, B. (1991) *Fostering Resiliency in Kids: Protective Factors in the Family, School and Community*. Portland, OR: Northwest Regional Educational Laboratory.

Bogotch, I.E., Miron, L.F. and Murray, J. (1998) 'Moral leadership discourses in urban settings: the multiple influences of social context', *Urban Education*, 33(3): 303–30.

Brooks, R.B. (2005) 'The power of parenting', in R.B. Brooks and S. Goldstein (eds), *Handbook of Resilience in Children*. New York: Kluwer. pp. 297–314.

Bryk, A.S. and Schneider, B.L. (2002) *Trust in Schools: A Core Resource for Improvement*. New York: Russell Sage Foundation.

Capper, C. (ed.) (1993) *Educational Administration in a Pluralistic Society*. Albany, NY: State University of New York Press.

Crowson, R. (1989) 'Managerial ethics in educational administration: the rational choice approach', *Urban Education*, 23(4): 412–35.

Cutrona, C.E. and Russell, D.W. (1990) 'Type of social support and specific stress: toward a theory of optimal matching', in B.R. Sarason, I.G. Sarason, and G.R. Pierce (eds), *Social, Support: An Interactional View*. New York: Wiley. pp. 319–66.

Davies, B. (2006) *Leading the Strategically Focused School*. London: Paul Chapman Publishing.

Day, C. (2005) 'Sustaining success in challenging contexts: leadership in English schools', *Journal of Educational Administration*, 43(6): 573–83.

Day, C. and Bakioglu, A. (1996) 'Development and disenchantment in the professional lives of headteachers', in I.F. Goodson and A. Hargreaves (eds), *Teachers' Professional Lives*. London: Falmer Press.

Day, C. and Leithwood, K. (eds) (2007) *Successful Principal Leadership in Times of Change: An international perspective*. Dordrecht: Springer.

Day, C., Harris, A. and Hadfield, M. (2001) 'Challenging the orthodoxy of effective school leadership', *International Journal of Leadership in Education*, 4(1): 39–56.

Day, C., Harris, A., Hadfield, M., Tolley, H. and Beresford, J. (2000) *Leading Schools in Times of Change*. Buckingham: Open University Press.

Evers, C.W. and Lakomski, G. (1991) *Knowing Educational Administration: Contemporary Methodological Controversies in Educational Administration*. New York: Pergamon Press.

Fielding, M. (2001) 'Taking education really seriously: four years' hard labour', in M. Fielding (ed.), *Taking Education Really Seriously: Four Years of Hard Labour*. London: Routledge. 1–14.

Fredrickson, B.L. (2004) 'The broaden-and-build theory of positive emotions', *The Royal Society*, 359: 1367–77.

Fullan, M. (2005) *Leadership and Sustainability: System Thinkers in Action*. Thousand Oaks, CA: Corwin Press.

Greenfield, W.D. (1991) *Toward a Theory of School Leadership*. Chicago, IL: American Educational Research Association.

Halpin, D. (2003) *Hope and Education: The Role of the Utopian Imagination*. London: RoutledgeFalmer.

Hargreaves, A. and Fink, D. (2006) *Sustainable Leadership*. San Francisco, CA: Jossey-Bass.

Henderson, N. and Milstein, M. (2003) *Resiliency in Schools: Making It Happen for Students and Educators*. Thousand Oaks, CA: Corwin Press.

Hobfoll, S.E. and Stevens, M.A. (1990) 'Social support during extreme stress: consequential and intervention', in B.R. Sarason, I.G. Sarason and G.R. Pierce (eds), *Social Support: An Interactional View*. New York: Wiley. pp. 454–81.

Hodgkinson, C. (1991) *Educational Leadership: The Moral Art*. Albany, NY: SUNY Press.

Jackson, P.W., Boostrom, R.E. and Hansen, D.T. (1993) *The Moral Life of Schools*. San Francisco, CA: Jossey-Bass.

Kohn, A. (1996) 'What to look for in a classroom', *Educational Leadership*, 54(1): 54–5.

Leithwood, K. and Duke, D. (1998) 'Mapping the conceptual terrain of leadership: a critical point of departure for cross-cultural studies', *Peabody Journal of Education*, 73(2): 31–50.

Leithwood, K. and Jantzi, D. (1999) 'Transformational school leadership effects: a replication', *School Effectiveness and School Improvement*, 10(4): 451–79.

Loehr, J. and Schwartz, T. (2003) *The Power of Full Engagement*. New York: Free Press.

Luthar, S. (1996) 'Resilience: a construct of value', paper presented at the Annual Conference of the American Psychological Association, Toronto.

Maxcy, S.J. (1995) 'Beyond leadership frameworks', *Educational Administration Quarterly*, 31(3): 473–83.

Noddings, N. (1992) *The challenge to care in schools*. New York: Teachers College Press.

Oswald, M., Johnson, B. and Howard, S. (2003) 'Quantifying and evaluating resilience promoting factors – teachers' beliefs and perceived roles', *Research in Education*, 70: 50–64.

Ribbins, P. (1999) 'Understanding leadership: developing headteachers', in T. Bush, L. Bell, R. Bolam, R. Glatter and P. Ribbins (eds), *Educational Management: Redefining Theory, Policy and Practices*. London: Paul Chapman Publishing.

Sergiovanni, T.J. (1992) *Moral Leadership: Getting to the Heart of School Improvement*. San Francisco, CA: Jossey-Bass.

Sergiovanni, T.J. (1993) 'Frames of leadership', *International Journal of Educational Reform*, 2: 19–26.

Sockett, M. (1993) *The Moral Base for Teacher Professionalism*. Columbia University: Teachers College Press.

Spillane, J.P. (2006) *Distributed Leadership*. San Francisco, CA: Jossey-Bass.

Starratt, R.J. (1991) 'Building an ethical school: a theory for practice in educational leadership', *Educational Administration Quarterly*, 27(2): 185–202.

Starratt, R.J. (1994) *Building on Ethical Schools: A Practical Response to the Moral Crises in Schools*. Bristol, PA: Falmer Press.

Stringfield, S., Ross, S. and Smith, L. (1996) 'Bold plans for school restructing: nine designs from New American Schools', in S. Stringfield, S. Ross and L. Smith (eds), *Bold Plans for School Restructuring*. Mahwah, NJ: Lawrence Erlbaum Associates.

Sugrue, C. (ed.) (2005) *Passionate Principalship: Learning from life histories of school leaders*. London: RoutledgeFalmer.

Tom, A. (1984) *Teaching as a Moral Craft*. New York: Longman.

Tugade, M.M., Fredrickson, B.L. and Feldman Barrett, L. (2004) 'Psychological resilience and positive emotional granularity: examining the benefits of positive emotions on coping and health', *Journal of Personality*, 72(6): 1162–90.

Waller, M. (2001) 'Resilience in ecosystemic context: Evolution of the concept', *American Journal of Orthopsychiatry*, 7(3) 290–7.

Walsh, F. (1998) *Strengthening Family Resilience*. New York: Guilford Press.

Weindling, D. (1999) 'Stages of headship', in T. Bush, L. Bell, R. Bolam, R. Glatter and P. Ribbins (eds), *Educational Management: Redefining Theory, Policy and Practice*. London: Paul Chapman Publishing.

Wenger, E. (1998) *Communities of Practice: Learning, Meaning and Identity*, Cambridge: Cambridge University Press.

Chapter 5

Sustainability of the status quo

Terry Deal

To onlookers, the dizzy carousel of change and reform goes round and round with little if any impact on their work. In recent memory, the endless cycle of trying to make things different has bounced off traditional ways like water off the back of a duck. Currently the field of organizations and policy is interested in sustainability, the ability of a system to maintain itself over the long haul. The new gambit focuses attention on the stability of reform and how a dismal track record might be improved. This tack seems somewhat ill-advised since, if sustainability is the centre of interest, the focus should be on the ability of schools to abide the onslaught of pressures that have attempted to remake them in the images of a revolving door of rational reformers.

The sustainability of traditional ways is robust even when a new wrinkle is obviously better. In the 1950s, the United States Congress formally adopted the metric system of standards and measurements. This seemed logical since most countries on the planet rely on this mode of operation. The fact that the US is out of step creates real problems in an ever so globalized world. The problems with the expensive Hubble telescope were attributed to two groups of engineers each following different standards. Having everyone on the same wavelength makes perfect sense to sensible people. But as Shakespeare wrote eons ago, 'Aye, there's the rub'. Since 1950, the ability of our (US) system of weights and measures to sustain itself is rather remarkable. Although our speedometers now feature both miles and kilometres in assigning speed it is obvious that people still judge their rate of travel in miles per hour. This situation is akin to the resilience of our education system in paying only lip service to the barrage of so-called 'improvements' launched with fanfares over the past several decades. Seymour Sarason's observation that 'the more things change, the more they stay the same' seems as apt now as when he coined the phrase many years ago. If we want to get a grasp on sustainability, we ought to be looking at the uncanny ability of the status quo to hold out against efforts to make it different – even if the changes might be better. What is there about schools as organizations that encourages a tenacious tendency to hold out against challenges to the existing state of affairs?

Loosely coupled structural arrangements

In technical organizations where there is clear link between work and product the main focus is on the means of production. Any innovation that improves how things are produced is quickly adopted. The bottom line is the difference in quality or cost, both relatively easy to measure. In institutionalized organizations, the relationship between efforts and outcomes is notoriously fuzzy and hard to pin down. Judgments about effectiveness are based more on faith and belief than on tangible results. As a consequence, appearance plays a significant role in judging how well an enterprise is performing. In order to be seen as doing well, organizations must project an image of being up to date. Innovations are therefore adopted ceremoniously but shielded or buffered from ongoing activities. This permits looking good while sustaining the status quo. Actually implementing changes could very well undermine people's belief and faith in the institution.

Buffering in institutional organizations is enhanced by loose linkages between levels and functions. What happens in schools is nominally affected by district policies or dictates. What teachers do in classrooms is largely independent from management at the school level. A command and control structure influences what happens on the factory floor in technical organizations. But in schools, the classroom is mostly immune to dictates from above, which promotes the sustainability of time-worn practices.

The success of the Polaris Missile Project provides a vivid example of the institutional logic at work in the US Navy. Unlike most federal projects Polaris was developed on time and under budget. Credit for the success was attributed to the modern management practices that were adopted early on. Technical specialists produced reams of information to guide decisions; frequent meetings provided a forum for making key decisions; a control room replete with PERT charts and other impressive graphs that indicated the projects progress. At the end, the admiral in charge received a commendation for 'bringing modern management to the Navy'.

A more close-grained look at the triumph of Polaris revealed a very different story. Modern management techniques were adopted in name only. Information produced by technical specialists went largely unheeded. Meetings served as revival occasions to keep people's spirits high rather than rational events to make clear-cut decisions. The control room, with its impressive array of documentation, had little to do with the progress of the project. Rather it served as a symbolic signal that Polaris was well managed and on track. The façade of modern management buffered the project from congressional interference, allowing the leadership to go about business as usual. Thereafter, other organizations were pressed to adopt the innovations without full knowledge of the real purposes served. Most, especially schools, got the brunt of the wrong lesson. But modern management devices such as behavioural objectives and PERT charts soon bit the dust, joining other threats to the sustainability of established ways.

The comfort of established routine

Work routines quickly become habitual. There are many reasons why this works to the advantage of individuals. Among other things, established routines of work are comfortable, free up people trying to master unnecessary details, and lessen stress on the job. The importance of sustaining routines becomes apparent when historically anchored ways are threatened by new demands.

Donald Burr found this out when he tried to make People's Express an example of rotating people among different jobs. On the surface, this seemed like a logical way to give people a break from repetitious chores and develop a holistic view of the business among people accustomed to seeing only their specialized function. The effort quickly backfired when stress and burnout accelerated among employees. They were overwhelmed trying to master the new demands of unfamiliar work. Their dissatisfaction soon reduced the quality of the airline's customer service. The values of specialization were reaffirmed by their now obvious contribution to employee morale and mental health.

Sustaining competence in organizations is vital to individual performance. Typically overlooked in changes designed to make things better is the problem of creating incompetence, which usually makes things worse. The status quo is preferred because people take comfort from the routines of work. Announcing a change means telling people that they are now incapable of doing their work and as a result are going to feel lousy. A large accounting firm computerized its records to reduce the amount of time required to process forms by hand. The sponsors of the change were surprised when the new system appeared to eat up more time than the old. A closer inspection revealed the reasons why. Clerical staff were first recording information by hand and then entering it into computers. Keeping two sets of books eliminated sacrificing old ways but undermined the rationale for making the procedural changes.

People go to great lengths to maintain their acknowledged skill set. Physicians are no exception. Jeff Goldsmith's landmark study, for example, set out to account for the number of surgical procedures performed in a particular locale. Controlling for other obvious factors – like demographics, income and characteristics of a given population – one variable accounted for the lion's share of the variance – the number of physicians in the immediate area trained to do a specific procedure Rather than learning new tricks, doctors were wedded to familiar techniques.

The obvious antidote for incompetence is training which should deal both with skills and feelings. But training rarely receives its share of resources allocated to reform. It is wrongly assumed people on their own will somehow get the hang of what they are now required to do. From this common-sense perspective, powerful pressures to perpetuate old routines seem blatantly obvious.

Avoiding conflict is a high priority

Politics play a central role in every organization. Resources are always in short supply and people inherently compete for their share. The competition has little to do with stated goals. Power, rather than authority, becomes the coin of the realm. People rely on who they are, what they know, who they know, persuasion and sheer might to triumph over opponents in an ongoing contest. The obvious by-product of this ongoing fracas is conflict. This is something most people seek to avoid. They smooth over obvious differences and flee rather than fight openly. Behind the scenes, they conspire, sabotage, and plot other strategies for getting even and getting their way. As a result, beneath the veneer of civility there is a festering bundle of turmoil and strife.

Change intensifies conflict. While proponents of change for the better are formulating plans, an army of status quo defenders are plotting a counter attack. The no-man's terrain separating the two factions remains in an unholy truce until the plans are launched. Then the war erupts. Very quickly it becomes evident to the backers of change that their adversaries are formidable and their supporters are lukewarm. Machiavelli describes this dynamic long ago in *The Prince*:

> *It must be realized that there is nothing more difficult to plan, more uncertain of success, or more dangerous to manage than the establishment of a new order of [things]; for he who introduces [change] makes enemies of all those who derived advantage from the old order and finds but lukewarm defenders among those who stand to gain from the new one. (Bolman and Deal, 2003: 320)*

Most often the outcome is the perpetuation of business as usual. The sustainability of familiar, conventional patterns and practices is reaffirmed.

The more promising political alternative of compromise and bargaining is a route seldom taken. Proponents of change remain steadfast in staying the course; resistors vow a fight to the death. Those who oppose the change are the most likely victors; sponsors typically lick their wounds in retreat. The creation of an arena where differences can be aired openly, compromises made and bargains struck carries the promise of a more positive outcome.

In the midst of the 1960s and 1970s zeal for social revolution, the Experimental Schools project was initiated in ten rural schools districts in the US. Ample federal resources were allocated to promote comprehensive change, to demonstrate the virtue of an entirely different approach to educating the nation's children. In the ten districts, planned reform was christened with ceremonial fanfare. But as ambitious plans were carried into action, detractors mounted stiff resistance. By the year's end, only one of the sponsoring superintendents was still in office. The survivor held out because he opened a dialogue with dissenting teachers, parents and community leaders. In the ensuing arena agreements were hammered out, balancing traditional and innovative ideas. Leaders of most successful change endeavours follow a similar course. They channel conflict into a forum where middle-ground pacts are created between promoters and opponents of the reform.

Symbols buttress cultural continuity

One of the most fundamental human needs is for life and work to have meaning. This existential yearning is satisfied by the creation of symbols that capture deeply held, historically anchored human values and sentiments. Cultural heroes, rituals, ceremonies, and stories pump life with purpose, passion and zest. For Forest Rangers, Smokey is more than a bear. The cartoon-like image captures the essence of what the Forest Service is all about. The cross stands for the spiritual core of the Christian faith just as the crescent represents the soul of Islam. Each religious following has its legendary founder, Jesus Christ for Christians; Mohammed for Muslims. Unique rituals and ceremonies bring believers into a cohesive flock. Different renditions of ceremonial traditions separate different sects within each faith: Catholics and Protestants in Christianity; Shiites and Sunnis within Islam. Stories for all faiths carry and reinforce values and beliefs. From a symbolic perspective, culture is the prime bulwark of sustainability both in religious and secular organizations.

Because of its bedrock role in undergirding individual and group meaning, culture erects a nearly impervious barrier to change. The more tightly knit the cultural fabric, the harder people will strive to perpetuate their mode of living. People sacrifice their bodies and souls to protect sacred symbols. Change alters people's attachment to values, heroes, ritual, ceremony and stories. When the bond is severed people experience an acute sense of existential loss. The emblematic pillars supporting their identity, of shoring up the meaning of life, are undercut. In *Hunger of Memory* Richard Rodriguez describes his reaction to the Church dropping Latin from the Catholic liturgy:

> *I cannot expect the liturgy – which reflects and cultivates my faith – to remain what it was. I will continue to go to the English mass. I will go because it is my liturgy. I will, however, often recall with nostalgia the faith I have lost ... I cling to the new Catholic Church. Though it leaves me unsatisfied, I fear giving it up, falling through space. (Rodriguez, 1982: 107–9)*

Rodriguez's reaction to the loss of the traditional liturgy is akin to changes made in secular organizations. Reactions to the introduction of New Coke were decidedly negative. Taste tests had confirmed that people preferred the new recipe to the old and rated it above Pepsi. But the company failed to take into account the symbolic meaning of Old

Coke. Customers were not shy about registering their rage: 'New Coke is for wimps', 'When they took old coke off the market, they violated my freedom of choice – baseball, hamburgers, Coke – they're all the fabric of America'. The company tried to rebound with Classic Coke, but learned a painful lesson about people's attachments to cherished symbols (Morganthau, 1985: 32–3).

More than anything else, sustainability is a cultural phenomenon. Our lack of progress toward switching to the metric system is caused by our historical attachment to ounces and pounds, inches and feet. It is more than learning the new system. We grew up with our system of weights and measurement. Imagine the pain of changing grandma's faded, handwritten, dog-eared recipe for the traditional family holiday stuffing. Somehow replacing tablespoons and cups with a European way of measuring ingredients seems almost sacrilegious. The end product will probably be the same but the cherished memories of grandma mixing the ingredients will suffer.

From a cultural view, changing a business is one thing; changing a church is a very different undertaking. Reforming education is somewhere in between. We can monkey around with peripheral practices, but messing with traditional values and rituals is going to create a strong counterattack of teachers, parents and students. In this case it is much better to think about revival rather than reform. As Albert Shanker, head of the American Federation of Teachers observed: 'There was something going on in one room schoolhouses that we need to dust off and bring forward.'

The issue of sustaining core values is well documented in the business literature. Kotter and Heskett's (1992) *Corporate Culture and Performance* and *Built to Last* by Collins and Porras (1994) are two well-documented examples. In top-performing organizations, widely shared values and beliefs serve as a moral compass to chart a steady course even when times are tough. Years ago, Johnson & Johnson were confronted with a severe crisis. Someone had poisoned bottles of Tylenol resulting in the deaths of several people. Chief executive officer (CEO), James Burke, was confronted with a tough decision. Do we assume that all the tainted bottles have been found and risk additional deaths? Or, do we pull all bottles of the product from retail shelves, incurring enormous economic costs. Burke's decision to recall Tylenol was based on a company value of putting customers first. The company emerged from the crisis stronger than before. Cultural benefits over the long haul towered over immediate short-term monetary sacrifices.

Often the lure of potentially more profits for shareholders encourages CEOs to tamper with historically, quasi-sacred cultural moral codes. Such tinkering typically carries the danger of a powerful backlash. Carly Farina's unwary challenge to the 'H-P Way' as Hewlett Packard's chief executive ended in the loss of her job. Home Depot's new head honcho's unwavering focus on the bottom line has eroded what was once a value-driven business. On his watch, the company has toppled from first place among competitors in customer satisfaction to last.

Symbolically savvy leaders pay reverence to the sustainability of important traditions. They will tackle peripheral practices but tread very softly around well-rooted cultural codes. Lou Gerstner's approach to remaking of IBM exemplifies this kind of leadership. IBM had fallen on bad times. The board was searching for a no-nonsense manager to get the company back on track. Gerstner's reputation as a cost-conscious, bottom-line-driven manager earned him the job. In his previous stints as CEO of RJR Nabisco and American Express he was a stickler for strategy, analysis and measurement. During his first press conference as an IBMer, he reinforced this rational image. When asked about his vision for the company, he told the assembled reporters, 'The last thing IBM needs is a vision'.

In his first days in the position, Gerstner laid out his strategy which outlined needed changes in the way IBM did business, including paying more attention to customers and becoming more market driven. As he began to learn more about the culture, he came to admire IBM's original values. But he also concluded that the company had drifted away from its cultural code and lost its way. His primary task was to reach back, pull forward and revitalize the company's soul. His leadership efforts resulted in one of the most dramatic corporate turnarounds in recent memory. He also learned a powerful lesson about sustaining traditions that work well historically:

> *I came to see in my time at IBM, that culture isn't just one aspect of the game – it is the game. In the end, an organization is nothing more than the collective capacity to crate value ... But no enterprise – whether in business, government, education, healthcare, or any other area of human endeavour – will succeed if those elements are not part of its DNA. (Bolman and Deal, 2003: 183)*

Sustainability must originate from within an organization. Very often, the current state of affairs can be attributed to cultural drift, as was the case at IBM. The responsibility of leaders is to ferret out what may have worked in the past that can improve productivity now. Renewal and revitalization sustain an organization over the long haul. External reform efforts will not be successful unless they take into account the culture of the place. It is symbols rather than rational strategies that tie together the past present and future in a meaningful cultural package.

Whither sustainability?

The concept of sustainability has captured the attention of academics and policy-makers. It is today's hot idea in good currency. If past is prologue, it will be around for awhile. It will be the subject of scholarly books and articles. It will be reflected in policies aimed at the improvement of education. It will hang on until the next fresh notion enters the management lexicon. Then sustainability will take its place on the shelf of old buzzwords, fashionable for awhile then removed from active service.

But the concept of sustainability carries some interesting implications for leadership and management. It becomes intriguing when we employ it to understand why organizations are so successful in perpetuating the status quo despite a relentless barrage of reforms. There are some interesting explanations for this remarkable staying power, which this chapter attempted to highlight. To the extent that we can accept plausible reasons for maintaining things as they are, we can capture the craft knowledge of those who labour in the trenches year after year. They know a lot more than we think they do.

The real challenge is how to encourage local talent to draw upon lessons they have learned and harnessing it to renew and revitalize education. An acupuncturist assumes energy in the human body and then uses needles to reduce blocks and stimulate the energy flow. That notion may be more apt than we think in our efforts to improve schools from within rather than trying to reform them from outside.

References

Bolman, L. and Deal, T. (2003) *Reframing Organizations*. San Francisco, CA: Jossey Bass.

Collins, J. and Porras J.I. (1994) *Built to Last*. New York: Harper Business Essentials.

Kotter, P. and Heskett, J.L. (1992) *Corporate Culture and Performance*. New York: Free Press.

Morganthau, T. (1985) 'Saying "No" to New Coke', *Newsweek*, 105(25): 32–3.

Rodriguez, R. (1982) *Hunger of Memory: The Education of Richard Rodriguez*. New York: Bantam Books.

Chapter 6

Developing and sustaining school leaders: lessons from research

Kenneth Leithwood, Scott Bauer and Brian Riedlinger

Introduction

Being a principal is tough work – rewarding for many, but tough for all. In some locations, attitudes toward school leadership seem paradoxical. Reformers, members of the public and many education professionals, for example, view principals as absolutely key to successful school improvement, even when such improvement is initiated by others (for example, Wikeley et al., 2005). At the same time, salaries paid to principals in many US states, at least, offer almost no material incentive for teachers to seriously consider volunteering to work the additional 15 or 20 hours per week that has become the norm for today's principals (*Harvard Educational Letter*, 2000). Not to mention being the person squarely in the sights of the accountability militia howling after what sophisticated analysts (for example, Linn, 2003) argue are often impossible 'annual yearly progress' targets for student achievement on high-stakes tests in schools set by states and districts.

While many principals like what they do and report high levels of job satisfaction (for example, Malone et al., 2001), working conditions notwithstanding, many also report feeling worn out by the job, isolated and under considerable stress, and seriously ponder the prospects of alternative employment (Whitaker, 2003). We cannot afford to have them leave; many districts are already forced to appoint people with minimal experience, at best. Nor can we afford to have them stay while feeling burned out. Burnout manifests itself in resistance to change and innovation, insensitive social relationships, and lack of care for others, among many other 'unleaderful' behaviours (see Byrne, 1991, for example). So it is past time that we attended more deeply to the problem of sustaining and further developing the principals we now have in schools.

In this chapter we describe the lessons learned about sustaining and further developing principals from the past six years' work of the Greater New Orleans School Leadership Center (SLC). With the support of a local foundation (the Baptist Community Ministries) the SLC's work was the object of an extensive, six-year external evaluation. This evaluation produced a series of quarterly reports about participants' or Fellows' experiences in Center activities, the influence of those experiences on their work in schools, and the effects of that work on student engagement and academic achievement. Evidence collected for that evaluation included direct observations of the Center's work, interviews with Fellows about the value they attributed to that work, surveys conducted with teachers in Fellows' schools, surveys of students about their engagement in Fellows' schools and analyses of changes in the achievement of students in Fellows' schools using the results of state-administered achievement tests.

Over that six-year period, the SLC found multiple ways of connecting its work to the professional and personal needs of an ever-expanding group of principals in the region. The Center also found increasingly effective ways of ensuring that its work made a significant contribution to the quality of teaching and learning in Fellows' schools. By any reasonable standard, the SLC must be judged a major success and one of the few organizations that can lay claim to having a sustained, long-term impact on a well-defined population of schools, teachers, administrators and students.

There is much to be learned from the SLC's work about building and sustaining the motivations, commitments and capacities of practising school leaders. Our first initiative to ensure lessons from that work did not go unnoticed focused on the relationship between SLC initiatives and student academic achievement (Leithwood et al., 2003). Our second initiative, described in this chapter, aimed to better understand the effects of the SLC's work on the type of leadership principals provided to their schools, as well as the energy and commitments they developed for carrying out that leadership. Evidence used for this purpose came from a series of 12 case studies of principals and schools. The 12 principals had participated in SLC initiatives for at least three years, during which time their schools had demonstrated improvements in teaching and learning. School staffs attributed a significant portion of that improvement to the principals' leadership and principals attributed much of their impact to participation in SLC experiences.

State-collected student achievement data were the starting point for selecting the 12 schools. All schools demonstrating increases in state testing results over a three-year period were included in the initial pool of potential schools for the study. Data from the larger external evaluation provided additional information, including results of teacher and student surveys conducted on two occasions several years apart in each school. These surveys captured teachers' judgements about the leadership and management of the principal, as well as the condition of school characteristics key to school improvement efforts. Student data, in addition to academic achievement, were about their engagement in their school. Interviews were conducted with principals and teachers in each of 12 selected schools during the fall of 2004. All interviews were transcribed and coded according to questions included in the interview protocol.

SLC initiatives for developing and sustaining principals

The SLC program reflects several sources of advice about leadership development strategies. One of these sources is the National Staff Development Council (Sparks and Hirsh, 2000). The Council recommends that leadership development programs have the following features: they should be long term rather than episodic; job embedded rather than detached; carefully planned with a coherent curriculum; and focused on student achievement. Programs should also emphasize reflective practice, provide opportunities for peers to discuss and solve problems of practice, and provide a context for coaching and mentoring.

Based on data provided by the University Council on Educational Administration (UCEA), Peterson (2001) argues that programs must have a clear mission and purpose linking leadership to school improvement; a coherent curriculum that provides linkage to state certification schemes; and an emphasis on the use of information technologies. He also suggests that programs should be continuous or long term rather than one-shot, and that a variety of instructional methods should be used rather than relying on one or a small set of delivery mechanisms.

The SLC's program explicitly reflects these sources of advice about the features of successful leadership development experiences. It is also unique among North American leadership centers in several important respects. First, the mission and goals of the SLC squarely connect the work of the principal to improving student achievement. In sharp contrast to traditional principals' centers, which typically focus on leadership development as an end in itself and take as an act of faith that participants will use new-found skills to improve schools, the SLC has been committed to school improvement through leadership development from the outset. The SLC places a strong emphasis on giving principals and other school leaders the skills, resources and tools that are needed to thoughtfully improve teaching and learning in their schools. This translates into a focus on changing how teachers teach and how they look at their teaching; an examination of supervision practices; and activities that focus on school change, school reform, and improving pedagogy. The Center deals with leadership skills and practices only insofar as a research-based theory of action can be articulated connecting these practices to school improvement. Significantly, the SLC's focus on leadership for school improvement is so deeply ingrained that it employs an evaluation design that looks at indicators of student performance and achievement as the ultimate litmus test of its efficacy.

The SLC is also unique because it has a full-time staff, and operates as an independent, not-for-profit organization governed through a partnership of the funder (BCM), the University of New Orleans, and Xavier University of Louisiana. Headed by the President/CEO, the Center staff also includes the Fellows Director, the Research Director and Research Associate, and a cadre of part-time graduate student interns. Support staff includes an Events Coordinator and Office Manager. The governance structure includes a board of directors made up of six representatives selected by the funder (BCM), and three representatives selected by each university. Each participant organization on the board has included experienced school principals among its board representatives. All significant decisions in the Center are made by a structure which includes Fellows, including a team which selects each new cohort of SLC participants.

The staffing and governance structure are a product of two key principles stressed by the original Center design team. First, the team stressed the importance of the Center 'being there' for principals. The norm experienced by most principals to be served by the Center was that support (when there was any at all) was sporadic and based on other people's notions of what principals need; there was a growing consensus that high-quality professional development needs to be continuous. In any case, the team's assumptions about the nature of school change suggested that if the goal was to improve schools, SLC initiatives could not be one-shot and disconnected from the experience of principals and their schools. The governance structure also aimed to ensure that Center activities were relevant by principals' standards. All programs have been designed with Fellows, guided by the expressed needs of principals and their schools, and each member of the Center staff is in contact with Fellows through shared decision-making teams. Indeed, the original design for Center programs was a product of a team of 13 'founding Fellows', who worked with university faculty and the foundation to conduct research on existing leadership development center models and create the initial model for the SLC.

The Center's program reflects a mix of traditional and somewhat novel activities and services. Programs have been designed around shared beliefs about the impact of leadership on school improvement, promotion of social justice, and the transformation of schools into learning organizations. The Center attempts to model for fellows the kinds of activities and practices that principals are encouraged to incorporate into their schools. There are four primary program areas.

The Fellows' program

The Fellows' program is the heart of the Center's activities. Rather than involving principals sporadically in isolated activities, a cadre of approximately 24 principals a year from area public, private and parochial schools apply to be fellows in the SLC. Fellowship reflects the primary way the Center strives to build a network among school leaders. Acceptance of a Fellow position carries significant rights and responsibilities.

Fellows are selected each January. Each Fellow signs a contract committing to participate in certain activities that are designed to focus his/her attention on leadership development for school improvement. In their first year Fellows participate in three pre-institute staff development programs that deal with vision building, school improvement and knowledge building through analysis of school performance data. Second, Fellows participate in two week-long summer institutes that build on the pre-institutes. These institutes focus on enriching leaders' ideas about quality teaching and how leadership can promote it.

Fellows are polled after summer institutes on their schools' needs so that post-institute sessions can be designed and conducted to have maximum impact on school goals. Third, Fellows are given a sizable grant ($10,000) to use to supplement the implementation of some facet of their schools' improvement plans. Center staff works with each Fellow to ensure that these moneys are targeted for significant student impact, and that plans have a sound evaluation component. Fourth, Fellows each receive a laptop (more recently, a tablet) computer and training in accessing the Internet in an effort to encourage them to develop skills in the use of technology.

Originally, the Fellowship was intended to last for two years. An indicator of the program's impact, however, is that past Fellows have essentially refused to leave. They created a membership category, 'veteran fellow' (some of whom call themselves 'fossil fellows'), structured an ongoing program (including their own summer institute), and serve as volunteers to help facilitate other SLC events.

Conferences and workshops

The SLC sponsors three types of conferences and workshops, which are open to all administrators in the five-parish region. Each fall and spring, the center sponsors a one- or two-day institute on a topic deemed important by Fellows. For example, in the fall of 2004 the Center sponsored a two-day session on teaching children of poverty. Over 200 educators attended. The SLC also sponsors more frequent 'conversations', small gatherings of principals who have an opportunity to speak informally to an acknowledged expert (who is typically visiting New Orleans for another reason). Finally, the Center staff also makes itself available for districts, schools and other professional organizations for customized workshops and acts as a conduit for schools to access university scholars and national experts for workshops.

Research services

In an effort to promote high-quality decision-making and the active use of school performance data, the SLC maintains a full-time research office, possibly the only school leadership center in the nation to invest significant resources in this fashion.

The research office provides several services, by far the most used of which is the preparation of research briefs on request. A research brief is a short literature review on any question or problem identified by a Fellow including an executive summary of research, an annotated bibliography and copies of one or two relevant papers. The SLC has a full-time research associate and a staff of graduate assistants from partner universities to provide this service. To date, the Center has developed over 180 briefs, and a library of briefs is maintained so that fellows can request reprints (which are updated after one year). This service allows Fellows to assess the extent of evidence available in support of the effects on student learning of initiatives they may be planning in their schools.

The research office also assists Fellows in two other ways. First, small research grants are available to Fellows' schools to conduct action research; about 20 grants were commissioned in the Center's first three years. Second, Center staff is available to schools and local districts to conduct research projects, prepare summaries of school performance data, and otherwise connect the schools to the services of partner universities. The research office also oversees maintaining the Center's modest lending library of books, videotapes, and other audio-visual material.

Learning initiatives

The newest facet of the SLC's program offerings is the Learning Initiatives (SLC-LI), started three years ago as a result of Fellows' input and ideas generated with the external evaluator. In the Learning Initiatives, which new Fellows must participate in as a part of their fellowship commitment, principals work together with their school leadership team on the design, implementation, and evaluation of their school's annual improvement plan. The SLC-LI schools work in loose collaboration with other SLC schools that have targeted similar, student focused, school improvement objectives, and receive facilitated training, data disaggregation services, and support for implementation and evaluation of school plans. Teacher leaders learn more about powerful forms of instruction. This learning is then shared with colleagues in the school and support for implementing such instruction is provided by schools leaders. Of all the components of the SLC program, this one addresses instructional improvement most directly.

Other activities

More recently the SLC has added to its repertoire a leadership development program for aspiring principals and teacher leaders, as well as a new program for superintendents and other central office administrators focused on the district's role in supporting school change. The Center is also working with school systems to develop a coaching and supervision program for new principals, which will replace the existing state-supported internship. These programs help leaders improve their schools by concentrating their leadership on teaching and learning.

Lessons about how to develop and sustain principal leadership

We identified 10 lessons for developing and sustaining principal leadership from our 12 case schools. These lessons, we believe, should be of considerable interest to the vast network of policy-makers, program developers, district leaders, foundations, universities, professional associations and staff developers across the world who are convinced that the success of their school reform efforts hinges on improving and sustaining the quality of school leadership. These lessons should be viewed both as a source of optimism that such improvement is possible and a source of guidance about how to go about the task.

Lesson 1: Dramatic individual change is possible

Extended and intensive professional development experiences for principals outside their own school and district environment can have a powerful influence on how principals approach improvement in their schools and their own leadership. Professional development of this sort seems capable of dramatically altering what are typically thought to be 'entrenched' leadership styles, often described as 'autocratic', in favour of much more democratic and participatory styles. Recent evidence in support of this lesson can be found in other, quite different, contexts (for example, Menter et al., 2005).

One of our case study principals, for example, had this to say about her approach to leadership and how it changed as a result of SLC experiences: 'Before SLC, I don't want to say that I was a dictator, but I definitely made all or most of the decisions here at school.' The SLC, she believed, taught her the importance of delegating authority and sharing decision making (although, ultimately she believed that it was still she who had to make the final decision). Because she began to understand that she could not do everything herself, she formed committees to handle many functions that were previously handled by her and the assistant principal; committees were formed to handle awards, discipline, grandparents' day, voluntary sponsorship, and social activities. This principal felt less stress because of shared leadership. She also believed that her faculty were more cohesive. Because they are more involved in decision-making, 'they are buying into what we are doing here at school'. 'We're all in it together.' The teachers we interviewed corroborated this view. 'Before, we did things because we were told we had to do them; now we have more input and our input is heard and valued.' The principal 'has made us realize that we all have to pull together as a team to be successful'.

Lesson 2: One good experience can 'jump start' the adoption of a continuous learning ethos

A small number of highly positive professional development experiences, most of our school cases suggest, can create a heightened interest in continuous learning on the part of principals and more self-initiated participation in subsequent professional development. Indeed, a few highly positive experiences seem capable of reversing the negative attitudes toward professional development that may have resulted from unhelpful prior experiences, of which most teachers and administrators seem to have had many. For example, when one of our case study principals first began to attend SLC initiatives, she was getting tired of her school leadership role; things had become 'difficult' for her. But, 'The School Leadership Center helped rekindle my spark.' Indeed, it reawakened her desire to go back to graduate school, something she did not think she was going to do. From her perspective, the SLC encouraged principals to be 'on the look out' for something that will keep them engaged when things get difficult. Following this advice, this principal found an issue that she felt the need to understand more fully – the impact on a child's life of having a mother who is in prison. She believed that the SLC was always there to encourage her to keep going – to develop a passion for something.

Lesson 3: Ongoing support is needed if leaders are to influence student learning

The change management literature is fond of telling us that change requires both pressure and support. But in the current context of accountability-oriented education policies, the balance between the two experienced by many school leaders, including Center Fellows, is radically one-sided. Professional development that helps principals cope effectively with the pressure may be the most defensible form of support for them.

The greatest efforts of high-quality, intensive, professional development for principals are realized when initial professional development experiences are extended and reinforced through well-planned follow-up support over several years. The school cases teach us the importance of ongoing relationships with the SLC staff, a network of other school leaders with similar challenges and, occasionally, 'outsiders' who bring unique perspectives to bear on the principals' work. As one of our case study Fellows noted, the opportunity to be with other school leaders and learn from them, was most helpful to her. To see that her struggles were no different from those of other principals, regardless of type of school (private, parochial, or public, urban or suburban) was a real eye-opener for her. 'We are all dealing with similar issues.' Another principal said, 'You have someone to call who understands the demands of being a principal. When you talk to another principal they know ... It may be that I'm calling about a particular program I know they have. SLC publishes a list of initiatives that their principals are working with in their schools. It's like a menu that I can look at to get help in an area and can call that person. Everybody is always willing to help each other.' The SLC staff, through the Learning Initiative (SLC-LI), in particular, not only provided skill-oriented training to principals and leadership teams, but also acted as a 'critical friend':

> *a trusted person who asks provocative questions, provides data to be examined through another lens, and offers critiques of a person's work as a friend. A critical friend takes the time to fully understand the context of the work presented and the outcomes that the person or group is working toward. The friend is an advocate for the work. (Costa and Kallick, quoted in Swaffield, 2005: 44)*

Lesson 4: Training should encompass the team as well as the individual principal

Follow-up experiences are most useful when they focus directly on issues in the principal's school and include direct training of school staff in addition to the principal, typically a cross-role leadership or improvement team. This more inclusive training is a way of sharing with the principal the job of developing leadership capacities among others in the school, as well as helping transform the school into a professional learning community. SLC's Learning Initiative adopted this inclusive focus and most of our school cases celebrate the outcomes of that focus.

One of the case study principals explained that from the distance of a few years, she realized that what was most helpful was participating in the SLC's Learning Initiative (SLC-LI) 'where we were given the time and space to work with our teachers on our School Improvement Plan'. The SLC-LI provided an opportunity, she noted, to share ideas and strategies with other teachers who had similar concerns. This sharing of ideas, the principal believed, helped to build teacher leaders who then took on more responsibilities at the school.

The SLC-LI combined sessions that encouraged cross-school and cross-district problem-solving with work in Fellows' own schools, thereby encouraging a level of sharing typically not experienced by principal and teacher leaders. Three outcomes seem noteworthy from this: a greater appreciation for the normalcy of problems and dilemmas faced across schools; an increased openness to alternative ways of looking at these problems; and a high level of transparency with regard to the discussion of problems and their possible solutions.

This lesson acknowledges our growing understanding about the contribution that shared leadership makes to school improvement (for example, Chrispeels, 2004), how shared leadership is best developed (Frost and Durrant, 2004) and, perhaps especially, how school improvement initiatives can be sustained during leadership transitions (Lambert, 2005).

Lesson 5: Direct, practical help in data-driven decision-making is especially critical in the current policy environment

Principals are being widely admonished to be data driven in their decision-making (for example, Earl and Katz, 2002) but are often constrained by lack of time, capacity and access to relevant data

(Bernhardt, 2005). Our case studies indicate that most principals felt quite uncertain about their understanding and use of numerical data for school improvement purposes as they began their work with the SLC. As one of our case study principals put it, 'No one showed us how to analyze test scores before. They just told us to analyze test scores.' And after their SLC experiences, most became highly data driven in their decision-making in the process of transforming their schools into data-driven organizations.

While the demand for data-driven decision-making on the part of school leaders is ubiquitous, the opportunities for suitable capacity development is not. A leadership center can contribute significantly to the data-driven nature of a principal's decisions – and their feelings of efficacy about this aspect of their job – by organizing hands-on training to build capacity. This was a core feature not only of the later SLC summer institutes, but eventually of follow-up workshops, as well. These initiatives focused primarily on the achievement data collected by the state – how to interpret such evidence and make productive use of it in setting school improvement priorities.

Using the SLC as an example, it also seems clear that a leadership center can contribute to data-driven decision-making by actually locating data relevant to the much broader array of policy decisions with which schools are faced, at the request of schools. This is a function performed by the SLC's research services and has served to greatly enhance the use of research evidence for improving practice. Noteworthy here is the encouragement of the use of relevant research in all phases of the school improvement process. Participation in SLC-LI taught Fellows to use data and connect to available research in identifying problems, analyzing their causes, developing action plans, and evaluating the implementation of these plans.

Lesson 6: Practice what you preach (and be nice)

We know that teachers' treatment of students is often influenced by how administrators treat teachers. Being the object of respectful behaviour inclines the recipient to treat others in a similarly respectful manner.

One of the lessons from our 12 cases is the remarkable influence on principals' relations with their staffs and students from the treatment the principals received from SLC staff. Becoming an SLC Fellow was to instantly enjoy the high regard of SLC staff. Your experiences were validated. Your ideas were listened to. Your successes were celebrated. Your challenges were appreciated. The SLC's staff modelled, in their relationships with Fellows, the meaning of transformative leadership, the value of shared decision-making, a commitment to evidence-based practice and openness to continuous learning. The principals in our 12 case studies noticed. As one remarked: 'SLC has been a real bright spot in my life as a principal ... it is rare [for principals] to be treated as the respected leaders of their business' (Principal). In fact, for several of them, the SLC example may have been a more powerful influence than the explicit training provided by SLC.

Lesson 7:A little bit of money goes a long way

We have long known that small amounts of discretionary money can have disproportionate consequences for school improvement (Louis and Miles, 1990). Such extra money not only has quite practical uses, it also symbolizes the importance the source of funding attaches to the work being funded, rewards people for initiative and encourages greater effort and commitment.

The SLC provided financial grants ranging from $5,000 to $15,000 to Fellows' schools to help with school improvement. While this is a tiny proportion of a school's total budget, it may be a huge proportion of the funds available to a school for discretionary activity. In the 12 case schools, the money was used for new teaching materials, time for school improvement planning and the like – not what one would imagine to be 'discretionary' activity in a highly functioning organization in a perfect world. But these schools – and many others across the world – do not find themselves in anything close to a perfect world. Helping find, or helping teach schools how to find, discretionary money is a very useful focus for the work of a leadership center for principals and their staffs.

Lesson 8: For a long-term impact, build a community of leaders

Efforts by a leadership center like the SLC, to create a culture of cooperation among participants in its programs can have far reaching, positive effects. The SLC's attention to mentoring, partnering and fostering communication among participants resulted in a 'networked learning community' of principals extending well beyond the boundaries of their individual districts. One of our case study principals cited as most helpful to her, the opportunity to be with other principals, to see that many of their struggles were no different from hers regardless of differences in schools. She explained that the SLC stresses the importance of networking and the power of conversation to 'help sustain, encourage and support us. They help us celebrate when good things happen and lift us up when bad things happen.' Members of this SLC-nurtured community now have access to extensive peer consultation, a menu of practical improvement strategies and a valuable source of social support in a job that often seems isolated and under-appreciated.

The advantages of participation in a community of principal-colleagues, as reflected in the 12 cases, overlap in large measure with the benefits of productive mentoring relationships reflected in research on this theme, for example: increased confidence and self-esteem; reduction in stress and frustration; practical advice and assistance; links to additional resources; a sounding board for new ideas; and improved communication skills (for a recent review of evidence, see Hobson and Sharp, 2005).

But the SLC learned, through hard experience, that networks of peers were far more acceptable to experienced school administrators than were mentoring relationships. Networks of peers provide equal-status access to many sources of advice rather than differentiated-status access to only one other source of advice. While mentoring may well be valuable for aspiring or novice school leaders, as Hobson and Sharp (2005) suggest, access to a peer network seems more helpful to experienced leaders.

Lesson 9: Use the community of leaders to retain successful leaders

While attrition in the principal ranks is endemic in the country at this time (for example, Whitaker, 2003), members of the networked learning communities created by the SLC and reflected in the 12 cases remain committed to their jobs and enthusiastic about what they are accomplishing. Building these communities through the work of leadership centers like the SLC may be one of the most promising responses to the attrition problem in sight. Most leadership centers should seriously consider including such network building as a key part of their overall mission.

How can centers do this community building? The sense of being valued and supported in their work, which principals developed through their SLC experiences, was a product of many initiatives, not all of which can be connected to school improvement work with a straight line. Consider, for example, the location of summer institutes in resort settings, the sincere and overt respect of Fellows demonstrated by SLC staff, the regular social events hosted by the Center, the affirming and inspirational tone of many of Brian's (SLC's CEO) Monday Messages,[1] the inviting physical atmosphere of the Center's offices and the attention paid to the work of individual principals and schools by Glenn (an SLC staff member).

None of this had been part of our case study principals' experiences in the other contexts of their professional lives. And none of these things added directly to the skills and knowledge they required for their school improvement efforts. But all of them helped to build the determination, persistence and commitment principals needed to be successful at improving their schools. These initiatives also helped principals develop a perspective on the value of their work that continued to make the job an exciting one for them.

Lesson 10: Use inspiring leadership models to recruit new leaders

As we mentioned in our introduction, there is a distinct lack of interest among teachers in aspiring to the principalship as a career goal at the present time (Educational Research Service et al., 2000). In contrast, an important feature of each of the 12 school cases was the development of teacher leadership and, in most cases, the adoption by these new teacher leaders of the principalship as a career goal for themselves.

While low administrator salaries, along with challenging working conditions, account for the widespread lack of interest in school administration, perhaps the most influential factor is teachers' perceptions of what it means to be a principal (for example, Sandham, 2001). Too many principals provide an uninspiring model of the principalship to their teachers. But when a leadership center dramatically alters a principal's style of leadership from one that is autocratic, perhaps not well informed and based on positional power to one that is more democratic, data driven and consensual, teachers experience a role that many find attractive. Our 12 cases illustrate just how powerful this effect can be.

In concert with Lesson 8, then, the justification for the work of leadership centers needs to be viewed more broadly than only leading to school improvement and increased student learning. While these are obviously central and necessary goals for leadership centers, in the current administrator recruitment and retention context, they are not sufficient. Leadership centers are in a powerful position to improve administrator recruitment and retention across the country and should explicitly aim to do so.

Conclusion

So this is what we have learned to this point. By promoting relational trust (Bryk and Schneider, 2002), and modelling the attributes of a learning organization, the SLC has been able to promote the creation of a culture of learning essential to the development of school leaders who take on the challenging puzzles associated with improving schools. Indeed, the SLC was founded on the belief that sound relationships must be built first – or early – and only then will individual leaders engage in the kind of transformational activities needed to promote change within their schools.

At the outset, the team that designed the SLC wrestled with how to develop (and model) such courageous leadership. The Center and its staff model many practices which improve the chances of success for school leaders: shared decision-making through, for example, the creation of structures to involve Fellows; risk-taking through the development of new programs and practices, and the importance of continuous evaluation through the Center's own evaluation practices. The stability of the Center; its focus on facilitative processes for school improvement; its balance of programming that empowers and develops individuals, teams, and networks; and the connectedness promoted through Center activities promotes the development of confidence among otherwise isolated professionals to be courageous leaders.

'What about the transferability of the SLC initiatives and the lessons we have drawn from our experiences?' you might be asking at this point. Much of what the SLC accomplishes, we want to emphasize, is by design. It is the product of a conscious effort by staff, the board, the evaluator, and Fellows themselves. Key to our design, for example, was commitment to a mission that makes 'courageous leadership for school improvement' the focus; having a full-time staff which makes it possible to devote the time and energy needed to continuously discuss and examine programs and practices, to incorporate feedback from Fellows, to nurture the network among Fellows, and otherwise act as steward of the mission; devoting resources to the external evaluation, and establishing a relationship with the evaluator(s) as a critical friend.

Creating a culture, as we have described it, has been vitally important for the SLC. In large part, however, SLC structures make this possible. Staff spent enormous amounts of time and energy in meetings making this explicit to one another. Furthermore, those facing the task of creating a leadership program need to understand that it just does not happen by chance. Like any other complex change effort, the SLC program was not all planned at the outset. The program that developed over time was the product of extensive discussions about the kind of leadership SLC staff wanted to model – risk-taking, dealing with ambiguity, using available research and actively encouraging and using feedback, and the like.

Sustaining the energy, commitment and enthusiasm of school leaders goes hand in hand with improving their capacities. Those responsible for this task might well be advised to think of capacity development as their primary goal, but one pursued in a way that also sustains school leaders' positive dispositions toward their work and continued willingness to do the heavy lifting we should all be grateful they are willing to do.

Note

1. He actually sends one out by email *every* week with only a very short interruption around hurricane Katrina.

References

Bernhardt, V. (2005) 'Data tools for school improvement', *Educational Leadership*, 62(5): 66–9.

Bryk, A. and Schneider, B. (2002) *Trust in Schools: A Core Resource for Improvement.* New York: Russell Sage Foundation.

Bryne, B. (1991) 'Burnout: investigating the impact of background variables for elementary, intermediate, secondary and university educators', *Teaching and Teacher Education*, 7(2): 197–209.

Chrispeels, J.H. (2004) 'Sharing leadership: learning from challenge – aiming toward promise', in J.H. Chrispeels (ed.), *Learning to Lead Together: The Promise and Challenge of Sharing Leadership.* Thousand Oaks, CA: Sage, pp. 363–76.

Earl, L. and Katz, S. (2002) 'Leading schools in a data-rich world', in K. Leithwood and P. Hallinger (eds), *Second International Handbook of Educational Leadership and Administration*, vol. 8. Dordrect: Kluwer.

Education Research Service, National Association of Elementary School Principals and National Association of Secondary School Principals (2000) *The Principal, Keystone of a High-Achieving School: Attracting and Keeping the Leaders We Need*. Arlington, VA: Education Research Service.

Frost, D. and Durrant, J. (2004) 'Supporting teachers' leadership: what can principals do? A teacher's perspective from research', in J.H. Chrispeels (ed.), *Learning to Lead Together: The Promise and Challenge of Sharing Leadership*. Thousand Oaks, CA: Sage, pp. 307–26.

Harvard Educational Letter (2000) www.edletter.org/index.shtml.

Hobson, A.J. and Sharp, C. (2005) 'Head to head: a systematic review of the research evidence on mentoring new head teachers', *School Leadership and Management*, 25(1): 25–42.

Lambert, L. (2005) 'Leadership for lasting reform', *Educational Leadership*, 62(5): 62–5.

Leithwood, K., Riedlinger, B., Bauer, S. and Jantzi, D. (2003) 'Leadership program effects on student learning: the case of the Greater New Orleans School Leadership Center', *Journal of School Leadership and Management*, 13(6): 707–38.

Linn, R. (2003) 'Accountability: responsibility and reasonable expectations', *Educational Researcher*, 32(7): 3–13.

Louis, K. and Miles, M.B. (1990) *Improving the Urban High School: What Works and Why*. New York: Teachers College Press.

Malone, B., Sharp, W. and Walter, J. (2001) 'What's right about the principalship', paper presented at the annual meeting of the Mid-Western Educational Research Association, Chicago, IL.

Menter, I., Holligan, C. and Mthenjwa, V. (2005) 'Reaching the parts that need to be reached? The impact of the Scottish Qualification for Headship', *School Leadership and Management*, 25(1): 7–23.

Peterson, K.D. (2001) 'The professional development of principals: innovations and opportunities', paper presented at the first meeting of the National Commission for the Advancement of Educational Leadership Preparation, Racine, WI.

Sandham, J.L. (2001) 'California faces a shortage of administrators, report warns', *Education Week*, 20(29): 5.

Sparks, D. and Hirsh, S. (2000) *Learning to Lead, Leading to Learn*. Oxford, OH: National Staff Development Council. Available from http://nsdc.org.library/leaders/leader_report.cfm.

Swaffield, S. (2005) 'No sleeping partners: relationships between head teachers and critical friends', *School Leadership and Management*, 25(1): 43–57.

Whitaker, K.S. (2003) 'Superintendent perceptions of quantity and quality of principal candidates', *Journal of School Leadership*, 13(2): 159–80.

Wikeley, F., Stoll, L., Murillo, J. and De Jong, R. (2005) 'Evaluating effective school improvement: case studies of programmes in eight European countries and their contribution to the effective school improvement model', *School Effectiveness and School Improvement*, 16(4): 387–406.

Chapter 7

Sustaining leadership in complex times: An individual and system solution

Michael Fullan and Lyn Sharratt

Introduction

Leadership energy has recently received greater attention as people grapple with the complexity, not only of achieving substantial improvement under challenging circumstances, but also of maintaining organizational momentum for continuous improvement (see Davies, 2005; Fullan, 2005; 2006; Fullan et al., 2006; Hargreaves and Fink, 2006; Loehr and Schwartz, 2003).

In this chapter we delve into the issues of leadership sustainability by examining a large school district with which we are associated. It is a particularly appropriate case for the topic, because the district has been intensively engaged in a district-wide reform for the past five years and has relied heavily on mobilizing leadership at all levels of the system. The question of interest is 'Under what conditions can leaders in the system sustain their efforts individually and collectively?'

We first provide some context in describing the district and the Literacy Collaborative (LC) model that has been the focus of reform. Second, we present the results up to this point. Third, we get into the substance of sustainability by drawing directly on data from school principals in the district. Finally we take up the implications for sustaining leadership presence as a continuous force for improvement, concluding that it is both an individual and a system responsibility. We note that if the latter two elements can operate in an interdependent manner the conditions for leadership energy, continuous renewal and sustainability have a greater chance of becoming embedded.

District context

York Region District School Board (YRDSB) is a large multicultural district just north of Toronto, Ontario, Canada. It is rapidly growing with a diverse sociocultural and linguistic population with over 100 different languages spoken in their schools. On average, the school board has been opening five elementary schools a year for the last five years and a secondary school every other year. There are a total of 140 elementary schools and 27 secondary schools with over 108,000 students and 8,000 teachers.

In 2000 when the district began its student achievement improvement strategy in earnest, Director of Education, Bill Hogarth, set out to develop the best possible model for reform drawing heavily on external ideas but developing a capacity from within the district to lead the reform with a critical mass of leaders at all levels of the district. The district decided the foundation for improving student achievement was to focus on improving literacy through a model which came to be known as the Literacy Collaborative. Key features of the approach included:

- articulating a clear vision and commitment to a system literacy priority for *all* students which is continually communicated to everyone in the system;
- developing a system-wide comprehensive plan and framework for continuous improvement (SPCI);
- using data to drive instruction and determine resources;
- building administrator and teacher capacity to teach literacy for *all* students;
- establishing professional learning communities at all levels of the system and beyond the district.

The district developed a strong team of curriculum coordinators and consultants, all focused on facilitating balanced literacy instruction. It also linked into external research development expertise, particularly with the Ontario Institute for Studies in Education of the University of Toronto (OISE/UT). Assessment of the effectiveness of the implementation was evaluated annually. Capacity-building focused on literacy assessment for learning, instructional strategies, and on change management. In this case, capacity-building means any strategy that develops the collective efficacy of a group to raise the bar and close the gap of student achievement through (1) new knowledge competencies and skills, (2) enhanced resources, and (3) greater motivation. The operative word is *collective* – what the group can do whether it is a given school or indeed the whole district to raise the bar and close the gap of student achievement.

The district has invested in ongoing, systematic professional development in literacy, assessment literacy, knowledge of the learner, instructional intelligence and e-learning, as well as professional learning focusing on change knowledge (understanding the change process, dealing with resistance, building professional learning communities, leadership and facilitation skills, and the like). The full-blown model is shown in Figure 7.1.

The model may appear overwhelming and we do not intend to explain it in detail here. In fact, the model was developed over time and is presented and discussed on an ongoing basis within the system to clarify the overall vision and to continuously improve the approach. Our point here is that the model is explicit, evolutionary (open to refinement based on ongoing evidence) and comprehensive. It reflects and guides the work of the district and is used by instructional leaders at all levels of the system.

More specifically, the Literacy Collaborative model involved developing and supporting school literacy teams, starting with an initial cohort in 2001–02 and adding schools over a four-year period until all schools in the district were involved, elementary and secondary. Each school team consisted of three people – the principal, the literacy teacher (a leadership role typically released for .25 to .5 time to work alongside the principal and classroom teachers during the school day) and the special education resource teacher (SERT). Note: the funding of the literacy teacher is from the school district's staffing using existing budget, not supported by provincial educational funding. The teams committed to participating in regional literacy professional development (PD) once a month and in change management sessions, led by Carol Rolheiser and Michael Fullan (OISE/UT) four times a year.

The cohorts joined LC, starting with the most disadvantaged elementary schools. In 2001–02, 17 elementary schools formed the first cohort; 21 schools were added in 2002–03; 45 in 2003–04, and the remaining 57 schools joined in 2004–05. Thus, by 2005 all schools were involved, including all 27 secondary schools. There is a longstanding saying in the change literature that 'change is a process not an event'. Such a process was actualized in York Region District School Board, not just because the professional development sessions were continuous over multiple years, but also because the strategy required school teams, working with their staffs, to apply ideas in between sessions and to continually build them into everyday practice. It was what

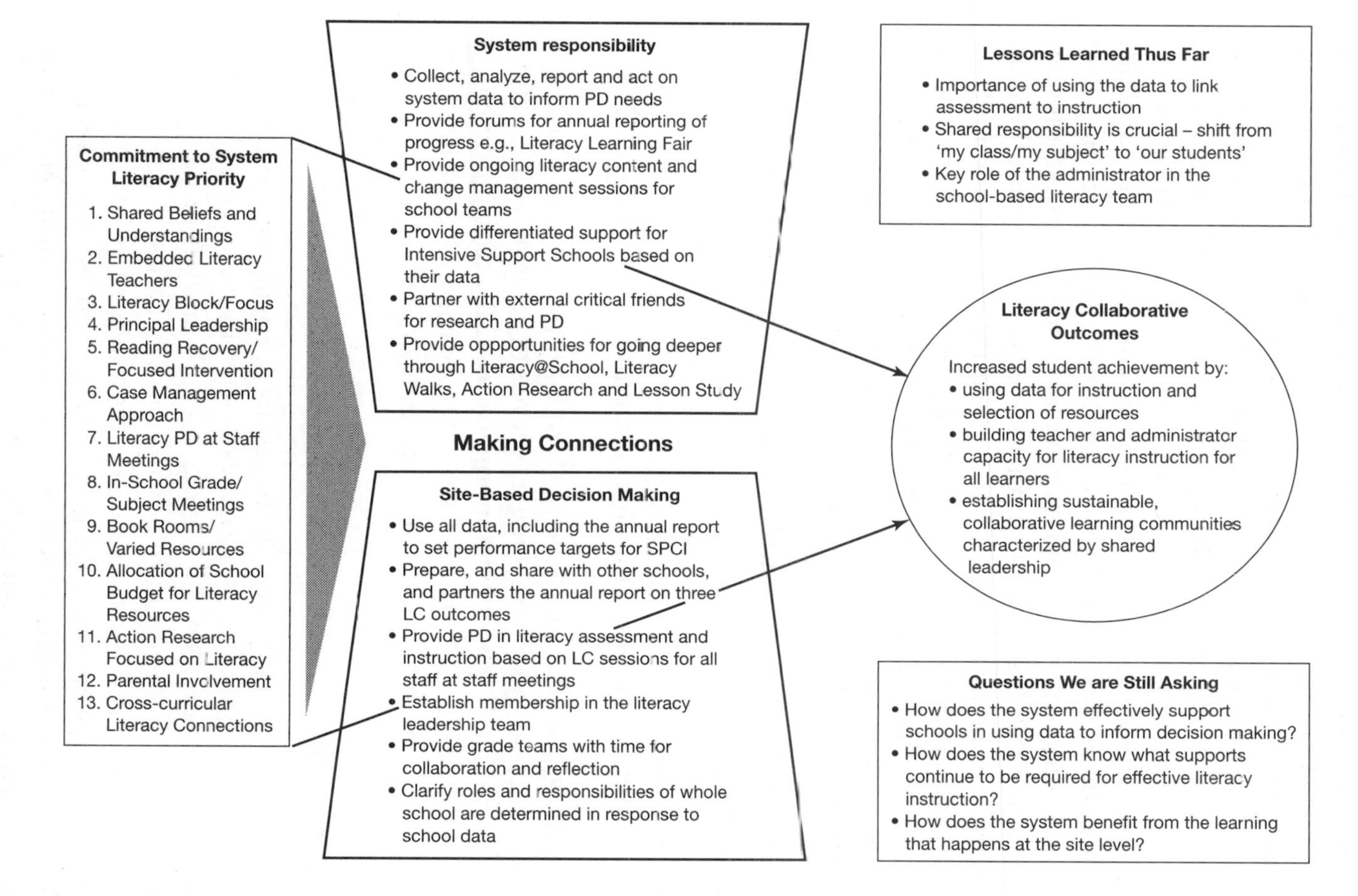

Figure 7.1 *The Literacy Collaborative vision*

happened in the schools in between sessions that counted. Ideas were constantly applied and discussed as the district emphasized 'learning in context', that is, learning by applying new ideas, building on them, and being re-energized by the successes achieved.

In short, the model was based on best knowledge. Comprehensive in coverage, the model was constantly shared and refined with all stakeholders – the school teams, the curriculum coordinator/consultant staff, the community, school board trustees, and the system as a whole. Moreover there was a multi-year commitment funded at the board table and outlined in a comprehensive system plan for continuous improvement (SPCI) so that the district stayed on course with the strategy. There was no mistaking that LC was clearly the system priority.

Each June the district organizes a Literacy Learning Fair in which the literacy leadership teams from *all* schools present what they have accomplished and learned. Schools must report on the three goals of LC: to increase students' literacy achievement by:

- using data to drive instruction and to select appropriate literacy resources;
- building administrators' and teachers' capacity for successful literacy instruction;
- establishing professional learning communities across the district.

The Literacy Learning Fair is part celebration, part peer pressure, and part peer support to keep reaching new levels of achievement. By annually sharing every schools' commitment to and accomplishment of increased student achievement, the 400 participants contributed to organization and individual leadership energy renewal.

Results so far

The intent here is not to explain the results in detail, but rather to convey enough detail that it is clear that YRDSB is a district on the move (see Sharratt and Fullan, 2005, for a more in-depth analysis of results). Our main question of interest in this chapter is, what are the issues in *sustaining* improvement – what are the key leadership issues for the immediate future in a system that is already highly focused and intentional?

Assessment of student achievement in reading, writing and mathematics for grade 3 and grade 6 children is conducted annually by the

Education Quality and Accountability Office (EQAO). The EQAO is an arm's-length government agency charged with assessing and communicating the results of all students in the province. To take grade 3 writing as an example, over the past five years (from 1999–2000 to 2004–05) York has moved from 66 per cent of the students reaching the provincial standard to approximately 75 per cent. During the first three years of this period the province as a whole was flat-lined at around 55 per cent until it launched in 2003 a province-wide strategy much along the lines of York's capacity-building but applied to all 72 districts in the province – latterly the province has moved from 55 per cent to 63 per cent (see Fullan, 2006). Table 7.1 describes these quantitative results in more detail.

Table 7.1 *Five-year span in EQAO results in YRDSB, 1999–2005*

EQAO (Method 2)	1999 (baseline year before district's literacy focus)	2005	% increase
Grade 3 Reading	59	69	10
Grade 3 Writing	66	75	9
Grade 3 Mathematics	70	80	10
Grade 6 Reading	61	75	14
Grade 6 Writing	59	72	13
Grade 6 Mathematics	63	76	13
% ESL/ELD Learners	Gr. 3 4% Gr. 6 4%	11% 6%	7 2
ESL/ELD Grade 3 Reading	34	56	22
ESL/ELD Grade 3 Writing	47	69	22
ESL/ELD Grade 3 Mathematics	62	75	13
ESL/ELD Grade 6 Reading	27	53	26
ESL/ELD Grade 6 Writing	27	62	35

ESL/ELD Grade 6 Mathematics	62	74	12
OSSLT (diploma Bearing assessment)	Oct. 2002 77%	Oct. 2004 87%	10
Reading at the end of Grade 1 (Reading Recovery™ site reports)	59%	83%	24

Source: Sharratt and Rolheiser, 2006

The aggregate figures mask the more fine-grained explanation of how results were achieved in specific schools. In Sharratt and Fullan (2006), we present data that show that those schools which had principal- and teacher-leadership that focused more specifically on all 13 parameters of the LC model in action achieved much greater results, including many of the most disadvantaged schools that began much below the YRDSB and the Ontario average, only to surpass both averages over the ensuing five years. The leadership teams in these schools:

- clearly understood the model and most importantly lived the shared beliefs and understandings;
- did continuous self-assessment, striving to align behaviour and beliefs among the principal, teacher-leaders and staff as a whole;
- did not let other 'distractors' divert their focus and energy. In fact they drew or renewed their leadership energy by means of understanding their improvement.

There are many schools in York Region that have these qualities and the system is now working toward greater consistency. For example, 28 elementary and six secondary schools were identified, using data, as 'stuck' or declining, and in 2005–06 received more intensive capacity-building support for school leadership teams from the curriculum and instructional services team (in the meantime, *all* schools in York Region continue to be engaged in district-wide reform, including all 27 secondary schools).

There is little doubt that there is widespread support for and understanding of LC in the district. In April 2005 we conducted a survey of all school teams in the district (each school leadership team consists of the principal, the lead literacy teacher, and the special education resource teacher). We received 387, or a 76 per cent return. The results from the survey showed that a very high percentage of school leaders perceived that LC had a strong, positive impact. The percentage scoring 4 or 5 on a five-point impact scale for selected questions is displayed in Table 7.2.

Table 7.2 *The Literacy Collaborative has*

1.	Provided teachers with a wider-range of teaching strategies	90%
2.	Helped ensure adequate resources to support students	78%
3.	Raised the expertise of teachers within their schools	88%
4.	Increased the school-wide focus on literacy	95%
5.	Clarified the role of all teachers in the support of literacy	78%
6.	Provided more attention and assistance to students at risk	83%
7.	Raised literacy expectations for all students	90%
8.	Produced more consistency and continuity in literacy across subjects	75%
9.	Fostered a more positive attitude among staff re literacy teaching	85%
10.	Facilitated sharing of expertise with teachers from other schools	69%

Granted that this survey does not tap into the perceptions of individual teachers but the leadership teams are very much in close interaction with classroom teachers. We conclude that it is accurate to say that the system as a whole has been energized by the strategy and the strong results being obtained. We get further confirmation from the fact that the provincial Literacy Numeracy Secretariat identified YRDSB as one of eight school districts which exemplified quality strategies in action. But our interest in this chapter is not about the results so far. Rather, what are the prospects for sustainability? How do individual principals sustain their commitment? How can the system help? Could it be that large-scale initiatives, even if successful, eventually take their toll and lead to diminished effort in light of relentless demands?

The nature and prospects of sustainability

Hargreaves and Fink (2006: 30) define sustainability in this way: 'Sustainability does not simply mean whether something will last. It addresses how particular initiatives can be developed without compromising the development of others in the environment now or in the future.' Thus, intentional reform models, like LC, must unfold in such a way that all schools benefit. The spirit underlying such approaches attempts to create a we–we mindset. As a result of purposeful interaction within and across schools, school leaders become more aware of, and indeed more committed to, the success of other schools in addition to their own.

It is our contention in this chapter that while individual leaders can and must work on their own sustaining energies, the conditions for sustaining large numbers of people can only be fostered if the organization as a whole is working in this direction. Moreover, we maintain that focusing on sustainability must become more deliberate and precise. It needs explicit attention – it must be worked on in a self- and organizationally-conscious manner.

This position is reinforced by the findings of two of the more informative books on organizational change which confirm the basic conditions for sustainability. Jim Collins (2001), in his well-known book, *Good to Great*, compares Fortune 500 companies that had 'good' performance with those that had 'great' performance as measured by 15 or more years of continuous financial success. Collins and his colleagues found five key themes associated with ongoing success. The first three, he claims, are more important early on because they build momentum. First, he found that we need more 'executive leaders' who can help build enduring greatness (leaders whose main mark is not only their contribution to success but also relative to how many leaders they leave behind who can go even further). Second, he emphasizes that organizations need to work on securing 'who' not just 'what'. The 'who' in this case are leaders who can help develop the five themes in question. The third theme is 'confront the brutal facts', that is, a relentless focus on examining data for making improvements. The fourth theme was the 'hedgehog effect' – a hedgehog is an animal that once it focuses, is hard to distract. Thus sustainable organizations learn to concentrate through passion, expertise and mobilization of resources in a way that keeps them going. The fifth theme is 'disciplined inquiry' – always problem-solving in relation to the central mission. Collins calls the overall effect the 'flywheel'. This is clearly related to sustainability because it takes less energy to keep the flywheel going once it is underway, permitting leaders to go deeper, which leads to greater success. More recently, Collins (2005) has confirmed that these ideas apply to the social sector, not because they come from business but because they focus on getting and maintaining greatness. The virtuous circle builds and further attracts believers and resources by getting and leveraging results.

An identical finding is contained in Kanter's (2004) study of *Confidence: How Winning and Losing Streaks Begin and End*. 'Confidence,' says Kanter, 'influences the willingness to invest – to commit money, time, reputation, emotional energy, or other resources – or withhold or hedge investments' (2004: 7). Kanter's solution is framed around developing three interconnected cornerstones – accountability, collaboration, and initiative. It is these conditions that generate sustaining investments of energy and commitment.

The system must also foster what we have come to call 'positive pressure' (Fullan, 2006). Positive pressure is one that is non-pejorative, that assumes that capacity is at the root of success, and that focused capacity-building strategies promote transparency in sharing practices and viewing results. In other words, one key to getting at sustainability is to bring issues out in the open in order to understand them, and in turn in order to address any problems.

In sum, the key concepts for us pertain to whether the system goes about its work in a way that helps people focus, that motivates and energizes people to make investments that are sensitive to the ebb and flow of energies, that uses success to beget more success, and that creates a critical mass of leaders who work together on these very matters.

Sustainability in York region

There are very little direct data available in the literature on what leaders in given systems think about in relation to the concept of sustainability. We decided then that a good place to start would be to go to the source and ask YRDSB principals three questions:

1. How do you sustain your school's literacy initiative as a leader?
2. How do you maintain energy/renewal for your staff to sustain the literacy focus?
3. How do you maintain your energy and renew yourself to sustain the literacy focus?

We set out to select a large number of principals on the basis of how active they were in the Literacy Collaborative. Thus, this is not a random sample but one in which the leaders identified were engaged in the reform. We wanted to know what active, purposeful principals thought about sustainability. We did not, it should be noted, select on a narrow basis a few exceptionally active principals. We wanted the sample to represent typical principals who could reflect what happens when 'regular' principals get immersed in ongoing change. We identified 61 elementary and 18 secondary school principals and asked them to respond in writing to the three questions. The response was overwhelming with 50 (82 per cent) of elementary and 17 (94 per cent) of secondary principals responding. This is admittedly a selective sample but is large and diverse, representing about 38 per cent of the total in the district. We found as expected that, although the questions were open ended, the vast majority of responses related to the components of the LC model. In other words, given that the model was intended to mobilize support at the school level for a sustained focus on literacy, and given that the model was developed in close communication with principals, we would expect that school leaders would gravitate to the content of the strategy when they thought (unprompted) about sustainability. We report below on the main themes that respondents spontaneously formulated, indicating the percentage of those who commented on the theme along with a representative quote or two relevant to the topic. Our interest here is in identifying the conditions or elements that are conducive to sustaining focus and energy on continuous improvement. Think of sustainability conditions as those that motivate people to continue to invest their energies in working with others to accomplish greater improvement.

Question 1: How do you as leader sustain your school's literacy initiative?

There were five major themes that attracted high numbers of comments:

1. Shared beliefs, goals, and vision.
2. Distributed leadership and professional learning cultures.
3. Data-based decisions/impact measures/celebrating success.
4. Resources.
5. School/community/home relations.

As we have found before, these are recurring themes (Sharratt, 2001); however, they are found here to be even more precise. We also note that shared beliefs is more of an outcome of a quality process than a precondition (Fullan, 2006). Put differently, one condition for sustainability involves working on defining, shaping and refining the shared vision of the school, in this case, using school data in relation to literacy improvement. The more that beliefs are shared, the greater the ongoing effort and the efficiency of the effort. Over 60 per cent of respondents identified shared beliefs as in the following three comments:

> *A common goal of improved student achievement and the attitude that* all *students can learn is embedded in the culture of the school.*

> *To sustain the school's literacy implementation, we try to maintain focus and assure that we have a common language. We try to set a few clear targets and we have an overall vision regarding where we want our students to be across the grades.*

> *When we reflect on the impact of our instructional decisions and what the data tell us that students are learning, it creates 'intellectual energy'. It becomes a craving to impact the learning of every student.*

A second key factor associated with continued success is what we have come to call the presence of dedicated 'second change agents' or what is sometimes referred to as distributive leadership – a critical mass of leaders led by the principal working on establishing a culture of ongoing learning. The principal is the first change agent. Having one or more 'second change agents' is crucial – for example, literacy lead teachers with direct responsibility and time during the school day to work with other teachers in their classrooms, to link teachers with each other internally and across schools, to help set up data management systems, and to work with principals on school improvement. Over 70 per cent of respondents highlighted this aspect:

> *Sustaining the momentum within the school is possible because of the many levels of support available to schools. The staffing made available for literacy coaches has been critical. This has given our school a teacher-leader who is working to increase the knowledge of those around her.*

We model processes and literacy content at staff meetings and build shared leadership by providing staff opportunities to take leadership roles in modelling and facilitating the use of information gained at LC sessions. As a principal, I fully utilize the concept of sharing leadership and creating a learning community. The sharing of leadership allows the administrative team and me to pace ourselves in terms of energy expenditure.

Administration communicates clear expectations to staff about why/how/when literacy instruction and focus occur in classrooms. Ensure that staff members have the tools, skills, etc. to use effective literacy practices i.e., no excuses.

Our primary learning team truly is a professional learning community with many teachers doing projects together and sharing ideas.

By using staff meetings, divisional meetings and grade partner planning times, teachers are encouraged to reflect on the needs of all students, generally, and at-risk students specifically.

Third, data driven instruction and the ubiquitous presence and use of data are core themes for promoting and maintaining effort. The case management approach is in place in all elementary schools where individual students are tracked with corrective action taking place on an ongoing basis. Over 40 per cent of responses related to this theme:

Student achievement in both literacy and numeracy is a focus for transition planning for students coming from grade 8 to grade 9. We make particular note of student achievement levels in grades 3 and 6 EQAO assessments. (Secondary principal)

It was a natural step for us to [use case data] to strive for differentiated instruction to provide for the diverse needs in each classroom.

Success breeds success. What we have done to date has proven to make a difference to increased student achievement. We celebrate this!

We have set aside time to review school results – to identify areas of weakness and to share successful approaches.

Fourth, resources are part and parcel of continued success, provided that they are part of a cycle of success. Kick-start the process with new resources, and then have success chase the money – this year's success is next year's additional resources (Fullan, 2006). Some 35 per cent highlighted this factor:

We have invested heavily in book rooms and appropriate classroom libraries for all three divisions.

We carry out decisions about the school resources in the area of literacy based on our school plan for continuous improvement. We allocate our financial, human, material resources in a way that makes literacy a priority.

The fifth theme for sustainability is probably one of the most important in the long run but also the most difficult to establish, namely, school to home community relationships. This element was reflected in comments from almost 40 per cent of respondents.

We have extended our partnerships with the parents and guardians from day one. This community has extended our understanding of cultural diversity – English as a second language, and economic and lifestyle impact on children's learning.

Finally, a kind of omnibus comment struck us as a particularly apropos summary with respect to question 1:

Support and encouragement are crucial. Pushing too hard never works. Magic happens when teachers take initiative within a framework which has been developed by the district. Incorporating PD into staff and division meetings needs to be led by staff not the principal. When teachers share their best practices, things happen. Providing both time and resources for mentoring/team teaching ensures that literacy becomes and remains a focus. Walking the fine line between push and pull is always an exciting challenge and worth the time to build strong leaders in a school.

Question 2: How do you maintain energy/renewal for your staff to sustain the literacy focus?

Our second question extended the school sustainability question more directly to focus on staff. As expected, there was overlap with the first question but more personally based aspects surfaced. We can use the same five categories to capture the comments.

First, with respect to shared beliefs about 30 per cent of the responses related to this category:

I have very high expectations for myself and others. I expect the best and then offer opportunities and experiences to help others improve.

Time to focus on the goals of the school as a team has been met in an improved way this year and is making a difference.

Talk about buy in – we all have a common message and again it gets linked back to that common vision.

Second, for leadership and learning cultures, principals talked about the day-to-day built-in support for what we call 'learning in context' – the kind of learning that occurs every day because it becomes part of the culture. About 45 to 60 per cent (depending on the subcategory) responded along these lines:

Teacher mentoring and team teaching have been important methods used to sustain the literacy implementation and energy in such a large school.

The literacy teachers (literacy coaches) have given staff many opportunities for support and role modelling. We give teachers time to collaborate with their grade partners.

Staff members need time to hear about a concept, learn about it, experiment with it, work it into everyday practice, consolidate it and, ultimately, sustain it as part of good teaching practice.

Probably the most effective means for sustaining something is the teacher's own enthusiasm when they see their students progressing and responding to strategies they are using. It's catching!

A culture of shared leadership is in place. We promote shared leadership in the school and teachers feel comfortable assuming these roles.

The external training provided by the district based on the LC model is a great motivator for me. I always bring back little seeds that I plant back at the school.

The opportunities available through the Literacy Collaborative have been excellent and the increased opportunities of more teachers attending workshops have provided great motivation and excitement at every level of the school.

Third, the use of data on student achievement as a tool for improvement, playing itself out in a learning culture, as crucial for maintaining focus and momentum was mentioned directly by 20 per cent of the respondents and by many more in relation to establishing sharing cultures:

We analyzed the data collected, charted the students identified as 'at risk' in the fall, and made plans to address their needs.

Our staff meeting agenda planning focus is on student data and related improvement ideas and activities, while keeping operational/informational items to an absolute minimum!

Fourth, about 25 per cent of the respondents mentioned resources:

Our book room is a central part of our school. Our teachers take tremendous ownership for it. They look forward to buying for it and keeping it up.

Budget for initiatives or simply having the resources in place is vital to ensuring that the change process is not interrupted or discarded and is integral to creating a culture of cohesiveness as staff members work and take ownership of literacy in their classrooms and in the school.

Timetabling, shared grade-level prep time, using curriculum instructional supply teacher days and, freeing up teachers to engage in professional learning are key to maintaining the focus.

Fifth, only a small minority (10 per cent) mentioned home–school relations as a sustainer, possibly because this is the most difficult aspect, and takes the longest to develop. In our experience, principals and teachers need to develop their own professional learning communities to a certain point first, before they reach out in a more proactive way to the community:

> *Key is engaging all educational partners and effectively using many volunteers, including: co-operative education students, tutors in the classroom and other community resources – human and non-human.*

Question 3: How do you maintain your energy and renewal for yourself to sustain the literacy focus?

The third major question in this research is the most personal because it asks principals what they, themselves, do to maintain their own energy and renewal. Three interrelated clusters stood out:

1. Personal renewal and challenge.
2. Passion expressed as student success (passion without success is a non-sustainer).
3. The social basis of sustainability.

Over two-thirds of respondents identified personal growth and stimulus as sustaining them:

> *It may sound trite but if we are asking our staff and students (and other employees) to read, read, read, then we had better be reading as well. I find that this is important in reminding me how important literacy is, so I read all the time, including professional reading, but more importantly expanding to novels, newspapers, etc.*

> *The personal satisfaction comes from learning new skills myself, and participating in PD provided by the curriculum department.*

> *Ongoing learning opportunities through the Literacy Collaborative, Literacy Walk training, in-school study groups and personal professional reading are some of the vehicles for energizing and empowering the sustaining focus on literacy.*

> *Attending the LC sessions with the teachers is another way to maintain my energy and renewal.*

I endeavour to never let the mood of others or the stress felt by others determine my mood. I strive to be positive, professional and set personal goals that I would like others to model.

The second theme was passion expressed through student success. Again, about two-thirds spontaneously expressed this theme:

But what really excites me is the children! Seeing their work displayed on the hallway walls, highlighting the reading comprehension strategy of the month, is very rewarding.

Watching amazing teachers work with students on something that you've taught them or that they have learned as a result of an opportunity that you have offered is energizing.

It is very easy to sustain the literacy focus when I see the positive results of the literacy practices our teachers implement in the school.

We focus on sharing and celebrating success that we're having. There is certainly an energy that comes from seeing that the instructional practices we are implementing are making a difference in the lives of all students.

Listening to success stories is encouraging and inspiring when one is occasionally faced with resistance or frustration.

The third theme – Working on and appreciating personal well-being and the social nature of sustainability in and outside of school – was featured by, again, some 60 per cent of the respondents:

My energy is sustained by watching and listening to dedicated staff that work hard and have fun doing it!

I spend time in classrooms to see literacy strategies in action (morning and afternoon walkthroughs).

I talk to staff, visit classrooms, am aware of how staff members are maintaining a literacy focus in their classrooms on a daily basis.

Renewal comes when I spend time with my family and friends. This allows me to keep life in perspective, appreciate the little things and not take myself too seriously.

I have learned to slow down (and that is hard for me) and digest the information from 'above'. I have learned how to prioritize the information and redistribute it to key staff for interpretation.

Finally, an overall comment seemed to capture the essence of personal sustainability:

I see literacy leadership as a never-ending cycle of learning and improvement. When you accept this idea it becomes easier to accept personal renewal as an essential component of effective leadership.

Implications for sustainability

Our chapter is clearly only one snapshot, albeit of a large district that is taking leadership sustainability seriously. We think that the personal perspectives of a large number of school leaders are both a unique and valuable contribution to our knowledge of personal perceptions on the question of sustainability. As we stand back and survey the overall LC model from the perspective of conditions that favour sustainability, four propositions stand out for us.

Proposition One: Sustainability is not about prolonging specific innovations, but rather it is about establishing the conditions for continuous student improvement.

Proposition Two: Sustainability is not possible unless school leaders and system leaders are working on the same agenda.

Proposition Three: Proposition Two notwithstanding, sustainability is not furthered by school and system leaders simply agreeing on the direction of the reform. Rather, agreement is continually tested and extended by leaders at both school and system levels putting pressure on each other. Sustainability is a two-way or multi-way street.

Proposition Four: We have a fair idea about what makes for sustainability within one district under conditions of stable leadership over a five or more year period, but we still do not know how sustainability fares when district leadership changes, or when state leadership changes direction.

We have been able to identify some of the main themes of sustainability. They amount to focus, consistency, and mutual reinforcement between the school and district levels, staying the course, and developing an attitude that continuity of good direction, and of increased student achievement is paramount. We know sustainability, as in continuous effort and energy, is always vulnerable. We know that sustaining cultures requires a lot of work to build and maintain, but can be destroyed quickly with different leadership, and change in political conditions. Yet by making what works explicit, and by enabling more and more leaders at all levels of the system to be aware of the conditions that energize them and those with whom they work, the chances for continued success are greatly enhanced.

Our general conclusion is to make the notion of sustainability transparent – foster open and continuous dialogue about whether system and school level discussions are focused and, thus, whether energy is flourishing. Finally, we do not see sustainability as linear. There are always ebbs and flows, a time to stand back and regroup, and so on. Sustainable organizations are more likely to see positive flow as cyclical and, thus, treat setbacks as temporary, and more likely, in turn, to find ways of re-energizing. Indeed, sustainable organizations do not experience and do not expect continued good fortune, but rather stay the course when things are not going well. Persistence and resilience are the hallmarks of individuals and organizations that are self-conscious and confident about their own capacities to win more than they lose, and to create their own self-fulfilling prophecies.

In short, it is not so much that people need to believe that sustainability is possible, but more that the only way to move forward is to be 'in the game' – to be engaged, seeking and helping to produce other leaders who are similarly disposed.

References

Collins, J. (2005) *Good to Great and the Social Sectors*. Boulder, CO: Jim Collins.

Collins, J. (2001) *Good to Great*. New York: HarperCollins.

Davies, B. (ed.) (2005) *The Essentials of School Leadership*. London: Paul Chapman Publishing.

Fullan, M. (2005) *Leadership and Sustainability*. Thousand Oaks, CA: Corwin Press; Toronto: Ontario Principals Council.

Fullan, M. (2006) *Turnaround Leadership*. San Francisco, CA: Jossey-Bass; Toronto: Ontario Principals Council.

Fullan, M., Hill, P. and Crevola, C. (2006) *Breakthrough*. Thousand Oaks, CA: Corwin Press; Toronto: Ontario Principals Council.

Hargreaves, A. and Fink, D. (2006) *Sustainable Leadership*. San Francisco, CA: Jossey-Bass.

Kanter, R.M. (2004) *Confidence: How Winning and Losing Streaks Begin and End*. New York: Crown Publishers.

Loehr, J. and Schwartz, T. (2003) *The Power of Full Engagement*. New York: Free Press.

Sharratt, L. (2001) 'Making the most of accountability policies: Is there a role for the school district?', *Orbit*, 32(1): 37–42.

Sharratt, L. and Fullan, M. (2005) *The School District that Did the Right Things Right*. Annenberg Institute for School Reform. Providence, RI: Brown University.

Sharratt, L. and Fullan, M. (2006) Accomplishing districtwide reform, *Journal of School Leadership*, 16: 583–95.

Sharratt, L. and Rolheiser, C. (2006) *Miracles in Progress: System Change and Coherence*. Toronto: York Region District School Board.

Chapter 8

Leadership and sustainability in an emerging market environment

Guilbert C. Hentschke

Overview

'Sustainability' has caught on in education as a characterization – not of what is, but of what ought to be. Scholars and writers in the field of compulsory schooling are looking to sustainability as a valued characteristic of leaders and organizations – and for understandable reasons. Why? Much of what is desired and valued in school settings has all too often been artificially cut short or terminated, requiring those remaining to 'start over'. Unfortunately, too many initiatives (and initiators) are not 'sustained' within the current system.

'Sustainability' appears to directly confront several fundamental and highly visible problems in current schooling systems, such as the unplanned and frequent turnover of key leadership personnel and teachers. Hence, the attractiveness of sustainability, especially as an attribute of leadership, is growing as a framework for improving the leadership of schools, an argument amply described in detail in other chapters of this volume. As a *normative* proposition, compelling arguments are being constructed around the inherent qualities of sustainability.

However, the concept itself, drawn originally from concerns about resource depletion in the built environment and, more recently, from studies of for-profit business behaviour, has been significantly modified during the course of its journey into the compulsory schooling world. Furthermore and at the same time, the environment within which those same schools operate is increasingly taking on characteristics of the marketplace, with increasingly fluid forms of financial support, attendance boundaries (markets), competing providers, 'bottom line' performance priorities, and alternative ways to organize and deliver schooling. As a *descriptive* proposition, the current operation of many schools is becoming less 'sustainable'. Change – for 'better' or 'worse' – trumps stability. The inherent attractiveness of *sustainability as predictable stability* in education, once assumed as a given, is increasingly a wistful longing.

So, as K-12 (compulsory-level, or kindergarten through grade twelve) educators embrace sustainability concepts for obvious and compelling reasons, the schooling environment is simultaneously morphing into one increasingly characterized by market forces and responses that more nearly characterize the environment of business organizations. To the extent that this is the case, and schooling organizations are required to be more flexible, nimble, cost-effective, innovative and opportunistic, 'sustainability' (at least some uses of that term) may continue to grow as a *desired* attribute of leaders and organizations and in reaction to market environments. As a *description* of schooling operations, however, sustainability will likely diminish. This chapter explores the implications of growing market environments on changing *descriptive* frameworks of sustainability in education.

The fundamental presumptions underlying this argument are as follows: (1) organizational behaviour is partially a function of organizational environment; (2) schools (some more than others) are gravitating to a more market-oriented environment; and (3) organizations in a much more market-oriented environment than schools are in at present should reveal some sense of where schools are headed – all with respect to 'sustainability'.

To the extent that educators (and their organizations) gravitate toward an increasingly market-oriented environment, they will face as many as six additional management issues where sustainability (at least some uses of the term) inevitably gets trumped by more pressing concerns. As such, sustainability, despite its normative allure, will likely have less (at least, different) descriptive value in those educational contexts where market forces are ascendant.

The chapter presents this argument through four distinct parts. Beginning with a brief synopsis and early summary of the definition of and arguments for sustainability, this chapter contrasts those ideas with the principal definitions of and normative arguments for sustainability made by educators applying the concept to education. Many of those arguments are much more deeply and elegantly presented in other chapters of this volume. They are highlighted here to provide a basis for comparison against the six 'realities' more typically associated with business behaviour in market environments. The second and third parts of the chapter address respectively the manifestations of growing market forces found in compulsory education and six 'non-sustaining' issues often faced by market-sensitive firms. Finally, the possibilities and limits of sustainability as a typical practice (descriptive efficacy) and as a worthy goal (normative efficacy) in market-related education environments are discussed.

Sustainability – sources of applications to education

'Sustainability', long associated with issues of the natural and built environments and, more generally, with global economic development, is increasingly being associated with issues of school leadership – and for arguably similar reasons. The first and most familiar source of inspiration for sustainability derives from growing popular concern of the natural limits to consumption of the earth's natural resources. The inherent limits of nature, both in quantitative dimensions and in propensities for renewal, dictate revising patterns of resource consumption to foster resource sustainability. The specific targets range from fish in the sea to forests to water to air, and arguments have extended from these to many other items of concern.

Arguments for sustainable development in the natural and built environment have emanated from a variety of sources, including a series of conferences and related reports which crystallized sustainable development as: 'articulating, integrating, and achieving social, economic, and environmental objectives and initiatives to protect humankind and the natural world' (Robinson, 1993: i). This particular perspective, call it *sustainability as organic preservation and conservation*, has been applied to the field of organizational behaviour, in a few instances, including educational institutions (Litten, 2005) and even school curricula (Wheeler and Byrne, 2003).

'Sustainable business development', directly derivative from this version of sustainability, entails a variety of normative arguments on how businesses should and can behave with regard to a variety of issues, including: 'their entire value system from the origins of the raw materials to production processes and customer applications to end-of-life

(EoL) solutions ... relationships with supply networks, customers and stakeholders, and support service providers for ... handling wastes, residuals, and impacts' (Rainey, 2006: 2–3). Within this conservation framework, sustainability in effect seeks to achieve 'sustainable outcomes' that 'balance the performance objectives of the present with the needs and expectations of the future' (Rainey, 2006: 3). Studies have addressed organizations in general (Hall and Vredenberg, 2003; Hart and Milstein, 2003; Pearce and Atkinson, 1993; Rainey, 2006), as well as firms in specific industrial sectors (Bell and Morse, 2000; Panico, 2004). As such it differs fundamentally from a second source of inspiration for sustainability in education which also emanates from the business community and the study of organizations – the study of how some (few) organizations seem to be able to sustain their dominant position in the long run. These studies of *sustainability as long run business success* have blended more descriptive, theoretical, and empirical perspectives with the normative perspective that has been associated with *sustainability as conservation*.

This second primary source of inspiration to apply sustainability arguments to compulsory education derives largely from studies of for-profit business endurance. Rarely featuring the term 'sustainability' as such, these large-scale, empirical studies of largely US publicly traded corporations seek to understand in their separate ways what enables some firms to endure over long periods of time when most firms do not. The illustrations, briefly cited here, are among the most heavily referenced by educators and others – *The Innovator's Dilemma* (Christensen, 1997), *Built to Last* (Collins and Porres, 1999), *Creative Destruction* (Foster and Caplan, 2001), *Good to Great* (Collins, 2001) and *The Innovator's Solution* (Christensen, 2003).

At the risk of excessive oversimplification and despite widely acknowledged differences among them, authors of these large-scale studies of for-profit businesses have uniformly premised their work on the widely acknowledged fact that the vast majority of businesses have *not* sustained themselves over long periods of time. For variations of 'sustained' read 'survived', 'sustained growth', 'remained as a distinct corporate entity', and 'stayed at or near the top of their industry'.

While the studies vary in research design, scope, scale, and even conclusions, each seeks to understand what takes place in those relatively rare instances when organizations manage to 'sustain themselves' over long periods of time. Brief characterizations of two of these studies illustrate both their variability of means and uniformity of purpose. In *Built to Last* the authors, Collins and Porras, argue that 'the vast majority of companies never become great, because the vast majority become quite good and that is their main problem' (1991; 1). The question they are asking is 'What has enabled some corporations to last so long, while other competitors in the same markets either struggle to get by, or fade away after a short period of time?' (1999). They examined 18 well-known, well-established and healthy companies ('visionaries'), and compared each to a counterpart in its specific area of business, and sought to find patterns between the visionary companies and their counterparts. They ultimately found that a company's 'core value system' is the determinant of its success.

The author of *The Innovator's Dilemma*, Clayton Christensen, focused greater attention initially on well-managed firms that ultimately did *not* sustain their leadership positions in order to understand why it appeared that '*good* management was the most powerful reason they failed to stay atop their industries' (1997: xii; emphasis added). Ultimately his in-depth analysis of numerous distinct industries, for example, computing and retail, revealed that most leading firms produced 'sustaining' innovations, but could not take advantage of 'disruptive' technologies without setting up separate business entities with economic models that differed from the parent company. The very small fraction of firms that undertook this strategy was able to sustain their positions in the long run.

Across these and similar studies the dimensions of sustainability and their measurement have varied, the normative versus descriptive implications have varied, and the analytical frameworks have certainly varied, but the fundamental premise remained uniformly constant. The vast majority of firms are not sustainable – and for well-understood, widely accepted reasons, ranging from leadership hubris (creative destruction), to the inherent difficulty of creating and adapting to 'disruptive innovations' (innovator's dilemma), to the lack of newly constructed organizational behaviours that appear to be associated with sustainability (for example, the 'hedgehog' concept in *Good to Great*). Of course, authors of these studies sought to understand how (the very few) firms sustained themselves, because the myriad examples and causes of non-sustainability were already widely acknowledged. Finding ways to sustain the business is inherently interesting to people in those businesses largely because it is so rarely achieved.

From these two sources of inspiration – concerns over long-run limits to developing the natural and built environment and large-scale studies of the performance of for-profit firms – 'sustainability' has gained a foothold in the schooling industry. Educators have drawn on both sources of inspiration, less as a descriptive framework than as a normative one: 'Sustainability does not simply mean whether something can last. It addresses how particular initiatives can be developed without compromising the development of others in the surrounding environment, now and in the future' (Hargreaves and Fink, 2000: 30). These and other scholars in education focus on organizations (the second inspiration) while applying normative arguments about the natural and built physical environment (the first inspiration). Most of these arguments are reactions to perceived problems in public school systems, especially traditional schooling processes which, though possibly achievable, even 'successful' in the short run, should not be *sustained* in the longer run. Several anecdotes illustrate this perspective.

Principal-led school reforms just begin to get traction when principal-turnover brings with it a new and different flavour of reform-of-the-day (Hargreaves and Fink, 2003a). Hence, leadership needs to be sustainable. School reforms themselves have an accretive, layered effect, with the most recent one piling on top of the next previous arrival, and so on back in time, resulting in unsustainable leadership and improvement efforts (Hargreaves and Fink, 2003b). Hence, school improvement initiatives require sustained attention over time to be effective. Reforms, from this perspective not only cannot be sustained, but the very belief that they will not be sustained is sufficient to doom their effective implementation and, of course, their sustainability (Fullan, 2005b). Finally, the hyper-pressurized, test-driven 'continuous improvement', 'high-stakes' accountability environments of today's schools bring with them added pressures to many schools – especially those labelled as failing (although usually stated more euphemistically) – that have great difficulty sustaining their frenetic survival activities.

So, to counter these problems, various forms of sustainable leadership are argued, including those which: 'sustains learning', 'endures over time', 'can be supported by available or achievable resources', 'don't impact negatively on the surrounding [school] environment' and 'promotes ecological diversity' (Hargreaves and Fink, 2003b: 694–6).

From these kinds of ecologically sensitive normative frameworks, authors in education have applied many interpretations, meanings, and implications from sustainability. 'If school improvement is to be sustainable, continuity of or longer tenure for the initial principal, or consistency in relation to those who follow him or her, is essential' (Hargreaves and Fink, 2003: 695). 'Sustainable success ... lies in ... distributed leadership ... not in ... an elite' (Hargreaves and Fink, 2003: 695). 'Sustainability is ... a moral and spatial issue as well as a temporal one.' As such sustainable leadership 'preserves sustaining learning ... [but not] learning that is trivial ... promotes continuity ... is socially just ... and [as such] is threatened by market-based parental choice and ... is patient and persevering ... [and therefore] defers gratification instead of seeking instant results' (drawn from Hargreaves, 2007).

Within this framework sustainability promises much and, as examined by writers from the business world, requires much – from listening skills (Eunson, 2003) to systems of measuring and reporting (Bell and Morse, 2000; Litten, 2005) to new methods of financial accounting (Chalk and Hemmings, 2000) to leadership development (Boyatzis et al., 2004). Notwithstanding these requirements, sustainability is an attractive concept within which to frame both the fundamental problems in schooling (like those named above), and to pose possible directions for improved leadership. Hence, over the last decade or so 'sustainable' leadership has logically been framed as a palliative for many of those public school ills, with 'sustainable' joining the panoply of adjectives modifying school leadership, including 'visionary', 'distributed', 'servant', 'entrepreneurial', 'strategic', 'turn-around' and others (Fullan, 2005b; Hargreaves and Fink, 2006).

Scholarship around these frameworks, largely theoretical and normative as opposed to empirical and descriptive, has defined these terms and framed schooling issues in ways that argue for the value of this particular brand of leadership. In most cases, the straw man in the argument is not any one of the other brands of leadership, for example, distributed leadership, but instead is the 'opposite' or ugly twin of the brand. Think, for instance, 'lack of vision', 'keeps the power to himself', 'in charge but doesn't help others', and 'tactical' or, worse, 'managerial', and 'not entrepreneurial'. The specific phrases used to deride problems of non-sustainability and to define and amplify sustainability's virtues, all derive from a reaction to the current state of public schooling – not its unchanging uniformity as so many other critics have noted, but the unplanned disorder that has grown out of a continuous cascade of accretive, partially implemented policy initiatives (Hargreaves and Fink, 2006). From the perspectives of many of these analysts the emerging market environment in education is compounding, not mitigating, these uncertainties.

Emerging market environments in education – manifestations, growth, and characteristics

The emerging market environment in education is far from well-developed and extremely uneven in its impacts on schools and schooling. It would be difficult to accurately characterize it beyond an observable variety of phenomena which we lump together and call 'market environment', which is the intent of this section. The market-oriented environment in schooling is easier to define than it is to measure. A number of its attributes in public schooling are increasingly visible, including increased reliance on multiple sources of revenue, and increased reliance on market, as opposed to hierarchical, transactions, greater consumer and provider choice, fewer protected student markets, and increasing varieties of educational providers (Davies and Hentschke, 2002).

In the context of US and UK compulsory schooling, these 'market environment' trends also characterize a service that is undergoing some degree of privatization, that is, an increasing proportion of services previously largely paid for and provided by government agencies are being supported and provided by private actors. Among the various possible forms of privatization (Hentschke and Wohlstetter, in press), three are particularly applicable to schooling. 'Supply side' privatization – wherein different levels of government outsource (or contract out) previously largely governmentally provided services to private (for-profit and non-profit) providers – is perhaps the most ubiquitous. In this instance government is permitting private businesses to provide or 'supply' the goods and services in question, while retaining *responsibility* for the service and *funding* of the service.

Increasingly school districts enter into relationships with education businesses to provide 'whole school operation', specialized tutoring services, transportation, and schooling services for individual students with specialized needs or challenges. Education analogues in the UK include City Technology Colleges (CTCs), Education Action Zones (EAZs), Public Private Partnerships (PPPs), and Private Finance Initiatives (PFIs). Charter schools illustrate this type of privatization (each charter school is usually chartered as a private organization), although charter school educators argue with some justification that they are 'public schools' because they are publicly funded, hence one of the sources of confusion.

The second form of privatization, 'demand side privatization', is really a variation of first with one important difference. Supply side privatization subsidizes the providers (that is, the *suppliers* of a service), whereas demand side privatization subsidizes the consumers (that is, the *demanders* of a service). Voucher plans are the most obvious type-two example in K-12 education.

The third form of privatization involves private individuals and organizations undertaking *both private funding and private provision*. Call these 'purely private' markets, in that governments did not formally act to foster privatization of either the demand or supply side. In this instance, governments are less directly involved, even though the purely private services in question may be closely associated with those already provided by governments. Purely private education services funded and provided by private individuals are growing and constitute an integral part of education's market environment, but are not necessarily new as such. Private schools and home schooling come to mind as two of the more obvious historic examples. More recently arrived purely private educational goods and services include educational toys and games as supplements to primary schools, individual private pay student tutoring services as supplements to school instruction, and private pay college advising and application services as supplements to school counselling.

Understandably, these purely private goods and services sometimes get confused with the publicly provided services they supplement as well as with other forms of privatization. These three types of privatization make up the 'growing market environment' in education, where they exist both in pure and in commingled forms. As an illustration of the latter, students attending a given private school can be paying their own way, while sitting right next to a student whose tuition is provided by a public agency – a realistic scenario with elements of all three forms of privatization.

From these diverse trends in schooling, three overlapping parameters are used here to define this emerging market environment: (1) growing choice (consumers and providers); (2) diversifying finance, including multiple revenue streams (for providers) and expenditure streams (for consumers); and (3) organizations from multiple sectors providing similar services within a governmental jurisdiction. Within these broad parameters, two dimensions of economic transactions provide a slightly narrower boundary around which to capture markets in education. They entail (1) transactions 'of choice' (2) across 'organizational lines'.

These parameters, while conceptually distinct, are neither mutually exclusive nor collectively exhaustive. Plus, within any geographic jurisdiction the presence of each will be a matter of degree, not kind. Nonetheless, in combination these three dimensions capture a large fraction of what we can arguably characterize as a growing 'market environment', and distinguish it from the public school stereotype of assigned attendance, standardized programming, and exclusively public funding and provision.

These theoretical parameters are made 'real' through organizations that operate well within this fuzzy, three-element boundary of the market environment. Schooling organizations operating well within this boundary include charter schools, home schooling families, home schooling service providers, district contract schools, voucher funding systems, virtual (distance learning) charter schools, private schools (for-profit and proprietary), and private businesses that supply the very wide range of goods and services to educational organizations (of all kinds). Still inside the 'market environment' boundaries, but nearer to the edge and closer to the traditional public school stereotype, are magnet schools, intra- and inter-district choice programs, and schools with substantial privately raised public education funds. Arguably at or over this boundary on the other side are the 18 million US students whose families have exercised their option of school choice through decisions to relocate their residence in what they believe to be a superior schooling environment. Finally, private businesses, in addition to private schools, that provide schooling and school-related services would be more inside the boundary than outside.

What is the approximate scope and scale of this 'market environment'? One estimate is in the range of 5 to 25 per cent of public schooling, depending on what you count and where you look.

'Markets' – not unlike 'sustainability' – are subject to a wide variety of interpretations and applications to a wide variety of phenomena. In education many initiatives have been linked to an increasing market environment, including but not limited to: charters, virtual charters, and vouchers in the USA, academies, private finance initiatives, CTCs in the UK, and in both countries home schooling services, educational toys, games and aids, privately provided schooling, tutoring, test preparation, and counselling – all sold either to private households or through contracts with government education agencies. Regardless of the label attached to these trends, the environment of schooling is increasingly fluid: current circumstances, positive and negative, are increasingly difficult to sustain.

Added organizational realities evoked in market environments

As desirable attributes of leaders and organizations, many of the diverse compelling arguments on behalf of sustainability, briefly summarized at the beginning of this chapter, could be applied without qualification to virtually all organizations. On the other hand, sustainability is arguably not at the top of the list as a descriptive perspective associated with understanding how organizations in particular (for example, emerging market) contexts actually behave and why. Reasons for this differ from the problem analyses of traditional publicly operated school contexts. Educational organizations (and their educational leaders) in emerging market environment are more likely to face at least four non-traditional issues at various points in their history where: the basic sustainability of the business is threatened; there is a drive to not sustain operations in their current manifestation; or there is a drive to increase operations in the short run to a point not sustainable in the long run.

The phenomenon of limited organizational life – 'creative destruction'

The assumption of continuity by firms in the marketplace no longer holds. Framed over half a century ago by economist Joseph Schumpeter, 'The problem that is usually being visualized is how capitalism *administers* existing structures, whereas the relevant problem is how it *creates* and *destroys* them' (from Foster and Kaplan, 2001: 15, emphasis in original). Destruction here is a means that allows the market to maintain freshness by eliminating those elements that are no longer needed, including collections of goods and services and the companies that produce them, 'old companies being replaced by new ones' (Foster and Kaplan, 2001: 139).

Schumpeter was referencing the 'destruction' of whole companies. Subsequent applications have included certain goods and services produced *within firms* as well. In both applications destruction is 'the end of the economically useful life'. This end may be due to the fact that the potential of the good or service has played itself out, or to changes in the mission and direction of the company, or to other causes. The core element from this perspective, nonetheless, is that in a market environment there may well be plausible arguments for ending (not sustaining) certain firms and the production of certain goods and services.

The closest analogue to recognition of creative destruction in public schools is perhaps the argument, policy, and practice of fostering the creation and growth of some charter schools while at the same time closing down less viable ones. The underlying premise here is that some educational enterprises should be closed down, not as a one-off, drastic, last-ditch option, but as an ongoing, 'routine' operation.

Not surviving through start up and initial growth

New businesses, in education or otherwise, face much more fundamental issues of early-stage survival. Sustainability here is more akin to continuing to exist. The vast majority of start-up organizations either never get operational or soon fail, and most entrepreneurs who start businesses are aware of this – either vaguely aware or acutely aware. Because survival is paramount in early stage businesses, many inherently unsustainable practices are considered and often undertaken, including burning out and turning over employees, undertaking excessive debt, and overly promising customers and investors. Theoreticians may rightly argue that business practices should be sustainable, but start-up circumstances may require that short-term unsustainable practices trump theoretically sound, long-run sustainable business practices.

Many start-up charter schools have had to begin operation in facilities that they knew in advance would not sustain their growth plans; they temporarily outsourced back-office operations with the intention of bringing them in house at a later date when scale and capacity made it feasible. In more than a few cases, temporary enrolment setbacks have necessitated deferring annual salary increases – another practice not sustainable in the long run, but accepted in the short run. If the firm manages to get beyond its inherent start-up challenges, it can then pursue a path of growth in sales and margins through innovation, where market-related threats and opportunities dictate improvements in business practices. Some forms of these threats never completely go away, necessitating reliance occasionally on drastic, non-sustainable survival tactics. This perspective is in contrast to many traditional public schooling environments where the basic survival threat does not exist, nor do the rewards presented by the opportunity for growth or change.

'Grow or die' – access to financial capital

Growth, both in scale and profitability, is closely associated with the behaviour of firms in market environments, and is often accompanied by fundamental transformations of the firm. The dynamics of most market-places, including parts of education, create imperatives for organizations in that market place to pursue models of growth. The implied sub-text of the major studies of for-profit businesses discussed earlier is that *all* firms sought desperately to grow, both revenues and margins, regardless of whether they were successful or not. Scale economies and increased profitability from increasing size still drives the decisions of many firms.

Investment capital finds its way into growing firms, facilitating further growth. In order to grow many firms require investment capital over and above any net revenues from sales, often followed in a future period by an 'exit strategy' whereby the fruits of the investment are harvested. The tactics and vehicles for capital flow are various – borrowing, issuing stock, going public, going private, taking on added investors, consolidating, merging, being acquired, being taken over – but the net effect is to direct and redirect the flow of investment capital into succeeding enterprises and away from enterprises that are less successful. These 'acute business moments', especially those accompanied by change in ownership, inevitably have major consequences for sustainability, representing inflection points between growth and decline. At a minimum they offer 'a great opportunity to reconsider assumptions about how a company gains and sustains its competitive advantage' (Gogel, 2006: A13).

Again, a number of (non-profit) charter schools provide an illustration of how infusions of investment capital (both profit-seeking and philanthropic) have fundamentally shaped the schools' trajectories. There are many more (less publicly visible) examples of for-profit education businesses whose fortunes have turned on whether they were able to secure sufficient investment capital to sustain the business and to grow.

Capturing sufficient market share through continual improvements in innovation and execution

Many providers of educational goods and services struggle to secure sufficient business to be able to sustain it, let alone to grow it. Market environments place a premium on educational providers addressing customers' problems through improvements (read innovations) in the goods and services it provides. Where wide choices among providers, and relative freedom to move among them, exists, firms are under pressure to provide what Christensen refers to as 'sustaining' innovations, which (at a minimum) respond to the interests of their current customers (1997; Christensen and Raynor, 2003).

In the context of market environments innovations that are brought rapidly to market ('first mover advantage'), that foster growth in volume and margins, and that increase market share are so fundamental to a firm's survival (sustainability) that they are 'routine' among firms that survive. Often the pressures to innovate and to grow rise to a level that is not sustainable over time.

The larger impact of education policy on organizational life

Education policy impacts educators in market environments as forcefully as it does in traditional public school environments, but in qualitatively different ways The pervasive presence and impact of public policy provides a basic platform around which to frame most problems and issues in traditional schooling, ranging currently from student testing pressures, to standards-based curricula, to adequate yearly progress, to sufficiently qualified teachers, to dropout rates. The ramifications between these kinds of issues and current policies and practices, which are almost definitional among traditional public schools, are amplified in market environments.

Policy and governance issues take on added, and qualitatively different, meanings in an increasingly market-oriented environment – from the perspectives of both traditional public schools and newer education service providers. Traditional schools, especially those labelled as chronically low-performing, are increasingly encouraged (at times required) to consider market-supplied goods and services to address those issues. For example, chronically low-performing schools in California are required to 'partner' with external 'support providers', and many US urban school districts are required to outsource tutoring services for kids in their lowest-performing schools, and on occasion provide tuition for them to attend other schools. Located somewhere between 'support' and 'external oversight', these schooling policies can contribute to, as well as mitigate, low school and student performance, depending on circumstances. Either way, they push, rather than pull, traditional schools into uncertain, fluid market environments.

From the 'partner' or 'support provider' perspective, such policies can either greatly enhance demands for services from firms in their niche if traditional schools and districts are required to purchase services. On the other hand, the same policies can effectively drain away demand for their services if those policies require purchases of *other* kinds of goods and services. In this case it depends on the match up between policy demands and what the firms produce.

Consider as an illustration the recent impact of US state and federal accountability legislation on the US for-profit education industry. Firms delivering K-12 educational (schooling) services, testing, and tutoring experienced unusually high year over year growth rates between 2000 and 2003, whereas firms providing pre-K educational services, computing hardware, and school supplies experienced unusually low growth among education firms during the same period (Hentschke, 2005). The former group of goods and services was required and funded in the accountability legislation, while the latter group was neither funded nor required. Public education policies impact the circumstances of private education firms at least as much as they do public ones.

Sustainability as typical practice and worthy goal in education

While sustainability may well provide a useful normative framework for improving education, its utility as a descriptive framework will likely be lessened as education gravitates more into a market environment. Large-scale studies of the continuity of (mostly very large, publicly traded, multinational) for-profit businesses provide significant descriptive understandings of the factors which enable a relatively small number of them to outlast their competitors, making the point that most do not. Although schooling is moving towards that market environment, it will likely be a very long time before the environment of the compulsory schooling industry could conceivably reflect the environment of those corporations.

Nonetheless, educators and their organizations will more frequently face some of the commonplace realities associated with organizational life in a market environment. Perhaps the more intriguing question at this point is, however, whether sustainability as a prized attribute and goal for education leaders and the institutions within which they labour will ever be replaced with normative goals such as flexibility, responsiveness, adaptability, short time to market, innovative and productive. As compulsory education gravitates further into a market environment, will the *desired* and *valued* attributes of educational organizations and their leaders evolve as well?

References

Bell, S. and Morse, S. (2000) *Sustainability Indicators: Measuring the Immeasurable*. London: James and James/Earthscan.

Boyatzis, R.E., Smith, M.L. and Blaize, N. (2006) 'Developing sustainable leaders through coaching and compassion', *The Academy of Management Learning and Education*, 5(1): 8–24.

Chalk, N. and Hemming, R. (2000) 'Assessing fiscal sustainability in theory and practice', *IMF Working Paper No. 00/81*. Available at http://ssm.com/abstract=879604.

Christensen, C. (1997) *The Innovator's Dilemma: When New Technologies Cause Great Firms to Fail*. Boston, MA: Harvard Business School Press.

Christensen, C. and Raynor, M. (2003) *The Innovator's Solution: Creating and Sustaining Successful Growth*. Boston, MA: Harvard Business School Press.

Collins, J. (2001) *Good to Great: Why Some Companies Make the Leap ... and Others Don't*. New York: HarperCollins.

Collins, J. and Porras, J. (1999) *Built to Last: Successful Habits of Visionary Companies*. New York: HarperCollins.

Davies, B. and Hentschke, G. (2002) 'Changing resource and organizational pattern: the challenge of resource educational organizations in the 21st century', *Journal of Educational Change*, 3(2): 135–59.

Eunson, L. (2003) 'Sustainable leadership requires listening skills, say executive of Royal Dutch/Shell'. Available at www.gsb.stanford.edu/news/headlines/vftt_vanderveer.shtml (accessed 22 January 2007).

Foster, R. and Kaplan, S. (2001) *Creative Destruction: From Built-to-Last to Built-to Perform*. London: Prentice Hall.

Fullan, M. (2005) 'Turnaround leadership', *The Educational Forum*, 69(Winter): 174–81.

Gogel, D.J. (2006) 'What's so great about private equity', *The Wall Street Journal*, 248(125): A13.

Hall, J. and Vredenburg, H. (2003) 'The challenges of innovating for sustainable development', *MIT Sloan Management Review* 45(1): 61–8.

Hargreaves, A. (2007) 'Welcome to Sustainable Leadership' (PowerPoint), Andy Hargreaves personal website. Accessed 22 January 2007. Available at www2bc.edu/~hargrean/docs/A.H.SustainLead.ppt.

Hargreaves, A. and Fink, D. (2000) 'The three dimensions of reform', *Educational Leadership*, 57(7): 30–4.

Hargreaves, A. and Fink, D. (2003a) 'The seven principles of sustainable leadership'. Available at www2.bc.edu/~hargrean/docs/seven_principles.pdf (accessed 27 November 2006).

Hargreaves, A. and Fink, D. (2003b) 'Sustaining leadership', *Phi Delta Kappan*, 84(9): 693–700.

Hargreaves, A. and Fink, D. (2006) *Sustainable Leadership*. San Francisco, CA: Jossey-Bass.

Hart, S. and Milstein, M. (2003) 'Creating sustainable value', *Academy of Management Executive*, 17(2): 56–69.

Hentschke, G. (2005) 'Characteristics of growth in the education industry: illustrations from US education businesses', paper presented at the seminar on New Areas of Educational Governance: The Impact of International Organizations and Markets on Education Policymaking, University of Bremen, Bremen, Germany, 23–24 September.

Hentschke, G. and Wohlstetter, P. (2007) 'K-12 education in a broader privatization context', in K. Buckley and L. Fusarelli (eds) *The Politics of Privatization in Education: The 2007 Yearbook of the Politics of Education Association*. Published as a special issue of *Educational Policy*, 21(1).

Litten, L. (2005) 'Measuring and reporting institutional sustainability', Annual Forum of the Association of Institutional Research, San Diego, 1 June.

Panico, R.C. (2004) 'Beyond results ... sustaining performance', *Global Cosmetic Industry*, 172(6): 66–7.

Pearce, D.W. and Atkinson, G.D. (1993) 'Capital theory and the measurement of sustainable development: an indicator of "weak" sustainability', *Ecological Economics*, 8(1993): 103–8.

Rainey, D.L. (2006) *Sustainable Business Development: Inventing the Future Through Strategy, Innovation, and Leadership*. Cambridge: Cambridge University Press.

Robinson, N. (1993) *Agenda 21: Earth's Action Plan*. New York: Oceana Publications.

Wheeler, K.A. and Byrne, J.M. (2003) 'K-12 sustainability education: its status and where higher education should intervene', *Planning for Higher Education*, 31(3): 23–8.

Chapter 9

Sustaining leaders for system change

David Hopkins

Introduction

By background and temperament I am a school improvement activist. Over the past 30 years or so I have self-consciously located myself at the intersection of practice, research and policy. It is here that I felt I could best contribute to the process of educational reform. Reflecting back over this time, one of the initiatives I am most proud of is the work I did with colleagues on the Improving the Quality of Education for All school improvement project where we collaborated with hundreds of schools in England and elsewhere in developing a model of school improvement that enhanced student outcomes through focusing on the teaching-learning process whilst strengthening the school's capacity for managing change. More recently, however, I found myself as a national policy-maker concerned not just with regional networks of schools but with a part responsibility for transforming a whole system. These two sets of experiences have convinced me that not only should every school be a great school, but that this is now a reasonable, realizable and socially just goal for any mature educational system. My time in government also helped me understand that realizing this aspiration is not in the gift of government but rather is achieved through a re-balancing of power in the system where, by and large, it is schools that lead the process of change. The inevitable conclusion from this line of thinking is that it is 'system leadership' that is the critical variable in transforming the landscape of education. The purpose of this chapter is to unpack the argument supporting this contention. In doing this I will discuss the:

- reasons why large-scale reform fails and the need for a systemic perspective;
- crucial policy conundrum in achieving sustained improvement;
- four key drivers that can build system capacity to deliver on standards;
- approach to 'segmentation' necessary to ensure that every school succeeds;
- the need to develop a form of system leadership necessary to sustain such an approach.

Why large-scale reform fails and the need for a systemic perspective

It is salutary at times to reflect on how much has changed in the study and practice of educational change even within one's own limited time in the field. Just over 15 years ago Milbrey McLaughlin (1990: 12) in her reanalysis of the extensive Rand Change Agent study originally conducted in the USA during the 1970s concluded that:

> *A general finding of the Change Agent study that has become almost a truism is that it is exceedingly difficult for policy to change practice, especially across levels of government. Contrary to the one-to-one relationship assumed to exist between policy and practice, the Change Agent study demonstrated that the nature, amount, and pace of change at the local level was a product of local factors that were largely beyond the control of higher-level policy makers.*

Her phrase 'policy cannot mandate what matters' captured the zeitgeist of the time and became the conventional wisdom for over a decade.

Perversely, the 1990s saw a resurgence in large-scale reform efforts in most western countries but, in line with McLaughlin's prediction, few had much impact on levels of student achievement. The failure of the reforms of the 1990s to accelerate student achievement in line with policy objectives has been widely documented (Hopkins, 2001).

For example, Ken Leithwood and his colleagues (1999) reviewed the impact of a number of 'performance-based' approaches to large-scale reform: an approach to centralized educational change had become widespread during the 1990s. The Leithwood review examined in a comparative manner, five cases of performance-based reform that are well known and have been widely documented – Kentucky, California, New Zealand, Victoria (Australia) and Chicago. On the basis of this review two striking conclusions were reached: (Leithwood, 1999: 40, 60–3)

- The first was that on the available evidence there was no increase in student achievement in any case except Chicago, and even that was 'slow in coming'.
- The second was the 'the disappointing contribution that performance-base reforms have made to improving the core technology of schooling'.

With the benefit of hindsight it is clear as to why these educational reforms did not in general have the desired impact and why McLaughlin's dictum was supported.

First, many reforms focused on the wrong variables. There is now an increasingly strong research base to suggest any strategy to promote student learning needs to give attention to engaging students and parents as active participants, and expanding the teaching and learning repertoires of teachers and students respectively.

Secondly, although the focus on teaching and learning is necessary, it is also an insufficient condition for school improvement. Richard Elmore (1995: 366) explains it in this way:

> *Principles of [best] practice [related to teaching and learning] ... have difficulty taking root in schools for essentially two reasons: (a) they require content knowledge and pedagogical skill that few teachers presently have, and (b) they challenge certain basic patterns in the organisation of schooling. Neither problem can be solved independently of the other, nor is teaching practice likely to change in the absence of solutions that operate simultaneously on both fronts.*

What is required is an approach to educational change that at the same time focuses on the organizational conditions of the school as well as the way teaching and learning is organized. The more the organization of the school remains the same the less likely will there be changes in classroom practice that directly and positively impact on student learning.

Third, most reforms did not adopt a systemic perspective. Focusing on individual classrooms or schools may improve performance for those limited number of students but if the concern is with social justice and whole populations then a whole-system perspective is required. It is helpful to think about this issue along two dimensions – reform efforts need to be both 'system wide' and 'system deep'. 'System wide' applies to the coherence and contingency across a policy spectrum, whereas 'system deep' refers to clarity and coherence at both the top and the bottom of the system – at the level of policy and in the minds of the majority of teachers – and all the levels in between.

For a country to succeed it needs both a competitive economy and an inclusive society. That requires an education system with high standards, which transmits and develops knowledge and culture from one generation to the next, promotes respect for and engagement with learning, broadens horizons and develops high expectations. It needs to ensure that all young people progressively develop the knowledge, understanding, skills, attitudes and values in the curriculum, and become effective, enthusiastic and independent learners, committed to lifelong learning and able to handle the demands of adult life. This is a pretty good description of an educational system committed to ensuring that every school is at least a good school and that most are on the journey to becoming great.

This aspiration, although easy to articulate, has implications that challenge the resolve of many national and local governments:

- First, this is an avidly social justice agenda redolent with moral purpose and needs to be communicated as such. Sadly many of our leaders feel uncomfortable talking about values that have concrete outcomes, yet without this one cannot build a consensus for social change.
- Second, it places the focus of reform directly on enhancing teaching quality and classroom practice rather than structural change. Government policy implementation has mostly commonly used the school as the unit of intervention, yet international research evidence shows that (a) the classroom is key in raising achievement and (b) the range of variation within any school dwarfs the difference between schools in the UK by a factor of three or four times.
- Third, it requires a commitment to sustained, systemic change because a focus on individual school improvement always distorts social equity. The evidence from the Charter School movement in the USA and Grant Maintained Schools in England suggests that although such initiatives may raise standards for those involved they depress standards in surrounding schools. This is not at all to argue against school autonomy, but to caution that it should be done within inclusive and collaborative settings.

With these key implications in mind, let me try and summarise the argument so far:

- The key paradox is that although large-scale reform is required to ensure a socially just and competitive society the performance-based

approach taken in the 1990s was largely ineffective in terms of raising standards and adjusting the organizational context of teaching and learning in schools.
- What is required if the goal of every school a great school is to be achieved is a systemic approach that integrates the classroom, school and system levels in the pursuit of enhancing student achievement.

What has only been implied in the preceding pages is that system change requires an entirely new approach to educational reform that has three key features:

- one that adopts a pedagogy designed to enable virtually every young person to reach their potential;
- the redesign of the landscape of schooling with independence and innovation, and networking and lateral responsibility its central characteristics;
- an approach to leadership that recognizes the necessity to shoulder wider roles that work for the success of other schools as well as one's own and a realization that in order to change the system one has to engage with it in a meaningful way.

This territory is not yet clearly charted so this chapter can at best only present an initial survey. But it is a terrain that is beginning to be explored by other educational change adventurers. The most prominent is the prolific Michael Fullan who in three recent monographs (2003; 2005; 2006) has given us increasingly precise insights as to what the new landscape will look like. Readers of his work will therefore find many of the concepts discussed in this chapter familiar. But there are two significant differences. The first is that Fullan refers to his 'tri-level solution' which is a similar idea to our three levels of classroom, school and system. Fullan's three levels, however, do not include a specific focus on the classroom but do distinguish between local and national system levels. Fullan also refers more generally to 'system thinkers' as a wider more encompassing role, whereas in this chapter we prefer to explore the role of the system leader. But these are differences of emphasis rather than substance, and there is clear agreement on the need for agency and leadership for system reform. In the following section I attempt to locate the role of the system leader within the broader context of system change as a whole.

Prescription or professionalism – the crucial policy conundrum

In describing the shift in policy and agency necessary for ensuring that every school is a great school I will locate the analysis within the context of educational reform in England. This is because it is the system I am most familiar with. I would also claim, however, that the direction of travel as well as the uncertainties seen in England are reflected in some way in most other educational systems.

The back story is well known. Most agreed that educational standards in England were too low and too varied in the 1970s and 1980s and that some form of direct state intervention was necessary. The resultant 'national prescription' proved very successful, particularly in raising standards in primary schools – progress confirmed by international comparisons. But progress plateaued in the second term of the Labour government, and whilst a bit more improvement might be squeezed out of prescription nationally, and perhaps a lot more in underperforming schools, one has to question whether it still offers the recipe for sustained large-scale reform in the medium term. There is a growing recognition that schools need to lead the next phase of reform.

Although this realization emerged from working on the educational reform agenda in England, it appears to have a wider relevance and seems to be a feature of most large-scale change efforts. Crucially, this implies a transition from an era of prescription to an era of professionalism. This is not to argue that 'top-down' is bad or 'bottom-up' is good, we now know to our cost that in isolation neither works. The key idea here is the change in the balance between national prescription and schools leading reform over time. However, achieving this shift is not straightforward. As Michael Fullan (2003) has said, it takes capacity to build capacity, and if there is insufficient capacity to begin with it is folly to announce that a move to 'professionalism' provides the basis of a new approach. The key question is 'how do we get there?', because we cannot simply move from one era to the other without self-consciously building professional capacity throughout the system. It is this progression that is illustrated in Figure 9.1.

This is a classic example of what Ron Heifetz (1994) has termed an adaptive challenge. An adaptive challenge is a problem situation for which solutions lie outside current ways of operating. This is in stark contrast to a technical problem for which the know-how already exists.

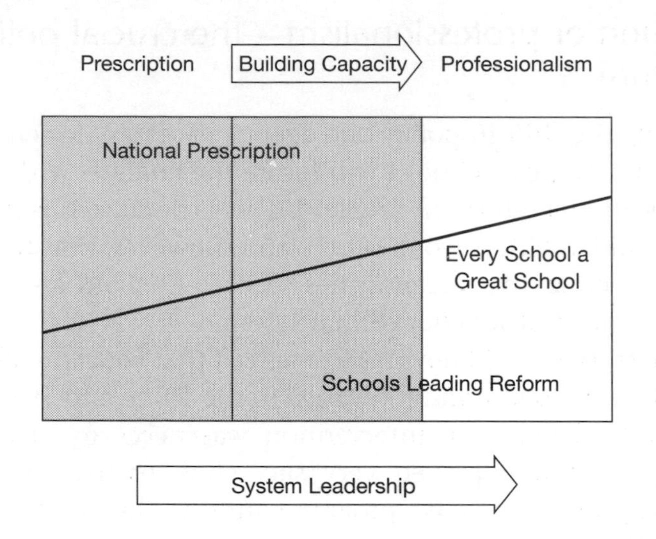

Figure 9.1 *Towards sustainable systemic reform*

This distinction has resonance for educational reform. Put simply, resolving a technical problem is a management issue; however, tackling adaptive challenges requires leadership. Often we try to solve technical problems with adaptive processes or, more commonly, force technical solutions onto adaptive problems. Figure 9.2 captures this distinction and illustrates how this issue underpins the policy conundrum of making the transition from prescription to professionalism and emphasizes the importance of capacity-building.

Almost by definition, adaptive challenges demand learning, because progress here requires new ways of thinking and operating. In these instances it is 'people who are the problem' because an effective response to an adaptive challenge is almost always beyond the current competence of those involved. Inevitably this is threatening and often the prospect of adaptive work generates heat and resistance.

Mobilizing people to meet adaptive challenges, as we shall see later, is at the heart of leadership practice. In the short term, leadership helps people meet an immediate challenge. In the medium to long term, leadership generates capacity to enable people to meet an ongoing stream of adaptive challenges. Ultimately, adaptive work requires us to reflect on the moral purpose by which we seek to thrive and demands diagnostic enquiry into the realities we face that threaten the realization of those purposes.

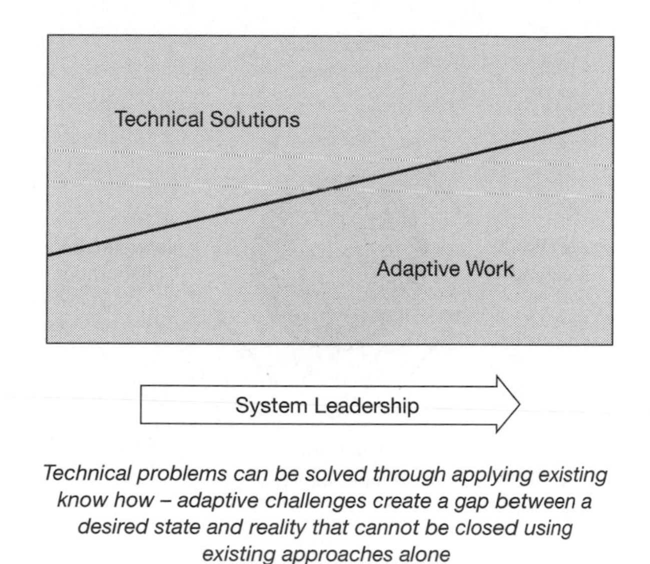

Figure 9.2 *System leadership as adaptive work*

But we are getting a little ahead of ourselves here. The purpose of referring to the 'adaptive challenge' has been to stress the point that in making the transition from 'prescription' to 'professionalism' strategies are required that not only continue to raise standards but also build capacity within the system. Hence the four drivers for system reform which I believe have a more general applicability as an approach to system-wide reform.

Four drivers for system reform

Building capacity demands that we replace numerous national initiatives with a national consensus on a limited number of educational trends. There seem to me to be four key drivers that, if pursued relentlessly and deeply, have the potential to deliver every school a great school. These are personalized learning, professionalized teaching, networks and collaboration, and intelligent accountability. As seen in the 'diamond of reform' Figure 9.3 they coalesce and mould to context through the exercise of responsible system leadership.

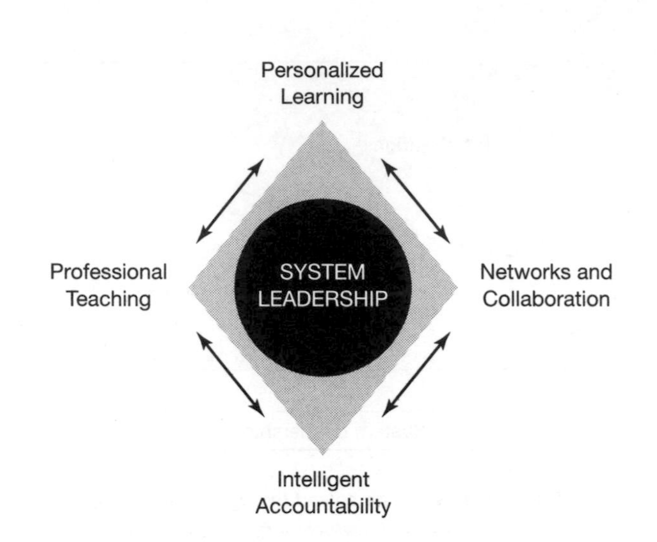

Figure 9.3 *The four drivers for system reform*

Together these key trends provide a core strategy for improvement. It would of course be tempting to provide instead more immediately digestible answers or to implement able initiatives. For instance, I am sometimes asked, 'Would more teaching assistants or greater use of ICT ensure learning is tailored to student need?' Although these are legitimate questions, they are actually second-order questions. We must first pursue the core trends, because with these in place teachers will be best able to decide how to deploy more teaching assistants or use ICT – funded overall by the centre, but determined by informed professionals.

On this I believe it is important to remember Jim Collins's argument in his book *Good to Great*: 'None of the good to great companies began their transformations with pioneering technology, yet they all became pioneers in the applications of technology once they grasped how it fit [with their core improvement strategies] and after they hit breakthrough' (2001: 162) and 'The comparison companies frequently tried to create a breakthrough with large, misguided acquisitions. The good to great companies, in contrast, principally use large acquisitions after breakthrough, to accelerate momentum in an already fast spinning wheel' (2001: 168). This is the approach being advocated here, it is the relentless focus on these four trends that lays the foundation for every school being great.

Driver 1 – personalized learning

The current focus on personalization is about putting citizens at the heart of public services and enabling them to have a say in the design and improvement of the organizations that serve them. In education this can be understood as personalized learning, the drive to tailor education to individual need, interest and aptitude so as to fulfil every young person's potential.

Personalized learning is an idea that is capturing the imagination of teachers, children and young people around the world. It is an idea that has its roots in the best practices of the teaching profession, and it has the potential to make every young person's learning experience stretching, creative, fun and successful.

In particular, personalized learning is:

- an educational approach that focuses on every individual achieving their potential and enhancing their learning skills;
- about designing teaching, curriculum and the school organization to address the needs of the student both individually and collectively;
- a system that is more accessible, open to customization and involves the learner in their own learning;
- a learning offer to all children that extends beyond the school context into the local community and beyond.

It is important to realize that personalized learning is not a new idea. Many schools and teachers have tailored curriculum and teaching methods to meet the needs of children and young people with great success for many years. What is new is the drive to make the best practices universal.

Driver 2 – professionalized teaching

As we strive for a high-equity, high-excellence education system, it is the continuing professional development (CPD) of teachers that is at the heart of the response. Put simply, unless teachers see their continuing development as an essential part of their professionalism the system will be unable to make the next big step forward in standards of learning and achievement. This is not just an 'academic' issue about making teaching more comparable to other great modern professions –

it is a highly practical, standards-based, issue about how we deliver personalized learning and fulfil the potential of every student. To personalize learning, teachers must increasingly focus on how they use data and evidence to apply a rich repertoire of teaching strategies to meet their students' needs. This in turn implies radically different forms of professional development with a strong focus on coaching and establishing schools as professional learning communities.

The key elements are:

- enhancing the teacher's repertoire of learning and teaching strategies to actively engage and stretch students;
- opportunities for teachers to engage newly learnt skills in the workplace through: immediate and sustained practice; collaboration and peer coaching; studying development and implementation;
- performance management systems that focus explicitly on learning and teaching in the classroom.

Achieving these goals would go along way to ensuring consistency of practice in all classrooms – creating a truly whole-school effect.

Driver 3 – networks and collaboration

Over the course of the past 10 to 15 years there has been a movement particularly in Organization for Economic Co-operation and Development (OECD) countries for schools to increasingly engage in collaborative activity. These have taken a range of forms. From 'clusters' to 'partnerships', 'collaboratives' to 'networks', schools across the country have been, and currently are, part of them. Frequently, schools are finding themselves belonging to three or more networks, with some schools in England listing as many as 10 in their portfolio.

The prevalence of networking practice supports the contention that there is no contradiction between strong, independent schools and strong networks, rather the reverse. Effective networks require strong leadership by participating heads, and clear objectives that add significant value to individual schools' own efforts. Without this networks wither and die, since the transaction costs outweigh the benefits they deliver. Nor is there a contradiction between collaboration and competition – many sectors of the economy both nationally and internationally are demonstrating that the combination of competition and collaboration delivers the most rapid improvements.

So it is clear that networks support improvement and innovation by enabling schools to collaborate on building curriculum diversity, extended services and professional support and to develop a vision of education that is shared and owned well beyond individual school gates.

Driver 4 – intelligent accountability

Over the past 10 years most educational systems have begun to introduce some form of educational accountability as a driver to raise standards. In this respect England has been ahead of the pack where a fairly sophisticated national framework for accountability has evolved since the early 1990s. That framework, which links together standardized achievement tests and examinations, target setting, publication of performance tables and independent inspection, has no doubt made a major contribution to the raising of standards during the period. There have, however, been criticisms of the accountability framework. Oft-quoted examples are of teachers 'teaching to the test' and schools increasing their 'competitiveness' through adjusting their admissions policy to boost their position in the published performance tables. Many would also argue that an overemphasis on external accountability increases the degree of dependence and lack of innovation within the system.

But the solution is not to abandon the accountability framework – that would be to throw the baby out with the bathwater – but to make it more 'intelligent'. In the move from 'prescription' to 'professionalism' any accountability framework needs to be able not only to fulfil its original purpose but also to build capacity and confidence for professional accountability. This is not just in terms of its own remit but also in supporting the capacity-building function of the other three drivers.

To better support progress towards 'every school a great school' a more intelligent accountability framework would achieve a more even balance between external and internal assessment with over time an increasing emphasis towards the latter. Critical to this shift is the operational clarity between formative and summative assessment to enable each to support more effectively their core purpose. In terms of formative assessment in particular, there is a need to develop increasingly precise methods for assessment for learning, pupil progress data, contextual value added and school profiles. These can become tools not just for personalizing learning and enhanced teacher professionalism, but also, for assisting school self-evaluation and holding schools open to public scrutiny.

Segmentation as the key to every school a great school

Each of these four drivers is integral to a social democratic settlement for education. Their system-wide impact, however, is both complicated and facilitated by the high degree of differentiation within most secondary school systems. Yet system transformation depends on excellent practice being developed, shared, demonstrated and adopted across and between schools.

So, in the move towards ensuring that every school is a great school, the four drivers provide a necessary but not sufficient condition. The missing ingredient is the concept of segmentation. The key idea being that all schools are at different stages in their improvement cycle, on a continuum from 'failing' to 'leading'. This opens up a highly differentiated approach to school improvement given that different schools will both need, and be able to provide, different forms of support and intervention at different times. An outline of this approach is set out in Table 9.1.

In the left-hand column is a basic taxonomy of schools that reflects the various stages of the performance cycle. This typology is based on an analysis of secondary schools in England. The number of categories and the terminology will vary from setting to setting, the crucial point being that not all schools are the same and each requires different forms of support. It is this that is the focus of the second column, where a range of strategies for supporting schools at different phases of their development are briefly described. Again these descriptions are grounded in the English context, but they do have a more universal applicability. There are two key points here:

- One size does not fit all.
- These different forms of intervention and support are increasingly being provided by schools themselves, rather than being imposed and delivered by some external agency.

To be successful however the segmentation approach requires a fair degree of boldness in setting system level expectations and conditions. There are four implications in particular that have to be grappled with:

- All failing and underperforming (and potentially low-achieving) schools should have a leading school that works with them in either a formal grouping federation (where the leading school principal or

Table 9.1 *A highly differentiated approach to school improvement*

Type of school	Key strategies – responsive to context and need
Leading schools	▪ Become leading practitioners ▪ Formal federation with lower-performing schools
Succeeding, self-improving schools	▪ Regular local networking for school leaders ▪ Between school curriculum development
Succeeding schools with internal variations	▪ Consistency interventions: such as Assessment for Learning ▪ Subject specialist support to particular departments
Underperforming schools	▪ Linked school support for underperforming departments ▪ Underperforming pupil programmes: catch-up
Low-attaining schools	▪ Formal support in federation structure ▪ Consultancy in core subjects and best practice
Failing schools	▪ Intensive support programme ▪ New provider such as an academy

head assumes overall control and accountability) or in more informal partnership. Evidence from existing federations in England suggests that a national system of federations would be capable of delivering a sustainable step-change in improvement in relatively short periods of time. For example a number of 'federated schools' have improved their five A*–Cs at GCSE from under 20 per cent to over 50 per cent in two years.

- Schools should take greater responsibility for neighbouring schools so that the move towards networking encourages groups of schools to form collaborative arrangements outside of local control. This would be on the condition that these schools provided extended services for all students within a geographic area, but equally on the acceptance that there would be incentives for doing so. Encouraging local schools to work together will build capacity for continuous improvement at local level.
- The incentives for greater system responsibility should include significantly enhanced funding for students most at risk. Beyond incentivizing local collaboratives, the potential effects for large-scale long-term reform include:

  - a more even distribution of 'at risk' students and associated increases in standards, due to more schools seeking to admit a larger proportion of 'at risk' students so as to increase their overall income.
  - a significant reduction in 'sink schools' even where 'at risk' students are concentrated, as there would be much greater potential to respond to the social-economic challenges (for example, by paying more to attract the best teachers; or by developing excellent parental involvement and outreach services).
- A rationalization of national and local agency functions and roles to allow the higher degree of national and regional co-ordination for this increasingly devolved system.

These proposals extend the previous discussion on networking but are consistent with the direction those recommendations were taking us. These current proposals also have a combination of school- and policy-level implications. This is consistent with the phase of adaptive change the overall system is currently in. If we are to move towards a system based on informed professional judgement, then capacity has to be simultaneously built at the school and system level as both schools and government learn new ways of working, establish new norms of engagement and build more flexible and problem-oriented work cultures.

But still there is a missing ingredient – the necessity for outstanding leadership as the system as a whole grapples with the challenge of adaptive change. As we shall see in the next section, it is system leadership that has the power to maximize the impact of both the four drivers and the energy of segmentation and make them work in different contexts.

System leadership as the catalyst for systemic change

I have argued that it is leadership that shapes the drivers to context, but this is obviously not a form of leadership that is commonplace. Traditional leadership and management approaches are well able to accommodate technical problems. The future, however, is about solving problems for which there is no immediate solution, and then to build the capacity for doing this into the medium and long term. This requires leadership of a different order.

The literature on leadership has mushroomed in recent years, as have leadership courses and qualifications. All seem to have a slightly different take on leadership and claims on truth, which I for one find a little confusing. In this section I will set out an approach to leadership, which

I am calling 'system leadership', that accommodates the arguments for sustainable educational transformation made in the preceding pages.

'System leaders' are those headteachers who are willing to shoulder system leadership roles: who care about and work for the success of other schools as well as their own. In England there appears to be an emerging cadre of these headteachers who stand in contrast to the competitive ethic of headship so prevalent in the nineties. It is these educators who by their own efforts and commitment are beginning to transform the nature of leadership and educational improvement in this country. Interestingly, there is also evidence of this role emerging in other leading educational systems such as Sweden and Finland (Hopkins, in press). These educational leaders seem to embody and share three striking characteristics:

1. System leaders measure their success in terms of improving student learning and increasing achievement, and strive to both raise the bar and narrow the gap(s).
2. System leaders are fundamentally committed to the improvement of teaching and learning. They engage deeply with the organization of teaching, learning, curriculum and assessment in order to personalize learning for all their students. It is this engagement and mastery of the teaching and learning process that gives the system leader the licence and currency with which to engage with other schools.
3. System leaders look both into classrooms and across the broader system, they realize in a deep way that the classroom, school and system levels all impact on each other. Crucially they understand that in order to change the larger system you have to engage with it in a meaningful way.

In terms of the argument here, this leads me to a simple proposition:

> If our goal is 'every school a great school' then policy and practice has to focus on system improvement. This means that a school head has to be almost as concerned about the success of other schools as he or she is about his or her own school. Sustained improvement of schools is not possible unless the whole system is moving forward.

Space precludes a full discussion of the system leadership concept. Indeed, we are still in the process of charting the movement as we work inductively from the behaviours of the outstanding leaders we are privileged to collaborate with (Hopkins and Higham, 2007). The following aspects of the role do, however, require some further comment:

- the moral purpose of system leadership;
- system leadership roles;
- the domains of system leadership.

The first thing to say is that system leadership, as Michael Fullan (2003) argued, is imbued with moral purpose. Without that there would not be the passion to proceed or the encouragement for others to follow. In England, for example, where the regularities of improvement in teaching and learning are still not well understood, where deprivation is still too good a predictor of educational success and where the goal is for every school to be a great school, then the leadership challenge is surely a systemic one. This perspective gives a broader appreciation of what is meant by the moral purpose of system leadership.

I would argue therefore that system leaders express their moral purpose through:

- understanding personalized learning, as the drive to tailor education to individual need, interest and aptitude so as to fulfil every young person's potential;
- measuring their success in terms of improving student learning and increasing achievement, and strive to both raise the bar and narrow the gap(s);
- developing their schools as personal and professional learning communities, with relationships built across and beyond each school to provide a range of learning experiences and professional development opportunities;
- striving for equity and inclusion through acting on context and culture. This is not just about eradicating poverty, as important as that is. It is also about giving communities a sense of worth and empowerment;
- realizing in a deep way that the classroom, school and system levels all impact on each other.

Although this degree of clarity is not necessarily obvious in the behaviour and practice of every headteacher, these aspirations are increasingly becoming part of the conventional wisdom of the best of our global educational leaders. It is also pleasing to see a variety of *system leader roles* emerging, within various systems that are consistent with such a moral purpose. At present, in England, these are:

- Partnering another school which is facing particular difficulties, that is, to run two schools. This role is now commonly referred to as being an Executive Head or, when more schools are involved in a federation, as the chief executive.
- Choosing to lead a school that is in extremely challenging circumstances, or becoming an academy principal.
- Acting as a 'civic leader' to broker and shape the networks of wider relationships across their local communities that can support children in developing their potential. In England this role currently relates to leading an education improvement partnership or a cluster of extended schools.
- Working as a 'change agent' within the system such as a consultant leader with a school leadership team to improve levels of attainment, or operating as one of the new School Improvement Partners.

No doubt these roles will expand and mature over time, as indeed these roles have evolved in response to the adaptive challenge of system change.

The third issue is what are the 'domains of system leadership', what does the task involve? One of the clearest definitions is the four core functions proposed by Ken Leithwood (2006) and his colleagues. These are:

- Setting direction: to enable every learner to reach their potential, and to translate this vision into whole school curriculum, consistency and high expectations.
- Managing teaching and learning: to ensure that there is both a high degree of consistency and innovation in teaching practices to enable personalized learning for all students.
- Developing people: to enable students to become active learners and to create schools as professional learning communities.
- Developing the organization: to create evidence-based schools and effective organization, and to be involved in networks collaborating to build curriculum diversity, professional support, extended services.

This outline stands up well when it is tested against existing approaches to school leadership that have had a demonstrable impact on student learning. Take, for instance, Richard Elmore's (2004: 66) contention that 'the purpose of leadership is the improvement of instructional practice and performance' and its four dimensions:

- Instructional improvement requires continuous learning.
- Learning requires modelling.
- The roles and activities of leadership flow from the expertise required for learning and improvement, not from the formal dictates of the institution.
- The exercise of authority requires reciprocity of accountability and capacity.

Finally, while it is true that 'system leadership' is a relatively new concept, it is one that is not only fit for purpose but also finds a resonance with the outstanding school leaders of the day. It is also not an academic or theoretical idea, but has developed out of the challenges that system reform is presenting us with and the thoughtful, pragmatic and morally purposeful responses being given by our leading principals and heads. Ultimately the test of system leadership is – is it having an impact where it matters? Can our school leaders answer the hard questions?

Michael Barber (2005) phrases them like this:

- Who are your key stakeholders in the local community? Do they understand your vision? Are they committed to it? How do you know?
- Have you established a core belief that every pupil (yes, every pupil) can achieve high standards? And then have you reorganized all the other variables (time, curriculum, teaching staff, and other resources) around the achievement of that goal? If not, why not?
- Is each pupil in your school working towards explicit, short- and medium-term targets in each subject?
- Does each teacher know how his/her impact in terms of results compares to every other teacher? Have you thought about whether governors or parents should have access to this data? And what do you do to make sure that teachers who perform below the top quartile are improving?
- How do you ensure that every young person has a good, trusting relationship with at least one significant adult in your school?
- What do you and your school do to contribute to the improvement of the system as a whole?

These are the types of questions that the best system leaders test themselves against and are now comfortable with. When all our school leaders can do so, then surely we are well on our way to every school being a great school.

Coda – realizing the vision of system leadership

There is no doubt that sustainable increases in student learning are possible with a boldness of vision and resoluteness of approach. Such transformation, however, is neither only nationally led nor only schools led, but necessarily both supporting each other within a system committed to raising the bar and to narrowing the gap. Crucially, a balance needs to be achieved between national prescription and schools leading reform, with the presumption towards the latter, except when schools find themselves in very challenging conditions.

In turn, through self-evaluation, schools will become increasingly aware of how to improve and how to contribute to improvement in other schools. For instance, in increasingly dynamic policy contexts, schools must use external standards to clarify, integrate and raise their own expectations. Equally schools, by themselves and in networks, must be enabled to lead improvements and innovations in teaching and learning with the support of highly specified, but not prescribed, best practices.

These are all glimpses of a new landscape for education which cannot flow simply from government legislation. Indeed, it is when schools help to lead reform of national educational systems that deep and sustainable progress occurs. This as I have argued in this chapter requires 'system leaders' within the profession – school leaders who are willing and able to shoulder wider roles and, in doing so, to work to improve the success and attainment of students in other schools as well as their own. At its heart, therefore, system leadership is about improving the deployment and development of our best leadership resources, in terms of both:

- greater productivity: with successful leaders using their own and their staff's knowledge and skills to improve other schools; and
- social justice: by using our most capable leaders to help deliver a national system in which every child has the opportunity to achieve their full potential.

In concluding it is important to remember that the challenge of 'system leadership' has great moral depth to it because it addresses directly the learning needs of our students, the professional growth of our teachers and enhances the role of the school as an agent of social change. The emphasis on transformation is key – sustaining high standards of learning and attainment for all of our students now needs to be seen within a systems context. It is this that will characterise the next phase of educational reform in England and elsewhere and the role of the system leader is crucial in this development. Unless we embrace such a leadership role then all the evidence suggests that society will continue to set educational goals that are, on current performance, beyond the capacity of the system to deliver.

References

Barber, M. (2005) 'A 21st Century self-evaluation framework', Annex 3 in 'Journeys of Discovery: the search for success by design', keynote speech, National Centre on Education and the Economy, Annual Conference, Florida, USA, 10 February.

Collins, J. (2001) *Good to Great*. London: Random House Business Books.

Elmore, R.F. (1995) 'Structural reform in educational practice', *Educational Researcher*, 24(9): 23–6

Elmore, R.F. (2004) *School Reform from the Inside Out*. Boston, MA: Harvard University Press

Fullan, M. (2003) *The Moral Imperative of School Leadership*. Thousand Oaks, CA: Corwin Press.

Fullan, M. (2005) *Leadership and Sustainability*. Thousand Oaks, CA: Corwin Press.

Fullan, M. (2006) *Beyond Turnaround Leadership*. New York: Jossey-Bass

Heifetz, R. (1994) *Leadership Without Easy Answers*. London: Belknap Press.

Hopkins, D. (2001) *School Improvement for Real*. London: RoutledgeFalmer.

Hopkins, D. (2007) *Every School a Great School*. Maidenhead: Open University Press/McGraw Hill.

Hopkins, D. and Higham, R. (2007) System Leadership: Mapping the Landscape. *School Leadership and Management*, 2(2) (in press).

Leithwood, K. (2006) 'Successful school leadership', report to the Department for Education and Skills, 30 March.

Leithwood, K., Jantzi, D. and Mascall, B. (1999) 'Large Scale Reform: What Works?', Unpublished manuscript, Ontario Institute for Studies in Education, University of Toronto.

McLaughlin, M.W. (1990) 'The Rand Change Agent Study revisited: macro perspectives, micro realities', *Educational Researcher*, 19(9): 12.

Chapter 10

Leadership succession

Geoff Southworth

Introduction

Leadership succession is one of the major challenges facing the profession. It is also a challenge which is likely to be with us for some time. In this chapter I shall examine the challenge and what can be done to create a systematic approach to succession planning. The ideas I set out are based on the work we have been doing, and continue to do at the National College for School Leadership (NCSL) in England. In NCSL's remit letter for 2006–07, the Secretary of State asked us to provide advice on the issue. To do this we consulted widely and examined the data we assembled to provide an evidence-based perspective on the issues. Drawing upon this work I shall begin by outlining the professional context for school leaders in England. Then I shall set out how I see the challenge, before looking at factors which might mitigate it. The following section then presents possible ways of responding to the challenge, arguing that a multifaceted approach is required which works at a number of levels of the school system.

The professional context of school leaders

During 2005 the NCSL conducted a major consultation exercise with school leaders. The Chief Executive, Steve Munby personally telephoned 500 headteachers and the college followed this up by hosting nine regional conferences for headteachers. One thousand headteachers attended these conferences. The Chief Executive set out his analysis of the challenges school leaders faced in the coming years. Using interactive technology, delegates discussed and provided feedback on the analysis. The four challenges set out in the analysis were overwhelmingly endorsed by the profession. The four challenges were:

- Transforming children's achievements and well-being.
- Developing leadership within and beyond the school.
- Identifying and growing tomorrow's leaders.
- Managing the accountabilities, complexities and relentlessness of leadership.

The first of these refers to the linking of the standards agenda to the requirements of the 2004 Children Act into a single, coherent approach. The Children Act, through its advocacy of extended schools and multidisciplinary working whereby education, social and health professionals work closely together to provide a unified service for children and parents, places new demands on schools to meet the needs of children's lives and their learning. For school leaders this means managing a new set of relationships and building new and flexible networks. This is not to say that school leaders alone manage these arrangements, but it is to say they and their senior staff will be participating in more extensive interactions than formerly, whilst continuing to improve the educational provision and outcomes for their pupils.

Developing leadership within and beyond the school is what Fullan (2003) calls system leadership. In recent years we have seen successful leaders playing a wider role than previously. We now have executive heads who have responsibility for more than one school. Federations of schools have also been created so that there is more shared leadership beyond the boundaries of the single institution. Consultant leaders have supported schools where the leadership has needed an injection of energy or a new focus, as well as supporting less experienced colleagues as they take on stubborn challenges or the most needy schools. It makes good sense for the most effective heads and leaders to play leading roles in improving the minority of schools that make only limited progress. New leadership roles such as mentors, coaches, consultant leaders, school improvement partners and executive heads are being developed to enable schools collectively to take more direct responsibility for their own and each other's improvement.

The third challenge was identifying tomorrow's school leaders. Research at NCSL has shown that there is a demographic 'time bomb' ticking away in education. Larger than average numbers of teachers and school leaders are over 50 years of age and the closer they are to retiring the more we need to think about replacing them. Without doubt, it is now time to prepare the next generation of school leaders.

Growing tomorrow's leaders is a task affected by the fourth challenge: accountability, complexity and relentlessness. Many heads experience the weight of responsibility as a heavy load and there are perceptions that the job is difficult. Moreover, in the next few years we will see a drive towards workforce remodelling with a more flexible and varied workforce. Schools will be more open to the community and have more members of the community working in them. Many schools will be rebuilt, or refurbished, as part of the government's Building Schools for the Future programme. This is a major investment bringing together the rebuilding, or refurbishment of secondary school buildings and significant educational reform with the aim of ensuring secondary pupils in every part of England learn in twenty-first-century facilities. Secondary schools will also need to form partnerships with further education colleges and other providers to deliver vocational provision and skills for 14–19-year-olds. Learning will become more personalized with an increasing focus on assessment for learning. Schools will become more data-rich and able to benchmark in a far more detailed way than ever before, and technology will continue to change teaching and learning. In other words, school leaders are inextricably involved in major changes. They need to lead and manage these changes and ensure their teams and workforces remain motivated and excited about them. Alongside everything else these changes combine to create a demanding agenda for school leaders.

This chapter is concerned with the third challenge, identifying and growing tomorrow's leaders. The need to ensure an orderly succession of school leaders is paramount. However, as this first section implies, the context in which succession planning is taking place influences perceptions of leadership and shapes what the next generation needs to be able to do. Succession planning is more than replacing one headteacher with another. It is about preparing individuals to be able to lead today and tomorrow in ways which are sensitive and responsive to their contexts.

The challenge of succession

It is important to start with the demographics since this is the root of the challenge. The NCSL has analysed the statistics carefully. Rather than reproduce them here I shall restrict myself to a few headline figures to give a flavour of the situation.

We know the number of headteachers who will retire in the future will increase. In 2004, 59 per cent of headteachers in the maintained sector were aged 50 or over, compared with 40 per cent in 1997. In 2004, 59 per cent of heads in nursery/primary schools were aged 50 or over (compared with 39 per cent in 1997) and 62 per cent of heads in secondary schools (compared with 48 per cent in 1997). In special schools and pupil referral units 60 per cent of heads were 50 or over in 2004 which compares with 37 per cent in 1997. Clearly, we have an ageing group of school leaders.

These headline numbers should be looked at in the light of other data. For one thing, the age profile of headteachers is similar to that in other work sectors in the UK. In other words, the situation is not unique to education. It reflects a national demographic trend. The so-called post-war 'baby boomer' generation is reaching the end of its working life. Nor is the issue peculiar to the UK. Across the developed world similar patterns exist. An examination of teacher flows shows that in France, Australia and the USA the picture is very similar, while in Scotland and Germany the problem is more acute and urgent as they have higher numbers of teachers and headteachers in the 55 to 59 age group.

What these figures also show is that the picture is much the same for deputy heads. This means that whilst we expect higher than average numbers of heads to leave, so too will larger numbers of deputies retire and, importantly, there are lower numbers of deputies following on behind them. This means there are not enough individuals in their thirties and early forties to fill the posts as senior colleagues leave.

Before turning to the recruitment challenge inherent in this situation, I want to say something about how we see this pattern unfolding over time. According to our analyses, at the time of writing, we believe the peak of the challenge will be reached between 2009 and 2011 – although it is difficult to be precise. There will be growing pressure to recruit to headships before then and for some time after too, but the greatest pressure on recruitment looks to be most likely to occur during 2009–2011.

The notion of 'pressure' also needs unpacking. At its peak we estimate there will be a need for an additional 15 to 20 per cent of senior leaders compared with the 2006 figures. However, and this is a critical point, we believe the demographic challenge can be resolved. There will be pressure and some recruitment 'hot spots', but through concerted action we are confident sufficient numbers can be found to prevent a crisis.

At 2005–06 rates we know that for every 100 middle leaders (for example, heads of departments, Key Stage leaders, subject leaders) 28 per cent, plan to take the National Professional Qualification for Headship (NPQH). Of this 28 per cent, 84 per cent graduate with the certificate. Of those who graduate 43 per cent are headteachers within five years. This translates into 10 headteachers for every 100 middle leaders. To resolve the succession problem we need to increase this conversion ratio and, if we double it, this alone will make a very significant difference.

So saying this is not to discount two other factors which also come into play and make the challenge both more urgent and complicated: recruitment and perception. Recruitment to headship has been tightening probably because the demographics are coming into play and not enough has been done, as yet, to counteract the issue. For example, we know from looking at shortages in local authorities and trying to gauge the severity and timing of shortages in each one we have studied that the problem is far from uniform across the country. We also know demand outstrips supply in three sets of schools: small rural schools; church schools; and schools in London. These are the schools with the highest rates of re-advertisements of headteacher vacancies. Therefore recruitment, while a challenge, is an uneven one with some areas and types of school finding it harder to recruit to than others. Nevertheless, no area will be unaffected by the challenge.

Furthermore, the logistics of recruitment mean that each and every school has to recruit and appoint its own headteacher when a vacancy occurs. Some turn to their local authorities for help and many are given very good advice and support. But this does not diminish the fact that every school has to find and appoint its own headteacher. Currently there are approximately 23,500 schools, and around 11 per cent in 2005 needed to recruit a headteacher (Howson, 2006). Leaving recruitment and the deployment of candidates to vacancies to 2,000 separate schools each year does not enable the situation to be 'managed'. What we might well have been seeing in the first few years of this century was not only a tightening of the supply side and recruitment to headship, but also the limitations of leaving it to every school to solve the problem on their own.

The second challenge which compounds the demographics of succession planning is that of role perceptions. From NCSL research into leaders' perceptions and those of other stakeholders we can see that many deputies and middle leaders do not aspire to headship because they see the job as too demanding. The reasons cited by respondents include dealing with the accountabilities, work–life balance and reduced contact with children and students. Yet these perceptions also look to be surprisingly monocular. From surveys conducted for the NCSL by the Market and Opinion Research Institute (MORI) we also know that serving headteachers are very positive about their role, with over 90 per cent saying they enjoy the work. It looks, therefore, as if those who are doing the job feel differently about the role from those who see it from the outside. Without doubt we need to work on these perceptions with the aim of improving how the job looks to those most likely to step into the role.

So far I have looked at the issue from three angles: the demographics; recruitment; and perceptions of headship. These three standpoints aim to deepen understanding of the challenges, but they also confine our understanding to an essentially school system perspective. As well as looking at other employment sectors and countries it is important to look and see if there are other forces at work which need to be borne in mind when trying to respond to the issues.

There are, without doubt, social factors which influence this issue and work conducted for NCSL by DEMOS drew attention to a number of trends. One of these was the move towards portfolio careers. As Figure 10.1 shows, this marks an important shift in attitudes towards

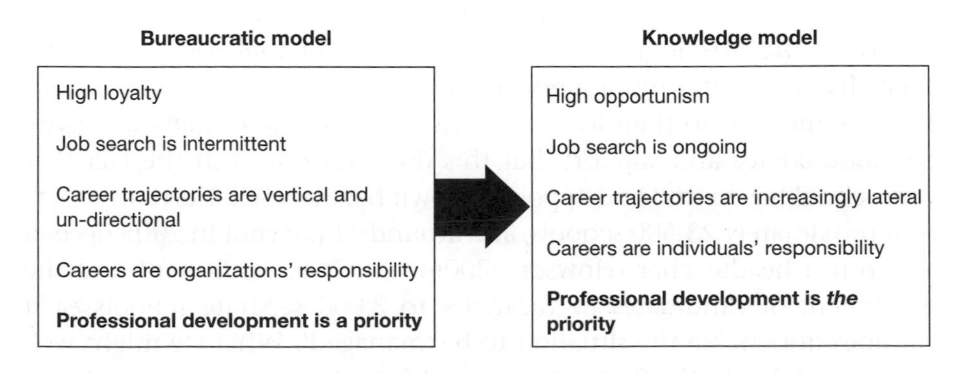

Figure 10.1 *Changes towards career planning (Bentley and Craig, 2006).*
Source: Reproduced with permission of DEMOS

career progression. It also implies that career planning needs to be more personalized than was the case in the past. Other forces at work include changes in family life, the fact that women are now half of the paid workforce and having children later in life, and that there is generally declining satisfaction with work, with most people saying they feel work has intensified in the recent past.

Although there is more to explore here, when these trends are put together they suggest that we should rethink how we grow tomorrow's leaders. The ways we have, until recently, developed individuals to become heads are no longer adequate to the challenges we face now and in the coming years. Expressed another way, how we manage leadership talent in schools needs to be not only improved, but re-engineered. Human capital is vital in education; indeed, in one sense it is what education itself is all about – maximizing human potential. Yet it may also be true that although schools are good in developing children and young people, they are not always so good in terms of managing their staff and their career aspirations.

In the past there were sufficient numbers of serving headteachers who prepared and promoted headship as the next career step for their deputies and assistant headteachers and who also identified middle leaders who should move to more senior positions. There have always been 'greenhouse' schools whose headteachers trained their deputies to go on and become successful headteachers themselves. What marked out the greenhouse schools was that their heads did this repeatedly so that three, four or five deputies who worked there moved on to headship. Moreover, the heads of these greenhouse schools claimed it as a prize that so many of their deputies stepped up to headship and did well.

There are still many heads who do this and such a stance needs to continue. However, because this approach is an act of individual commitment, as against a system-wide norm, it was not managed across large numbers of schools. Now we need to consider other ways of promoting headship and moving people on. If individual and informal ways of creating talent pools and pipelines to headship served schools well in the recent past, it is too weak a solution for what is needed in the next period. We need to rethink and regroup our efforts.

We also need to think of the issue as being more than a supply-side challenge. It is both a quantitative and qualitative issue. We certainly need to increase the supply of eligible candidates, but we also need to ensure we have enough of the right people, ready for what the job will demand of them in this century. That is why I set out in the first section the challenges school leaders face today and tomorrow. There is an opportunity here, but only if we face it full on and avoid walking into the future facing backwards. This means looking at how we prepare and develop leadership talent in each school, across groups of schools and have clarity about what are the key skills they need to serve their schools. What must not happen is that the quantity demands lowers the quality of school leadership. We must use the supply challenge as a chance to improve quality as well as produce sufficient numbers of prospective school leaders.

Mitigating factors

Whilst the challenges over headteacher supply are testing they are not insurmountable. For one thing, as noted in the previous section, we believe we can make up the numbers by a combination of increasing supply and reducing demand through retention. There are two other factors which also work to reduce the size of the problem and here I shall briefly set them out.

The first factor which will help is that pupil numbers are declining. Rolls in school are falling, with 155,000 fewer pupils in primary schools and 50,000 fewer students in secondary schools by 2008 compared with 2004. Such declines, particularly in the primary sector mean that there will be some school closures, or amalgamations. Over the last 10 years there has been a move to amalgamating separate infant and junior schools when one head leaves, or as pupil numbers have declined. This pattern has reduced the total number of schools. The forecasts about falling rolls suggest that the trend of amalgamating infant and junior schools will continue, thereby reducing the number of headteacher vacancies.

Another trend likely to continue and to impact on the need to recruit will be federations of schools. In some cases, where small rural schools are finding it difficult to recruit headteachers, the formation of federations led by a combination of site leaders and an executive head is likely to increase in popularity. Such arrangements are common in other countries. For example, the NCSL conducted research into such arrangements in the Netherlands (NCSL, 2005) and found that there are considerable advantages to federating for both schools and school leaders. Federations can save schools with falling rolls and provide headteachers with more time for reflection, preparation and organization, as well as reducing strain and leading to a better work–life balance.

Taken together falling rolls, amalgamations and federations will reduce some of the supply strain, but they will not solve it. To resolve succession planning and all that it involves we should not rely on chance, or good fortune, but move to a more managed and systemic strategy.

Opportunities

It is too simplistic to regard succession planning as a 'problem'. Whilst leadership succession is a major challenge, it is also an opportunity. There are at least three positive aspects to the challenge.

First, as intimated above, succession represents a major chance to bring in a new generation of school leaders. Some commentators are arguing for a process of leadership succession which skips a generation and brings in to headship a much younger cohort of headteachers. We have done this before. In the 1970s many young headteachers were appointed, most of them to primary sector headships. Some were appointed in their late twenties, others in their early thirties. It might be time to return to such a pattern. To do so would mean accelerating their leadership development and, importantly, ensuring they are supported once in post. Mentoring would be a key way of providing support, but there is likely to be a need to provide coaching as well.

Second, with the turnover in heads we expect there is a real chance to improve the gender balance in headship. Proportionally there are currently too many men and not enough women heads, although the situation has been improving in the last 15 years. As increasing numbers of headteachers take retirement there is a real opportunity to appoint many more women to headships. This means ensuring we have enough women willing to take on the role and providing advice to school governors to consider gender as a factor when making appointments.

Third, there is an opportunity to improve the mix of headteachers by appointing more candidates from minority ethnic groups. We urgently need to improve the ethnic mix and balance, and the changes envisaged provide the chance to do this. Again this has implications for preparation so that there is a flow of such candidates and for governors to heed this as an opportunity.

Towards a response

Before presenting some of the ideas which have been developed and continue to develop in the light of growing awareness and understanding around leadership succession, it is important to say something about the nature of any solutions to this problem. As I have suggested at a number of points, the issue is not simply one of finding a headteacher for every vacant post and leaving it to each school to recruit and appoint the best candidate. The problem is a system-wide one and warrants a systemic response.

Simply stated, we can already see that some schools working alone are struggling to appoint headteachers. Likewise, there are limitations to what government can decree. At heart this is a demographic problem, and legislation alone cannot resolve the riddle of insufficient 30- and 40-year-olds. In my view we need to develop alliances, at all levels to resolve the problem and to capitalize on the opportunities. I shall return to how we might do this in the section looking at developing leadership learning communities.

Increase the supply and flow of those ready to become headteachers

A number of tactics are needed to increase the supply of prospective headteachers. We can begin by focusing on middle leaders and assistant and deputy headteachers. Some of the work conducted by the NCSL into distributed leadership and leadership succession has paved the way for this emphasis (Hartle and Smith, 2003; NCSL, 2004). We need to prepare middle leaders to step into the vacant deputy headships that will be coming in the next five years. And we need to be ready to move many of these through to headship more quickly than we have in the past. At the same time, we need to make deputy headship a more valuable role in its own right and much more of a preparation for headship.

Some heads and governors have always regarded deputy headship as a training role. Indeed, some think deputy headship only has merit in so far as it prepares individuals to become heads. My own view (Southworth, 1998) is that we need to make deputy headship less about deputizing and more concerned with headship. As far as I can see, all deputies are headteachers; the only thing that prevents them from being the headteacher is that their colleague head keeps coming to the school each day! If we viewed deputy headship as headship now, and expect post-holders to play a fuller part than simply waiting in the wings and being an understudy when the head is absent, this would fulfil a number of goals all at once.

For one thing it would encourage deputies to play more of a leading role. For another it would foster shared leadership – heads and deputies, especially in some primary schools would need to work more closely and collaboratively. Both can be seen in many of the schools that have adopted this approach, along with the rise in the number of leadership teams. What all of this is about is redesigning deputy headship, in part to relieve some of the load heads feel and to ensure deputies take on aspects of headship all the time, rather than for some of the time and then only when the head is away. Such arrangements are already happening in many schools. It is relatively common in secondary schools, rather less so in primaries. If more schools adopted this approach it would help prepare deputies for headship in another school and enhance their contribution to their present school. In short, it deals with both the needs of today and tomorrow.

In addition, heads should actively create times for the deputy to lead the school. One factor which inhibits some deputies and assistant heads from applying for headships is that they lack the confidence to do the job. Often this is because they have not had the chance to do so. Building and sustaining confidence is a key factor in growing the next generation of leaders. Ensuring that those most likely to move to headship have the confidence to do the job is about creating the self-belief and the motivation to take on this demanding role. We therefore need to increase opportunities for deputies and assistant heads to be acting heads and, when they do, we must ensure it builds their confidence rather than undermines it. Therefore they must also be mentored during the period they take on these responsibilities. It is, as one head has advised the NCSL, all about helping deputies to 'try before they buy'.

When planned leadership opportunities are created it can be highly beneficial. It enables deputies to see headship from the inside, to experience the responsibilities and to learn first-hand that the work is doable and enjoyable. As one deputy wrote about his period of acting headship – 'I would recommend it as a way of finding out if headship is for you'. For this individual it confirmed that it was for him. Significantly, this was a planned opportunity with mentoring and support designed into the experience at the outset so that the deputy did not feel he was on his own.

In addition to increasing confidence we should also provide opportunities for deputies to lead in other contexts. In the past many deputies and assistant heads moved to a headship in a different school with experience of only a few schools and a limited number of role models to base their leadership on. Typically, deputy heads move into headship with just three or four role models to draw on. Furthermore, the lack of experience in many schools often means that individuals have not encountered some types of school, or a range of contexts to equip them to perform well in the school to which they are appointed.

If we take the learning from acting headships a step further, then we ought to consider ways of providing placements and internships so that members of leadership teams and deputies gain experience of a wider than otherwise range of schools and settings. These assignments would need to be time limited to reduce disruptions to their own schools. But given that arrangements can be devised to minimize such disturbance then the potential is considerable.

With careful planning and preparation it should be possible to create the conditions whereby the individual deputy, the host school and the deputy's own school all benefit. If the assignment in the host school was aimed at a specific need then that school would be advantaged by having targeted analysis and action. The individual would benefit from the planned deployment, as well as gaining all manner of insights into another school and the opportunity to work alongside another head and be a member of a different leadership team. The 'donor school' could benefit from other staff stepping up to take on the responsibilities of the deployed colleague. We need to see such movements around and between schools as creating opportunities which strengthen leadership at all points in the pipeline to headship.

The evidence we have of heads and senior leaders working beyond their own schools shows that this creates a 'win–win' form of development. What the individual learns whilst working away from their own school pays dividends when they return and apply their new knowledge and skills in their own school. At the same time, the individual gains knowledge of different contexts and develops insights into how other headteachers operate. Such learning is invaluable because these future school leaders learn *how* to do the job. Such craft knowledge is premium learning for future school leaders and we should try to ensure that everyone has as much access to it as possible. Therefore, it is important for prospective headteachers to be paired up with effective and successful heads who provide positive role models and who act as coaches whilst the two work together.

Some of this is already happening; therefore we need to move to a larger scale. Increasing the numbers involved is one thing, but we also need to accelerate the learning processes too. This is why the Fast Track scheme is so important. It challenges assumptions about how long it takes for someone to become a headteacher. Moreover, it relies on the early identification of potential leaders. This too is something we need to focus on. If we are to create talent pools, then we need to be able to spot suitable candidates at an early stage in their careers and then ensure they are given a range of development opportunities and support, as well as some stretching tasks to move them towards headship.

At the same time we need to learn the lessons from those schools I earlier called 'greenhouse' schools. What do the heads and governors of these schools do to develop so many future leaders? We need to look in some depth and detail at these schools and their headteachers, and we should also follow up those who were deputies there and have moved on to become heads, to see how they have fared and what the most valuable and pertinent experiences actually were.

Address how headship is perceived

From what was said earlier we also need to address how headship is being perceived by those who might step forward to take it on. Undoubtedly there is a need to accentuate the positive. At the time of writing, too much attention may be being paid by the media to the demands of the role and too little to the joys of the job.

Almost all the heads I know were attracted to the job because they saw it as the best position from which they could make a positive difference to children's and young people's lives and learning. Of course, some days events conspire to divert attention towards more mundane matters of organizational management. All leaders need to watch that they do not become victims of chronic executive busyness whereby they spend too much time on the 'merely urgent' and too little time on what is really important. Most of this can be avoided by careful time management, and by using personal assistants, administrative support and school business managers or bursars to share the load and look after the bureaucratic demands of the work. Workforce remodelling has an important part to play in making schools and school leadership fit for purpose.

Therefore, we need to look at how remodelling the workforce can provide better support for headteachers and leadership teams. At the same time we also need serving heads to be more vocal about the joys of the job and to talk it up rather more than at present. Without doubt headteachers need to be positive, passionate and optimistic people. No one wants to follow a cynic.

In addition, perhaps school governors should be considering ways of providing better support for their senior staff. At a time when work–life balance is being highlighted and when well-being is becoming a concern for all professionals, school governors and heads themselves might think about how they deal with them. Occupational psychologists, for example, highlight the need for senior managers to have what they call coping strategies. These are often simple and practical ways of managing one's workload and dealing with the occupational stresses that come with the job (see Cooper and Kelly, 1993; Southworth, 1995). It can be as straightforward as protecting time at the weekend for family and friends, going to the gym regularly, or being focused on a leisure pursuit or interest which provides a respite from the work. Such strategies are a necessary antidote to intensely active and busy work patterns.

Remodel leadership

Another possibility is to remodel the very nature and form of headship and senior leadership in schools. Two things can be said about this. First, a number of new models of headship have emerged in the last few years. There are growing numbers of co-headships, for example, although these are still proportionally very small. There are rather more executive school leaders who have responsibility for more than one school or a federation, as noted above. In other words, headship is no longer the same job in every school; it is becoming more diverse. Indeed, given the models which have emerged in the recent past, headship and school leadership is likely to continue being more varied than previously.

Increase support

There is a strong case for increasing the support for all school leaders. Some, such as new heads, already can work with a mentor. This may need to spread to many more leaders, and schools should be willing to commit funding for this to happen. Similarly, there is a good case for increasing coaching for leaders. For a headteacher to be able to work with a coach can be very beneficial. We know that the very best athletes and sportsmen and women rely on coaches. Increasingly, executive coaching is becoming the norm. They enable individuals to examine their performance, identify development needs and help them to unburden themselves of some of their most pressing concerns and doubts. Even the most successful can lose confidence when faced with an apparently unfathomable problem or dilemma. A coach can ensure that such a loss in confidence is a short-term occurrence and can prevent it from becoming deeply corrosive. In short, we need to ensure through a variety of means that being at the top of the profession does not create such a sense of loneliness that heads become professionally and socially isolated from their peers and colleagues and have no one to turn to for advice and counsel

Develop leadership learning communities

I now want to turn to some of the mechanisms by which the supply and flow of large numbers of high-quality candidates for senior leadership posts can be generated.

To start with, using local authorities and networks of schools, such as federations and trusts, as well as diocesan groups and other collaborative arrangements, sets of schools must be encouraged to take responsibility for creating leadership talent pools. If groups of schools did this they would quickly be able to train and develop, with external support from a range of providers, including the NCSL, a group of individuals who were looking to move into headship. These could become a resource to all the schools and they could be deployed to support and develop specific needs in many of the participating schools. At the same time, these tasks and assignments would develop their leadership skills and provide them with greater awareness of schools' needs and contexts.

One of the things which mark out successful leaders is their understanding of the context in which they operate. Providing future leaders with the opportunity to work in a range of settings increases their contextual literacy, their ability to diagnose environmental needs and to act on their analyses. Such skills lie at the heart of effective leadership. They need to be learned – as the discussion has previously emphasized – applied and honed.

Talent pools could also enable a better match between person and post. Some people struggle in a job because they are not well suited to the particular demands of that post. We all have specific skill sets and making sure my skill set is adequate to needs of the job I am doing is a major determiner of whether I will succeed or struggle. Groups of schools could create the capacity for a small panel of headteachers, say, to provide career counselling to those individuals looking to move towards senior posts. This is but one possible way of doing this. The key issue is using local arrangements to improve the deployment and match of candidates to available posts.

This last point introduces the idea of using local knowledge to improve local provision. Such an intention would be considerably strengthened by local data on staff being used to create local solutions and priorities. Local authorities have a key role to play here. Many have such data and are acting on it. All might be able to take a part in organizing local groupings. In the case of unitary and smaller authorities they would be the local grouping. In larger authorities sets of groups might be put in place. Whatever the basis of the groupings, encouraging them to see the issue as a shared responsibility and working together to create ways best suited to their needs could prove a winner in resolving the issue.

As a system-wide issue the challenge needs to be addressed at several levels within the school system. Individual schools have a part to play, in managing talent within the school. So, too, is there a role for central government to champion the need for action. Between these two there is a need for a mediating level of action too. This middle tier could ensure there is engagement with the issues and broker local solutions which are informed, over time, with what other groupings are doing and what looks to be working well. It would also be the best place to encourage a data-driven response. Local authority data (which could show the age profile of leaders, the size of leadership teams, recruitment forecasts and where these are likely to occur – type and size of school) could be key in not only moving schools to act, but in identifying exactly what is needed in a specific locality because the data would show where the greatest needs are likely to be (for example, secondary schools, Catholic schools, small rural primaries) and how other factors – falling rolls, federations – might mitigate some of the demands and needs. The middle level has a truly central role to play.

So, too, do the professional associations. The Association of School and College Leaders (ASCL) has, for example, been looking into sustainable leadership. Its report (Hill, 2006) concluded that sustainable leadership rested on 10 principles. Of these, four are closely related to the challenge of leadership succession:

- Believe in the power and purpose of learning – valuing the achievements of all their students and seeking to embed a love of learning and the skills for learning in every student and staff member.
- Share and foster leadership – both within schools and across schools.
- Build and sustain a learning community – investing in all staff and continually evaluating a school's work and effectiveness.

- Renew themselves by taking time out to think, to learn and relax and also by preparing the next generation of leaders (Hill, 2006: 79).

There is much here which is in common with what I have presented and it is most encouraging. The professional associations, like government, have a part to play in ensuring there is a call to action, in drawing attention to leadership development and by promoting learning communities in which learning to lead is an integral part.

Conclusion

Those leaders who are currently coming to the close of their careers in schools have a responsibility to ensure that there is a well-prepared and motivated generation of new leaders ready to step up to headship and senior leadership posts. This responsibility is not theirs alone. It is one shared with governors, local authorities, diocesan colleagues, the professional associations and groups of schools. The National College for School Leadership has a part to play, as do other organizations such as the Specialist Schools and Academy Trust. Together the challenge can be met and turned so we see it as the chance to bring on a new generation of leaders.

I have suggested that a range of strategies can be devised and deployed to increase leadership development, accelerate career progression, accentuate the rewards of leading a school, and build and sustain individuals' confidence in their abilities to be school leaders. These and other ideas need to be implemented in a new climate and framework. The climate should promote leadership development and a sense of shared responsibility for bringing on the next generation. The framework should create pools of leadership talent from which prospective heads can be drawn. Schools and central government and its agencies have parts to play. There is also a need for activity at an intermediate or middle level. This level needs to be carefully designed and co-ordinated.

All this will rely on serving headteachers thinking about the legacy they will leave when they retire. After so many years of unstinting service to their schools and the system, they and we cannot allow their hard work to be undone by failing to ensure they are succeeded by high-quality and well-prepared new leaders. It is as simple and stark as that.

Jim Collins in his book *Good to Great* (2001) reported on the research he and his team conducted into companies that had been high performers for many years and had continued to succeed year on year. In the book he identified the characteristics of those who led these successful companies. He called these executives level 5 leaders and they were distinguishable from other leaders by a number of characteristics. These included displaying a compelling modesty and being self-effacing and understated. Yet they were also 'fanatically driven, infected with an incurable need to produce sustained results' and resolved to do whatever it took to make the company great. One characteristic though stands out in the context of this chapter's focus. It was that: 'Level 5 leaders set up their successors for even greater success in the next generation, whereas egocentric level 4 leaders often set up their successors for failure' (Collins, 2001: 39).

These level 5 leaders wanted to see the organization even more successful in the next generation, and were comfortable with the idea that most people will not necessarily know that the roots of that success trace back to their efforts (Collins, 2001: 26). That is what we must hope the current crop of headteachers want too, and we all have a part in ensuring that this happens right across the school system. If we can, together, meet this challenge then we have every chance of not only bringing in high-quality school leaders, but of ensuring the school system moves from being good to great. If we can make a success of succession planning then that is the prize we will achieve; and it will be rooted in what those who are about to leave did just before they left.

References

Bentley, T. and Craig, J. (2006) PowerPoint presentation to NCSL Advisory Board, London, DEMOS, www.demos.co.uk.

Collins, J. (2001) *Good to Great*. London: Random House Business Books.

Cooper, C. and Kelly, M. (1993) 'Occupational stress in headteachers: a national UK study', *British Journal of Educational Psychology*, 63: 130–43.

Fullan, M. (2003) *The Moral Imperative of School Leadership*. Thousand Oaks, CA: Corwin Press.

Hartle, F. and Smith K. (2003) *Growing Tomorrow's School Leaders: The Challenge*. Nottingham: NCSL.

Hill, R. (2006) *Leadership that Lasts: Sustainable School Leadership in the 21st Century*. Leicester: Harcourt.

Howson, J. (2006) *Annual Survey of Appointments in Schools in England and Wales*. Oxford: Education Data Surveys.

National College for School Leadership (NCSL) (2004) *Meeting the Challenge: Growing Tomorrow's School Leaders*. Nottingham: NCSL.

National College for School Leadership (NCSL) (2005) *Does Every Primary School Need a Headteacher? Key Implications from a Study of Federations in the Netherlands*. Nottingham: NCSL.

Southworth, G. (1995) *Talking Heads: Voices of Experience – an Investigation into Primary Headship in the 1990s*. Cambridge: University of Cambridge, Institute of Education.

Southworth, G. (1998) *Leading Improving Primary Schools: The Work of Headteachers and Deputy Heads*. London: RoutledgeFalmer.

Index

A
academic achievement 74
accountability 11, 12, 125, 142, 151, 165
achievement, improved 4, 60–1
achievement data, as tool for improvement 131
achievement targets, short-term 13, 52, 54, 55
acting appointments, headship 27
activist leadership 77–9
acute business moments 149
adaptive challenge 159–61, 171
administrative work 33, 34, 35
administrivia 38, 41
Adventures of Charter School Creators 42–4
advocacy 75–6
Association of School and College Leaders (ASCL) 190–1
'at risk' students 168
atomic energy 59
authentic learning 69
autocratic leadership 104
autonomy 37, 38

B
Baby Boomers 49, 178
behavioural issues 76
belief(s) 16, 67, 127, 130
best practice 156
breadth, of sustainability 24, 51, 52
'broaden-and-build' theory 69
Brundtland Report 51
'building blocks' metaphor 80
Building Schools for the Future programme 177
Built to Last 93, 140, 141
burnout 97–8
business development, sustainable 139–41

C
capacity, for resilience 69
capacity-building 20–1, 125, 159
care 67, 73–4
career planning/progression 180–1
central government 190
change
  and conflict 91
  culture as barrier to 92–3
  need for pressure and support 106
  see also climate change; individual change; organizational change; repetitive change syndrome; strategic change; system change
Change Agent study 155
change agents 127–8, 171
charter schools 42–4, 144, 146, 148, 149
Children Act (2004) 176
'Chronos' time 19
civic leaders 171
climate change 61
closed systems 55–6
co-ordination, national and regional 168
coaching 164, 188
coaching and supervision program (SLC) 104
collaboration 32, 79, 125, 164–5
communities of practice 69
community, exhilarating leadership 32, 37
community of leaders
  building 109–10
  using to retain successful leaders 110–11
community-school relations 129, 131–2
competence, sustaining 90
compromise 91
conferences (SLC) 102
confidence 57–8, 67, 74, 185
Confidence: How Winning and Losing Streaks Begin and End 125
conflict, avoiding 90–1
conservation 52
constraints 34, 35
consultant leaders 176
consultation 73–4
continuing professional development (CPD) 163–4
continuous improvement 116, 142, 149–50
continuous learning ethos 105
conversation 15, 16, 21
  see also dialogue
coping strategies 188
core values 93, 141
Corporate Culture and Performance 93
courage of conviction 75–6
cradle-to-cradle approach, resources 56
cradle-to-grave process, entropy 54
craft knowledge 95, 186
creative destruction 147–8
Creative Destruction 140
cultural continuity, symbols 92–5
culture
  as barrier to change 92–3
  of learning 112–13
  see also school culture
curriculum, hurried and narrowing 54

D
data-driven decision-making 107–8
data-driven instruction 128
decentralization 28
decision-making 105, 107–8
deep learning outcomes 12–13
delegation 105
demand side privatization 145
demographic 'time bomb' 177
demographics, leadership 49–50
DEMOS 180
depth, of sustainability 24, 51, 52
deputy headship 184–7
dialogue 67, 135
  see also conversation
disciplined inquiry 124–5
discretionary money 109
distributed leadership 67, 73, 127, 143, 184
diversity 52, 53

E
education
  basic provision 13
  demographic 'time bomb' 177
  market environments 144–6
  sustainability in 137–8, 139–43, 151–2
Education Data Surveys (EDS) 27
education policy, impact on organizational life 150–1
Education Quality and Accountability Office (EQAO) 121
educational reform 52, 54, 56, 59, 93
  see also system change
educational standards 1
'emetic' leadership 40
emotional managers 48
energy depletion 54
energy release 59–60
energy renewal 55–8, 61, 129–32
energy restraint 53–5, 56, 61
enhanced learning 76
entropy 53–4
ethnic mix, headship 183
execution, market share 149–50
executive leaders 124
executive stress 55
exhilarating leadership 27–9
  aspects of 31–3
  expert commentaries on research findings 38–42
  implications for policy and practice 42–4
  leader voice 29–30
  shifting the balance to 35–8
Exhilarating Leadership 29
existential loss 92
Experimental Schools' project 91
external factors, discouraging aspects of work 34, 35, 40–1
external testing 12

F
Fast Track scheme 186–7
federated schools 167, 182
Fellows' program 101–2, 103
financial capital 149
'flywheel' effect 125
for-profit business 140–2
for-profit education 151
formal conversation 21
formative assessment 165

G
gender balance, headship 183
Generation X 49, 50
Gerstner, Lou 94
Good to Great 18, 124–5, 140, 141, 162, 191–2
government initiatives, achieving 77–8
government-imposed results-driven agenda 81
greedy work 47–8, 49
'greenhouse' schools 181, 187

H
Hall, Sir Iain 38–9
happiness 58
headship
  acting appointments 27
  addressing perception of 187–8
  attracting and maintaining appointments 26
  ethnic mix 183
  gender balance 183
  quality of candidates for 27
  remodelling nature and form of 188
  vacancies 27
  see also deputy headship
headteachers
  age profile 178
  growing pressure to recruit 178–9
  salaries 27
  see also leaders; principals
hedgehog effect 124, 141
hierarchy of needs 39
high-trust systems 57, 58
higher order needs 39
home schooling 145, 146
home-school relations 129, 131–2
hope 81
human resourcefulness 57–8
human resources, depletion of 54
humility, personal 18
Hunger of Memory 92

I
IBM 94
ICT 76
improved achievement 4, 60–1
improvement see school improvement; sustainable improvement

incompetence 90
individual change 104–5
individual conversation 15
informal conversation 21
informal learning 15
initiative 125
innovation 88, 149–50
Innovator's Dilemma, The 140, 141
Innovator's Solution, The 140
inspiring leadership models 111–12
institutional conversation 15
institutional organizations, structural arrangements 88–9
intelligent accountability 165
intra- inter-district choice programs 146
intuition 19
invitational leadership 15
involvement, creating 20–1

J
justice
  sustainable leadership 51, 52
  sustaining resilience 75–6
  see also social justice

K
'Kairos' time 19

L
lack of support 33
large-scale reform 56, 155–8, 167–8
leader voice 29–30
leaders
  Baby Boomers 49, 178
  of charter schools 42–3
  Millenials 50
  professional context 175–7
  shortages 49–50
  successful 18, 19
  support for 188–9
  symbolic roles 17
  see also community of leaders; executive leaders; headteachers; middle leaders; principals; system leaders; women leaders
leadership
  charter schools 43–4
  crisis in 26–7
  energy 116
  intuition 19
  new roles 176
  purpose of 171–2
  role perceptions 180
  see also activist leadership; distributed leadership; exhilarating leadership; headship; principalship; sustainable leadership
leadership development program (SLC) 104
leadership learning communities 189–91
leadership succession 175–92
  challenges 178–82
    mitigating factors 182
    positive aspects 183
  international crisis in 47–8
  solutions 183–91
Leadership and Sustainability 2
leading schools 166–7
Leading with Soul 16
learner-focused 76–7
learning communities 67, 69
  see also leadership learning communities; networked learning community; professional learning communities
learning in context 130–1
Learning Initiatives (SLC) 103, 106, 107
learning outcomes, importance of deep 12–13
learning-centred perspectives 68
learning-focused 76–7
length, of sustainability 24, 51, 52
level 5 leadership 18, 192
limited organizational life 147–8
Literacy Collaborative model 117–20
  implications for sustainability 134–5
  leaders' perspectives 125–34
  results 120–3
Literacy Learning Fair 120
local authorities 190
long-term objectives, balancing short-term and 13–14
loosely coupled structural arrangements 88–9
low-performing schools 150, 166
low-trust systems 57
lower order needs 39

M
McSchools 56
magnet schools 42, 146
market environments
  in education 137–8, 144–6
  impact of education policy 150–1
  organizational realities 147–50
Market and Opinion Research Institute 180
Marshall, Steve 38, 39–40
Maslow's hierarchy of needs 39
meaning
  yearning for 92
  see also sense of meaning
measures, of success 22–3
mechanically-driven reform 54
meetings 16
mentoring 183, 185
middle leaders 48, 184
Millenials 50
ministrivia 38
modern management 89
moral purpose(s) 66–8, 77, 78, 170

N
National College for School Leadership (NCSL) 175–7, 178, 180, 184, 189, 191
national policy, balancing demands of 77–8
National Professional Qualification for Headship 179
National Staff Development Council (NSDC) 99
natural environment, sustainability 139
networked learning community 109–10
networks/networking
  energy renewal 58
  exhilarating leadership 32, 37
  importance of 110, 167
  improvement and innovation through 164–5
New Enterprise Logic of Schools, The 28–9
new professionals 50

O
objectives, balancing short- and long-term 13–14
Odyssey Charter School 43
ongoing support, need for 106
open systems 56
organizational change 124
organizational life
  impact of education policy 150–1
  limited 147–8
organizations
  energy-depleting environments 54
  reactions to change 92–3
  realities, market environments 147–50
  structural arrangements 88–9
  sustaining core values 93–4
output measures 12
outsourcing 144, 150

P
partnership 42, 171
party politics 40–1
passion 16–17, 133
performance of staff 33, 34
performance-based reform 155–6, 157–8
personal factors
  discouraging aspects of work 34, 35
  exhilarating leadership 32, 36, 41
personal humility 18
personal renewal and challenge 132–3
personal resources 69
personalized learning 163
planned deployment 186
planned leadership opportunities 185–6
Polaris Missile Project 88–9
portfolio careers 180
positive emotions 69, 81
positive pressure 125
'pragmatopian' 14
predictable stability 138
prescription, or professionalism 159–61
principals
  attitudes towards 97
  need to sustain and develop 97–8
  salaries 97
  SLC *see* School Leadership Center
  teachers' perceptions 48–9
  see also headteachers
principalship
  resistance to 49
  stress of 46–7
private schools 145
privatization 144–5
Privilege and the Price, The 26
processes, importance of 15–16
professional associations 190–1
professional context, school leaders 175–7
professional development 104, 105, 106
  see also continuing professional development
professional learning communities 58, 164
professional will 18
professionalism 36, 159–61
professionalized teaching 163–4
pupil numbers, declining 182
'purely private' markets 145

R
Raising Achievement/Transforming Learning project 58, 60
Re-Imagining the Self-Managing School 28, 29
recognition 37
recruitment, of headteachers
  growing pressure 178–9
  inspiring leadership models 111–12
reform *see* educational reform; school reforms; system change
relational trust 112
repetitive change syndrome 54
research services (SLC) 102–3
resilience 65–82
  case study
    methodology 69–70
    findings 70–81
    discussion 81–2
  concept of 68–9
  definition 65
  moral purpose 66–8, 77, 78, 170
  sustaining 79–81
resilience-conserving strategies 80
resourcefulness 52, 57
  see also human resourcefulness
resources
  cradle-to-cradle approach 56
  exhilarating leadership 37
  as part of continued success 129, 131
  see also human resources; personal resources
respectful relations 108–9

responsibility 73–4, 167
reward and success, culture of 22
role perceptions, leadership 180
routine, comfort of established 89–90

S
salaries 27, 97
satisfaction/dissatisfaction surveys 35
school, home/community relationships 129, 131–2
school culture 22, 73
school improvement
achievement data as tool for 131
SLC focus on 100
sustainable 142–3
through networking 164–5
see also continuous improvement; sustainable improvement
school leadership see leaders; leadership
School Leadership Center (SLC)
culture of learning 112–13
focus on school improvement 100
lessons for developing and sustaining principals 104–12
building a community of leaders 109–10
continuous learning ethos 105
data-driven decision-making 107–8
discretionary money 109
individual change 104–5
inspiring leadership models 111–12
ongoing support, need for 106
practising what you preach 108–9
retaining successful leaders 110–11
training 107
mission and goals 100
programs
coaching and supervision 104
conferences and workshops 102
Fellows' program 101–2, 103
leadership development 104
Learning Initiatives 103, 106, 107
research services 102–3
sources of advice 99–100
staffing and governance structure 100–1
work 98–9
school reforms 142
school renewal 56–7
school-based management 28
schools
closures and amalgamations 182
factors of success 78–9
federated 167, 182
marketplace environment 137–8
open systems 56
privatization 144–5
segmentation approach 166–8
self-evaluation 173
shaming and blaming 54
strategically focused 15, 22–3
see also charter schools, private schools; 'greenhouse' schools; low-performing schools; magnet schools
second change agents 127–8
segmentation 166–8
self-evaluation 173
self-management 28
senior staff, support for 187–8
sense of meaning, creation of 16
shared beliefs/vision 127, 130
shared leadership 105, 107, 184
short-term accountability 11, 12
short-term achievement targets 13, 52, 54, 55
short-term objectives, balancing long-term and 13–14
sink schools 168
skills, sustainable leadership 17
SLC *see* School Leadership Center
social change 173–4
social factors, leadership succession 180–1
social justice 17, 67–8
social nature, sustainability 133–4
specialist college status 76
Specialist Schools and Academy Trust 191
specialization 89
Spinks, Jim 38, 40–2
sports, obsession with 22
staff
discouraging aspects of work 33, 34
exhilaration associated with 31
support for senior 187–8
standardized McSchools 56
start-up organizations, non-survival of 148
status quo, sustainability of 87–95
strategic abandonment 19–20
strategic capacity 21
strategic change 15, 24
strategic conversations 16, 21
strategic timing 19–20
strategically focused schools 15, 22–3
strategy 13, 16
stress 46–7, 55
structural arrangements, loosely coupled 88–9
student success, passion expressed through 133
student voice 29
students
exhilaration associated with 31
releasing latent energy of 59, 60
success
core values 141
exhilaration associated with 31
factors of 78–9
strategic measures of 22–3
see also student success
successful companies 192
successful leaders 18, 19
succession planning 177
supply side privatization 144, 145

support
  lack of 33
  need for 106, 129
  for school leaders 188–9
  for senior staff 187–8
support networks 80
support providers 150, 151
sustainability
  concept of 95
  as cultural phenomenon 93
  definition 23
  in education 137–8, 139–43, 151–2
  nature and prospects of 124–5
  principles of 24
  of the status quo 87–95
  as sustainable improvement 1–2
sustainable business development 139–41
sustainable development 51, 139
sustainable improvement 1–2, 66
sustainable leadership
  definition 11, 51
  energy release 59–60
  energy renewal 55–8
  energy restraint 53–5
  factors 11–24
    balancing short- and long-term objectives 13–14
    building capacity and creating involvement 20–1
    building in sustainability 23–4
    deep learning outcomes 12–13
    developing strategic measures of success 22–3
    importance of processes 15–16
    passion 16–17
    personal humility and professional will 18
    strategic timing and abandonment 19–20
  market environment 137–52
  principles 51–2, 190–1
  research 116–35
    district context 117–20
    implications 134–5
    leaders' perspectives 125–34
    nature and prospects of sustainability 124–5
    results 120–3
  resilience 65–82
  skills 17
sustainable learning 22
sustainable society 51
Sustaining Leadership 2
sustaining resilience *see* resilience
symbols, cultural continuity 92–5
system change 154–74
  four drivers for 161–5
  need for systemic perspective 155–8
  prescription or professionalism 159–61
  segmentation 166–8
  system leadership 168–72
system deep reform 156
system leaders 169, 170–1
system leadership 154, 176
  as catalyst for change 168–72
  domains 171
  realizing the vision of 173–4
system level, energy renewal 58
System Thinkers in Action 2
system wide reform 156

T
talent pools 186–7, 189, 191
teachers
  intellectual and emotional renewal 58
  perceptions of principals 48–9
  releasing latent energy of 59, 60
  see also headteachers
technical organizations, structural arrangements 88
testing 12, 14
thermodynamics, finite view of energy 53
'toxic' language 40
training 90, 107
transformational leadership 19, 66, 109
tri-level solution 158
trust 57, 67, 74, 112

U
University Council on Educational Administration (UCEA) 99

V
vacancies, headship 27
values 17, 66, 67
  see also core values
Vaughn Next Century Learning Centre 43

W
whiteboards 76
'whole school operation' 144
women leaders 48
work
  boring, depressing and discouraging 33–5, 44
  environments, energy-depleting 54
  exhilarating *see* exhilarating leadership
workforce remodelling 187
workload 26–7, 38
workshops, (SLC) 102

Y
York Region District School Board
  Literacy Collaborative model study 117–20
    implications for sustainability 134–5
    leaders' perspectives 125–34
    results 120–3